"Ryan LaMothe ranks among the most penetrating, wide-ranging and illuminating interpreters of the onset of the Anthropocene age. No one surpasses him for crafting an acute and balanced analysis of the many political, ethical and moral issues that this turbulent new era entails. His sharp psychoanalytic insights make this an especially valuable contribution to our understanding of the unfolding crisis."

–**Kurt Jacobsen and David Morgan**, *co-editors of Free Associations*


"In his at once expansive and finely detailed exposé of the illusions that are killing us and destroying our planet, Ryan LaMothe puts psychoanalysis, philosophy, and political science on the couch and arrives at a revolutionary understanding of a new *psychoanalytic political theory*. Radical to its Aristotelian roots and with all the 'Urgency of Now,' LaMothe's carefully argued masterpiece of interdisciplinary scholarship is more than a riveting read. It is essential to our survival as a species."

–**Hattie Myers, PhD**, *Training and Supervising Psychoanalyst at the Institute for Psychoanalytic Training and Research (IPTAR), Editor in Chief of* ROOM: A Sketchbook for Analytic Action


"LaMothe makes a compelling case for the fierce urgency of bringing political philosophy into heated, constructive conversation with psychoanalysis. Crossing these and other boundaries, he shows, can allow us to begin to understand and address the multiple catastrophes of the Anthropocene. Philosophers, psychoanalytically minded practitioners, and anyone prepared for a bracing investigation ranging from theories of capitalism to theories of care, among other areas, will benefit from this interdisciplinary book. Our psychic stability and the stability of our planet make thinkers like LaMothe required reading."

–**Susan Kassouf, PhD**, *Licensed Psychoanalyst (National Psychological Association for Psychoanalysis)*

# A Political Psychoanalysis for the Anthropocene Age

*A Political Psychoanalysis for the Anthropocene Age* presents an evaluation of the politics of climate change and considers how psychoanalysis can contribute to this discourse.

Presented in two parts, this book first uses a psychoanalytic approach to interrogate political-economic realities and their impact on shaping Western political selves in the Anthropocene age. Ryan LaMothe identifies core illusions of the Western psyche and how they shape behavior and relations, as well as how they are implicated in various emotional responses to climate change like eco-mourning and eco-denial. Topics such as political dwelling, sovereignty, political violence and change, climate obstacles such as capitalism, nationalism, and imperialism, and the problem of hope are explored using psychoanalytic and philosophical perspectives. LaMothe then considers the role of psychoanalysis in the public-political realm, as well as how a psychoanalytic political perspective invites reforming the education and practice of psychoanalysis.

*A Political Psychoanalysis for the Anthropocene Age* will be thought-provoking reading for psychoanalysts and psychotherapists, as well as anyone interested in the politics of climate change.

**Ryan LaMothe** is a professor of pastoral care and counseling at Saint Meinrad Seminary and School of Theology, USA. Over the last three decades, he has published books and articles in the areas of psychology of religion, psychoanalysis, pastoral counseling, and political theology and philosophy. He is Past President of the Society for Pastoral Theology and has served on several editorial boards.

# A Political Psychoanalysis for the Anthropocene Age

## The Fierce Urgency of Now

Ryan LaMothe

R Routledge
Taylor & Francis Group

LONDON AND NEW YORK

Designed cover image: Getty | Nastco

First published 2024
by Routledge
4 Park Square, Milton Park, Abingdon, Oxon OX14 4RN

and by Routledge
605 Third Avenue, New York, NY 10158

Routledge is an imprint of the Taylor & Francis Group, an informa business

British Library Cataloguing-in-Publication Data
A catalogue record for this book is available from the British Library

ISBN: 9781032193618 (hbk)
ISBN: 9781032193625 (pbk)
ISBN: 9781003258827 (ebk)

DOI: 10.4324/9781003258827

Typeset in Times New Roman
by codeMantra

For Cyn
and all those who labor to care for the earth and its
residents

In memory of
Bill and Pat LaMothe

# Contents

# Acknowledgments

While a book may represent the unique voice of the author, it is in fact a chorus of voices. For instance, we consider the Republic to represent the singular mind of Plato, and in many ways it is. However, it also comprises the many voices of philosophers who preceded and were contemporaries of Plato. While far from displaying the scholarly acumen of Plato, this book has also emerged from listening to and reading other authors from diverse fields, who I have endeavored to cite. I also have had opportunities to test out some of the ideas in these chapters in varied venues, such as Princeton Seminary's Jacob Neumann Lecture, a series of three lectures on climate change at Fordham University, three lectures at the National Psychological Association for Psychoanalysis and Appalachian Psychoanalytic Society. I am particularly grateful to Claire Steinberger, Tony Pipolo, Susan Kassouf, Kurt Jacobsen, David Morgan, and Panu Pihkala for their interest in my ideas and for their comments about them. Since I straddle more than one discipline, I have benefited from conversations with and support from Robert Dykstra, Nancy Ramsay, Bruce Rogers-Vaughn, Carrie Doehring, Jaco Hamman, Kirk Bingaman, Phil Zylla, and others. I also want to thank Susannah Frearson, Senior Editor at Routledge Press, who supported this project. The constructive comments and suggestions of two anonymous outside readers were deeply appreciated. A special thanks to Mary Jeanne Schumacher and Cindy Geisen for their editorial corrections and comments on this and other works. Cindy, over the months, also offered relevant sources for my consideration. So, while any errors are mine alone, this book represents past and present voices of people who are concerned about the well-being of a biodiverse earth and its inhabitants.

# Introduction

## Psychoanalysis, the Political, and the Anthropocene Age

Martin Luther King Jr. (1998, p.205) used the phrase "the fierce urgency of now" to point to the long history of slavery, racial segregation, and other forms of economic and political injustices and the imperative to act now for freedom and justice for all people of color. This phrase continues to have meaning, given the prevalence of racism and classism in the United States and elsewhere. Yet, King's fierce urgency of now also has particular relevance when we consider the present and future catastrophes associated with climate change (e.g., massive storms, desertification, rising seas, coastal erosion, record flooding, collapse of coral reefs and fish populations, collapse of insect populations, heat domes, and enormous fires).[1] These disasters will accompany mass movements of desperate people seeking safety and provisions, which will place enormous pressures on states and, in worse-case scenarios, destabilize states and increase political violence within and between nation-states—likely outcomes that CIA and Pentagon reports cite (Davenport, 2014).[2] Never before in history have human beings been faced with a global existential threat and crisis of their own making. (Western nations share most of the responsibility, given the history of colonialism and global capitalism.) To be sure, one could point out that human beings faced (and face) an existential crisis with the proliferation of nuclear weapons during the Cold War, which continues to be a threat to the planet. But nuclear winter is a possibility that so far has been avoided. Human-caused climate change, however, has been going on for decades, having real impacts on human beings and millions of other species (Klein, 2014; Kolbert, 2014; Wilson, 2005). Indeed, as Joseph Dodds (2011) notes, "Climate change embodies a world of unpredictable, multi-level, highly complex, non-linear interlocking systems, and to fully grasp the threat…is more than one intellectual field can encompass" (p.15). The complexity and dangers of climate change are reflected in the move in discourses from discussions about global warming to discourses on the "climate emergency," which reinforces the phrase "fierce urgency of now." Climate discourse is also shifting away from stopping the rise of global warming to adapting to it—as if adapting is, in the long run, a viable strategy.[3] While the fierce urgency of now concerns all human beings and other species, my focus is narrower. I am using this phrase to refer to psychoanalytically informed practitioners and educators, as well as analytically knowledgeable philosophers, cultural critics, etc.

DOI: 10.4324/9781003258827-1

This may raise a question. A therapist/educator may agree that climate change is an immediate threat and that we need to act now, but what does this have to do with psychoanalytic theorizing, education, or psychoanalytically informed therapies? Relatedly, what does the given climate emergency have to do with psychoanalysis' relation to the public-political sphere?[4] In short, what do psychoanalytic theories and practices have to do with global warming and the attending social-political discourses regarding climate change? Perhaps the most immediate answer is that therapists are already dealing with patients' eco-anxiety, eco-guilt/debt, eco-betrayal, eco-despair, eco-denial, eco-mourning, etc. (Budziszewska & Jonsson, 2021; Fredericks, 2021; Grouse, 2020; Kassouf, 2017; Orange, 2017; Pihkala, 2019; Weintrobe, 2021).[5] There are also ecologically concerned psychoanalysts and others who use psychoanalytic theory as a critical hermeneutical framework to understand and critique the social-political apparatuses[6] that contribute to or produce psychosocial resistances to climate action (Hamilton, 2012; Hoggett, 2012; Tollemache, 2019; Weintrobe, 2021; Westcott, 2019). In my view, these approaches have clinical relevance ala Frantz Fanon in that they can illuminate the real social-political and economic sources of psychological distress so that patients can choose an action(s) in relation to these sources (Gibson & Beneduce, 2017).[7] And then there is Donna Orange's (2017) engaging and important work, wherein she uses psychoanalytic theory and philosophy[8] to propose a radical ethic for the climate emergency.

Perhaps my imaginary therapist/educator is now convinced of the urgent need to engage climate change, both with regard to the consulting room and the public-political spheres. While this is a happy occasion, I want to press further. Most psychoanalytic approaches to climate change use psychoanalytic theories to understand psychosocial experiences of, resistances to, and actions toward climate change (e.g., Hoggett, 2019, p.9). As mentioned above, a critical analysis often includes critiques of hegemonic political-economic apparatuses (Hoggett, 2013; Weintrobe, 2021), like neoliberal capitalism, that shape subjectivities by mystifying the real sources of climate change and subverting climate action. What is consistently overlooked in these approaches is the latent presence of political philosophies that are integral to and embedded within psychoanalytic engagement with these larger realities. That is, using psychoanalytic theories and concepts to interpret public-political phenomena is necessarily informed by the analyst's political philosophy,[9] though this is rarely acknowledged. For instance, Sally Weintrobe's (2021) prophetic book on climate crisis and psychoanalysis is, in my reading, shaped by feminist-liberative political theories, as well as by political philosophies (e.g., liberalism) that undergird social democratic societies. Another example is Michael Rustin's (1991) work in which he approaches Klein's work from a socialist perspective. In a later work, Rustin (2021) argues "that there can be nothing more vital for a progressive, deliberative, universalist, and democratic politics than to understand the preconditions of reason itself." Psychoanalysis, he continues, "has a major contribution to make to understanding the developmental foundations and the continuing social precondition of rationality" (p.113). To return to the climate crisis, Joseph Dodds (2011) notes that eco-anxieties "related to Klein's depressive position involve mourning for the damage done and a reparative drive to restore, repair, and recreate the lost and damaged world" (p.69). Of course, this involves recognizing the damage that already has been done and continues to occur. Anticipatory mourning for Dodds is related to acknowledging "the fact that nothing is permanent and everything, including our civilization and even the wider natural system of the Earth, will eventually disappear" (p.72). Weintrobe's, Rustin's, and Dodds' analytic approaches share the belief that psychoanalysis can contribute to understanding the social-political realm (see also Roazen, 1999), which, in the case of Weintrobe and Dodds, includes the relation between the climate emergency and the political. Their approaches also accompany stated and unstated political philosophies. This is not a critique, but rather a challenge. Can psychoanalysts intentionally develop psychoanalytically informed political philosophies that they can use to engage in public discourses around climate change? Philosopher-psychoanalyst Donna Orange (2017), who knows of Aristotle's uniting ethos and polis, does so in proposing a radical ethics. Her radical ethics is not simply for psychoanalysts or those interested in psychoanalytic theories. It is also for the larger public-political interlocutors who are engaged around issues of climate action. In this approach, psychoanalysis is not simply a critical "scientific" methodology for understanding the psyche in relation to the polis; it is also a political theory of human belonging and dwelling that includes other species and the earth.

While Orange privileges ethics over politics, my approach is the reverse. Part I of this book develops a psychoanalytically inflected political philosophy, which is radical in the senses of being rooted in both the existential realities of human dwelling in nature and psychosocial development. Stated differently, the fundamental, often implicit, existential question in most political philosophies is: how shall we dwell together? Yet, the answers to this question, in Western political philosophies, have excluded Othered human beings, other species, and the earth—more on this later. Psychoanalytic theories of development, I contend, also implicitly address this question as well. Parents' unstated query of how shall "we" dwell together founds and precedes any answers to the question of how shall "I" dwell posed (unconsciously) by children. As will become clearer, these questions, while usually anthropocentric, necessarily include other species and the earth, which is increasingly evident in the context of the Anthropocene Age.[10]

There are several reasons for taking this approach. First, with some qualifications, I agree with Sally Weintrobe's (2021) comment that "(M)ost discussions of psychology take insufficient account of politics" (p.13). Not only do members of the helping professions need to take politics (includes economics) into account with regard to psychosocial sufferings and the suffering of other species; we need to engage in public-political discourse around climate change. This includes not only using psychological theories as hermeneutical critical lenses for understanding (1) collective conscious and unconscious motivations that contribute to climate change and climate inaction, and (2) psychosocial suffering associated with climate change; it also includes being cognizant of or constructing political philosophies that attend our theories and practices. Second, one of the fascinating aspects about psychoanalysis over the last century or so is its use by people in other disciplines (literary critical theories, sociology, philosophy, etc.). My hope is that the approach taken in this book will invite audiences from other disciplines, because when it comes to climate action, diverse groups need to engage in speaking and acting together if we are to cooperate and sustain each other in this emergency. This also suggests that while I see psychoanalysis as concerned about human psychosocial suffering in the consulting room, I consider the consulting room to be integrally associated with the public-political realm. This means not only a psychoanalytic critical engagement with politics, but also attending to the political theories and notions of the good that undergird our approaches to the political (or explicitly constructing a psychoanalytic political philosophy). I add that there is an urgent imperative for therapists and educators to engage in political-public discourse and action regarding climate change because of the psychosocial harms that arise from climate change. This includes concerns about harms to other species and the earth, since any answer to the question how of shall we dwell together depends on a bio-diverse earth. That is, our psychological, physical, and political well-being depend on a habitable earth. The earth, as Terry Eagleton (2016) notes, "is the first condition of our existence" (p.228). To embrace this imperative requires being clear about the political philosophy that informs our analytic critiques and discourses.

This perspective may raise questions about how I understand psychoanalysis, and so a few thoughts are needed for clarification. Freud and many of his disciples clearly believed and promoted the idea that psychoanalysis is a science, which tended to separate the consulting room from political realities (Cushman, 1995, 2019). And yet, what is intriguing about Freud is that he relied on a patriarchal political myth (Oedipus Rex) to construct a putative universal view of human (male) psychosocial development. In addition, Freud (1950), not unlike Hobbes, Locke, and Rousseau, constructed a story or myth regarding the origins of civilization that Freud believed to be recapitulated developmentally. The birth of civilization is clearly related to the political and, in this case, civilization is portrayed as thoroughly patriarchal, with violence as a means of attaining political position and power. Add to this Freud's (1939) last work, *Moses and Monotheism*, wherein he takes for granted patriarchal sovereignty as the organizing principle of the Israelite polis. From a different angle, Freud (1915, 1927, 1930) was not shy about addressing what were ostensibly macro political realities, such as war, human progress, and religion (see also Frosh, 2020). The thread in this is not simply to point to the connection between psychoanalytic theorizing and the political realm, but rather to highlight that psychoanalytic theorizing is understandably wedded to anthropological (political) views, theories, or myths, which are not universal and timeless objective truths or scientific facts. This points to the view that psychoanalytic theories and therapies, in part, are moral-political discourses because they possess visions of the good rooted in a polis (Cushman, 2019, pp.117–121; see also Kovel, 1988).

Psychoanalysts (and psychoanalytically informed cultural critics and philosophers, e.g., Adorno, Benjamin, Eagleton, and Marcuse) who have addressed political and economic matters, using psychoanalytic theories, clearly have a vision of the good, which is not extraneous or a mere addition to their theories. Indeed, their visions of the good life are, in my view, both political and psychoanalytic. To return to Sally Weintrobe's work, it is obvious that psychoanalysis and the political are intertwined and both are informed by a vision of the common good. If one agrees that psychoanalysis possesses a vision of the good, it is not simply or solely a moral discourse. Indeed, Phillip Cushman, in my view, would place moral discourse within the realm of political life. In surveying psychoanalytic history, we also observe a number of psychoanalysts who were, in varied ways, politically engaged, using psychoanalysis to interpret political realities and to engage in political discourse (e.g., Alfred Adler, Franz Alexander, Gordon Allport, Frantz Fanon, Erich Fromm, Joel Kovel, R. D. Laing, Wilhelm Reich, Donald Winnicott, to name a few).[11] Indeed, the works of Frantz Fanon have given birth to a great deal of literature that examines the intersection of politics and the psyche (Laubscher, Hook, & Desai, 2022; see also Samuels, 1993). Psychoanalysts have addressed political issues concerning war (Freud, 1915; Winnicott in Lejeune, 2017, p.255), racism (Altman, 2000, 2004; Dalal, 2002), classism (Gherovici & Christian, 2019; Layton, Hollander, & Gutwill, 2006), and decolonization (Swartz, 2019). As Paul Roazen (1999) contends, psychoanalysis is not only relevant to political life, but it is necessary (see also Bowker & Buzby, 2017). Comparably, Eli Zaretsky (2015) argues, psychoanalytic thought has been used to understand the political conflicts and struggles of the 20th century, not simply to understand, but also to engage in the polis' spaces of speaking and acting together (Arendt, 1958). Like Socrates, both Roazen and Zaretsky who believe that moving toward realizing the good in the polis required the engagement of critical reflection in the public sphere. In addition, Adam Phillips (2021b) has written, "If all life is group life, psychoanalysis must be politics by other means" (p.49).

All of this does not necessarily imply that psychoanalysis is simply a political venture and not a science. There are, for instance, decades of psychoanalytic scientific qualitative and quantitative research on infant-parent interactions. Like other research, these studies can be assessed in terms of whether they can be replicated. Of course, science itself is not completely separable from the political, not only because it is a human endeavor that takes place within a polis, but also because science is often used for both bad and good political aims, such as using climate science to develop political and economic policies to reduce greenhouse gas emissions or the use of science in the development of massively destructive weapons. In addition, science often has a vision of the good, which may conflict with political visions of the good. That said, in this book I emphasize the political-moral aspects of psychoanalysis, because (1) political philosophies and their visions of the good are often latent in psychoanalytic theorizing, shaping critical discourses, and (2) psychoanalytically philosophically informed therapists and educators can better engage in larger political discourses around climate change with those who hold different anthropological views or different visions of the common good. The latter point implies a certain humility in that this approach is not about making scientific claims, but instead offers claims about the good—local and universal goods associated with the global reality of climate change.

Given the centrality of the concept "political" to this book and the fact that it is contested, the next section addresses some of the features of "political." This section is the skeleton or bones of a political philosophy, and Part I of the book will put flesh on the bones of a psychoanalytic political philosophy. The remaining section of this introduction provides a brief description of the following chapters.

## The Concept "Political" and Its Features

The notion of "political" has its roots in the Greek concept "polis." The polis or city-state, broadly speaking, comprises particular human-created institutions, rules, regulations, and laws necessary for living a life in common. Stated another way, the political can be understood as referring to the communicative activity of the polis' residents that is concerned with issues and questions of living a life in common. Naturally, this communicative activity is shaped and legitimated by human-created public-political institutions and their attending policies, programs, laws, etc. (Arendt, 1958, p.198). These public-political institutions are artifices, which are inextricably linked to shared narratives and rituals that reflect people's beliefs, expectations, hopes, or visions (assumptive world) that found their communications with each other (Honneth, 2007, pp.218–239). These shared narratives and practices reveal how residents of the polis understand and live out the common good or how the group understands and ideally works together toward the survival and flourishing of its members.

Hannah Arendt (1958) uses the notion "space of appearances" in her depiction of the communicative activity of the polis. Arendt writes that the polis is "the public-political realm in which [human beings] attain their full humanity, not only because they are (as in the privacy of the household) but also because they appear" (Arendt, 2005, p.21). To appear is to engage in the polis' discourse, which requires interlocutors who recognize and treat each other as persons—unique, valued, inviolable, and responsive subjects (singularity: Macmurray, 1991). Axel Honneth (2007) points out that Arendt

> claims that human subjects are naturally dependent on being perceived and affirmed in a public sphere, for it is only in this way that they can acquire the measure of psychic stability and self-confidence needed to cope with their existential problems and risks.
>
> (pp.30–31)

Added to this is Honneth's view that "individual subjects are only capable of experiencing themselves as free beings if they have learned to be actively engaged in public discussion of political affairs" (p.30). To return to Arendt (2018), she contends that "public freedom is a tangible reality, created by [persons] to enjoy together in public—to be seen, heard, and known, and remembered by others" (p.375). Political agency, in other words, depends on the polis' apparatuses that support mutual-personal recognition (Honneth, 2021; Macmurray, 1991; Nussbaum, 2019), which founds the space of appearances, and for Arendt, spaces of appearance are spaces of speaking and acting together.

Of course, some individuals can be recognized as persons in the polis, but this recognition does not include being allowed to engage in political discourse, which, for Honneth and Arendt, means they are denied full humanity and political agency. Aristotle and many political philosophers (and political theologians) who followed him, for instance, viewed women as being part of the polis, but not part of the space of appearances associated with the political. Women were constructed such that they were recognized as not possessing political agency—less than full persons. Add to this those who are not recognized as persons, such as those human beings constructed as slaves or barbarians. They reside in the polis, but they are not recognized as persons or as citizens, and they are not believed to be capable of political agency and not permitted to exercise it. When these Others attempt to exercise their political agency, the apparatuses of the polis that privilege adult males use violence or the threat of violence and public humiliation to squelch the exercise of political agency. So, personal recognition associated with the polis' space of appearances includes laws, policies, and practices that indicate who exactly is allowed the political agency to engage in a polis' communicative spaces of speaking and acting together.

Five other features of the space of appearances and recognition are important to highlight vis-à-vis the political. First, political agency develops and is sustained in spaces of appearances, wherein members obtain a sense of self-esteem, self-respect, and self-confidence that is derived from mutual-personal recognition (Honneth, 1995). Put another way, these senses of the self found political agency vis-à-vis speaking and acting together. The polis' shared narratives, rituals, and institutional apparatuses serve to produce and maintain political agency and the space of appearances. From a negative perspective, a polis can possess narratives and apparatuses or disciplinary regimes that attempt to restrict or deny self-esteem, self-confidence, and self-respect of those who reside within the polis (e.g., Aristotle's polis and the exclusion of women). Orlando Patterson (1982) illustrates this in the context of the U.S. polis. He uses the term "social death" to refer to enslaved persons in the United States who were restricted from public-political spaces even as they resided in them. Worse, political non-recognition could include the ultimate, which is expelling some individuals from the polis, namely, death. Similarly, Giorgio Agamben (1998) adopts the term *homo sacer* to refer to someone who can be killed, although their death is not considered a homicide or sacrifice. In these cases, the polis possesses apparatuses that violently attempt to deny the self-esteem, self-confidence, and self-respect of the victim, confirming that the individual possesses no political agency and is not a part of the polis' space of appearances.

All of this may seem more consciously intentional than what we note in history. That is, a person born into a particular polis internalizes (Schafer, 1990)—in varying degrees—the meanings, beliefs, values, and expectations ensconced in collective narratives and rituals, which leads to the formation of what Lynne Layton (2020) calls the normative unconscious or what Timothy Zeddies (2002) calls historical unconscious. Both normative and historical unconscious are imbricated with conscious political constructions of reality, yet they omit the present and past sufferings of marginalized Others (including the lives and sufferings of other species). For millennia, few Western philosophers, for instance, recognize the political agency of women, which meant that the polis' apparatuses attempted to debase women's self-esteem, self-confidence, and self-respect. Women, in other words, were (and continue to be, in some places) not deemed to be politically normative or relevant and, therefore, not remembered.

A different way to understand how assumptive political visions can marginalize some groups is Donnel Stern's notion of weak dissociation, which is indebted to Herbert Fingarette's (1969) philosophical analysis of routine self-deception. Fingarette wrote,

> it is when we judge that there is a purposeful discrepancy between the way the individual really is engaged in the world and the story he tells himself that we have the complex but common form of self-deception in which we are interested.

> (p.62)

This self-deception, from Fingarette's perspective, results from not spelling out (narrating) one's engagement in the world or, better, spelling out one's engagement such that one does not avow one's actions or the consequences of these actions. Stern (1997), building on Fingarette's analysis of self-deception, argues that weak dissociation entails narrative rigidity, which means that individuals organize their experiences so that their actions and consequences are narrowly spelled out, leaving out actions and consequences that do not "fit" the dominant, rigid story. Inflexible narration, in other words, means that those ideas, meanings, values, and affects that are unconsciously (normative unconscious) perceived to contradict the dominant-conscious narrative are excluded or unformulated and therefore outside of awareness. In weak dissociation, Stern argued, we spell out only what

> we believe we can tolerate, or that furthers our purpose, or that promises a feeling of safety, satisfaction, and the good things in life; we dissociate the meanings that we believe we will not be able to tolerate, that frighten us and seem to threaten the fulfillment of our deepest intentions.

> (p.128)

In terms of the polis and political agency, the historical exclusion of women (and other groups, including other species) from the political realm of speaking and acting together reflects the intersection of conscious and unconscious processes, which psychoanalysis, through the notions of normative unconscious, historical unconscious, and weak dissociation, can illuminate. In short, our conscious political constructions of the "good" are imbued with unconscious processes, which beg for analysis. In addition, this psychoanalytic rendering of political agency vis-à-vis the polis' apparatuses points to the first step toward the possibility for political liberation—a liberation that relies on the political-public work of raising what is unconscious to consciousness.[12]

A second feature implicit in the view of the political as communicative activity is social cooperation. For a polis to be viable, the space of appearance must include individuals cooperating together—shared exercise of political agency—to address the varied questions, issues, and problems that come from living a life in common. Even when we think of a dystopian polis, such as one depicted in the television series *Deadwood*, we see in the midst of conflict, competition, and violence a semblance of cooperation, even if it entails various factions vying for control. Or we could turn to the deep and deepening political polarization in the United States with all of the fractured spaces of speaking and acting together. Nevertheless, sufficient cooperation exists, so far, to maintain a relatively stable polis—at least for now. Of course, for cooperation to be possible in the polis' spaces of speaking and acting together, there must be shared beliefs, values, and visions that are ensconced in collectively held narratives and practices.

Political cooperation necessarily presumes some level of civic trust, which is the third feature of "political." For Thomas Hobbes, cooperation is enforced through the leviathan that enforces a social contract. If there is trust, it emerges from a shared fear of the leviathan's violence—a fear that accompanies the desire for security and stability. This view reflects the turbulent times in which Hobbes lived and is certainly a political philosophy that acknowledges the need for cooperation. Unfortunately, cooperation is ensured through the leviathan's apparatuses of political violence. Yet, other political philosophers (e.g., Løgstrup, 1997; MacIntyre, 1983, 2007; Macmurray, 1991; Sandel, 1998, 2005) argue that civic mutual-personal trust is necessary for the communicative cooperation of citizens, and that fear and anxiety undermine political agencies and cooperation. One might say that a decent polis, to use Avishai Margalit's (1996) notion, entails sufficient mutual-personal recognition to produce and maintain the civic trust necessary for cooperation in living a life in common.

As suggested above, even the communicative activity of a good-enough polis entails contestation and relational failures amidst civic trust and cooperation. This is why Arendt (2005) and Desmond Tutu (1999) argue that a polis must have narratives that promote and institutions that facilitate practices of forgiveness. These invite the possibility of repairing the space of appearances, which is the fourth attribute of the political. Forgiveness implies remorseful acknowledgment of and responsibility for harms caused and includes actions that are aimed at repairing the social-political fabric and restoring the political agency necessary for collective trust and cooperation. Public apologies by political figures for the harms done to African Americans and Native Americans, while welcome, fall short because they are not followed by political actions aimed at addressing how past harms continue to be present in the political-economic practices today. A clear example is the political apology of President Clinton for the usurpation of Hawaii's government in 1983. This apology did not involve federal recognition of native Hawaiians, which meant a continued lack of legal protections.[13] A slightly more positive illustration is Germany's taking political accountability for the Holocaust, providing the victims who survived with reparations, which obviously could not fully repair the harms done.[14]

The fifth and related feature of the political is civic care, which is elaborated in the next chapter. For now, let me acknowledge that numerous political theorists (Bubeck, 1995; Engster, 2007; Gilligan, 1982; Hamington, 2004; Løgstrup, 1997; Macmurray, 1991; Noddings, 1984; Oliner & Oliner, 1995; Robinson, 1999, 2011; Sevenhuijsen, 1998; Tronto, 1993, 2013) have argued that care is fundamentally a political concept. Recently, Shawn Fraisart (2021), in his analysis of Plato, Rousseau, and Godwin, argues that care has been a key concept in Western political philosophies. Indeed, Aristotle (Barker, 1971) argued that "It is friendship which consists in the pursuit of a common social life" (p.120). Later he wrote that the political community "depends on friendship" (p.181), which suggests that mutual person-recognition and *care* founds experiences of rapport and forms of dialogue, as well as civic trust and cooperation. We can also point to contemporary philosophers, such as John Macmurray (1992), who argues that a flourishing polis is one "in which each cares for all others and no one for himself" (p.159). Similarly, Sheldon Wolin (2016a) contends that "The political emerges as the shared concerns of human beings to take care of themselves and the part of the world they claim as their lot" (p.248). And Michael Hardt and Antonio Negri (2005) claim that care or "love serve(s) as the basis for our political projects in common and the construction of a new society. Without love, we are nothing" (p.352). This makes sense since the polis' apparatuses undergird the recognition of citizens as persons who possess the political agency to speak and act together. Personal recognition in the polis then necessarily accompanies a degree of civic care. By contrast, failures of recognition attend varied forms of social-political carelessness and civic distrust are evident in marginalization, oppression, and the maldistribution of resources (Fraser & Honneth, 2003; Margalit, 1996). In brief, political or civic care can be understood as everything we do to help individuals, families, communities, and societies (1) meet the vital biological, psychosocial, and existential or spiritual needs of individuals, families, and communities, (2) develop or maintain basic capabilities with the aim of human flourishing, (3) facilitate parity of participation in the polis' space of appearances, and (4) maintain a habitable environment for all.[15]

Naturally, each good-enough polis produces and lives out idioms of civic care— unique expressions of care that emerge from the particularity of the symbols systems and practices associated with a specific polis. This civic care is founded on mutual-personal recognition and intertwined with civic trust, which make possible sufficient degrees of vulnerability and dependency that are needed to accept personal recognition/care and political cooperation. In other words, to receive care in the public realm and to act cooperatively in civic spaces of appearance, there must be enough trust and vulnerability to risk appearing and acting in political-public spaces. While ultimately impossible and contradictory, a polis that promotes invulnerable and independent (neoliberal) subjects would be a failed polis, because it would deny the existential realities of being human (vulnerability and dependency) and naturally lack both the sufficient civic care and civic trust necessary for speaking and acting together.

The centrality of civic trust and care with regard to the political is difficult to grasp given the polarized political situation in the United States. Yet, political polarization and the rifeness of social-political enmity simply prove the point. By this, I mean that the absence of civic care and trust means that an existing polis devolves into chaos or into an indecent society (Margalit, 1996). Aristotle, for example, believed that the absence of friendship in the polis results in "a state, not of freemen, but only slaves and masters; a state of envy on the one side and on the other contempt" (p.181). Turning to the work of John Adams, Hannah Arendt (2018) notes the will to power "tends to destroy all political life" (p.375), because it represents the absence of friendship, trust, care, and the cooperation necessary for a thriving political life. That the United States continues to function politically means that, for now, there continues to be a modicum of civic care and trust, even in the midst of political polarization and alienation, though we certainly need more practices of forgiveness and repair.

Listed below are some basic, existential attributes of the political, which can be framed in terms of functions vis-à-vis the political. Above, I noted that "political" refers to socially held and publicly expressed symbols, narratives, and rituals. These are embodied in a polis' socially created apparatuses that *function* to:

a  Shape subjectivity and legitimate an individual's political agency in the public realm (Arendt, 1958).
b  Facilitate collective discourse and action in the public realm (D'Entreves, 1994).
c  Distribute power and resources (Ransom, 1997).
d  Legitimate authority and governance.
e  Adjudicate claims, discipline, and repair breaches of both social order and the laws governing social arrangements and the distribution of resources.
f  Provide an overarching social-political identity that supports collective action and discourse, and maintain a shared sense of continuity and cohesion.
g  Facilitate mutual trust and care of citizens (and non-citizens) for the sake of survival and flourishing.

Before moving on, it is helpful to say more about the political in relation to governing institutions or state apparatuses and the notion of citizenship. Leo Strauss and Joseph Cropsey (1987) indicate that modern people tend to view the state "in contradistinction to 'society'" or the public realm (p.6). This distinction is inconceivable, they argue, for classical political philosophers like Plato and Aristotle. Aristotle, for instance, viewed the city-state as "a kind of partnership, association, or community, that is, a group of persons who share or hold certain things in common" (Lord, 1987, p.134), which necessarily comprises governing structures. These governing structures, Macmurray (1991) notes, are human creations and, as such, can be altered or overthrown (p.137). He also argues that "The State has no rights, no authority, for it is an instrument, not an agent; a network of organization, not a person" (Macmurray, 2004, p.106). As a created instrument, the state ideally "exists to make society possible, to provide mechanisms through which the sharing of human experience may be achieved" (p.106). Put another way, while the "State is merely a mechanism, and therefore a means to an end, [it has] no value in itself" (p.106).[16] The state's value as a mechanism vis-à-vis the political is its ability to facilitate mutual-personal recognition that founds civic trust and civic care, which, in turn, are yoked to political agency and communicative spaces of speaking and acting together—cooperation and forgiveness. Ideally speaking, the state is created for the people, for the polis, and not the people for the state, though history is littered with states subjugating people for the purpose of securing the state.

This is important for discussions of psychoanalysis and the political in subsequent chapters. For now, I simply acknowledge that if people identify the state with "political," then what ensues is splitting off other aspects of social or public life from the political. For example, the idea that the consulting room has nothing to do with the political because politics has to do with concerns of the state is a distortion of both the consulting room and politics. For Aristotle and many other philosophers, this would be a mistake, because political life, while including the state, is broader, concerning spaces of speaking and acting together in daily life.

Any discussion of the state and the political necessarily implies the notion of citizen—a legal resident of a bounded geographical territory (e.g., sovereign nation) who participates in a shared national identity and who, ideally, has legitimate political agency.[17] This is our typical understanding of citizen, but that will be questioned in subsequent chapters given the realities of the Anthropocene Age, such as mass migrations and the exclusion of other species from the political. For now, I turn to political philosopher Sheldon Wolin (2016b), who argues that

> A political being is not to be defined as the citizen has been, as an abstract, disconnected bearer of rights, privileges, and immunities, but as a person whose existence is located in a particular place and draws its sustenance from circumscribed relationships: family, friends, church, neighborhood, workplace, community, town, city.
>
> (p.377)

He continues, "These relationships are the sources from which political being draws power—symbolic, material, and psychological—and that enables them to act together" (p.377). In this view, anyone who resides within the polis is a political being, which avoids the legal anchoring of political agency/identity with an exclusive view of citizenship.

Giorgio Agamben (2000), from a different angle, takes up the juxtaposition of citizenship with political agency. Agamben invites us

> to abandon decidedly, without reservation, the fundamental concepts through which we have so far represented the subjects of the political (Man, the Citizen

and its rights, but also the sovereign people, the worker, and so forth) and build our political philosophy anew starting from the one and only figure of the refugee.

(Agamben, 2000, p.15)

"The refugee must be considered for what he is," Agamben (1998) writes,

nothing less than a limit concept that radically calls into question the fundamental categories of the nation-state, from the birth-nation to the man-citizen link, and that thereby makes it possible to clear the way for a long-overdue renewal of categories.

(p.134)

Like Wolin, Agamben challenges us to locate political agency/identity with anyone who resides in our locales. This is especially important when we consider that there are and will be millions of climate refugees seeking shelter and aid.

This reimagining of the political and citizenship does not imply that in the Anthropocene Age we should adopt the idea that all human beings are citizens of the earth, which is a laudable goal, but flawed. While I will say more about this in the coming chapters, Western political philosophies have excluded not only Othered human beings from the political, but also other species and the earth. Western philosophies (and theologies), Claire Colebrook and Jason Maxwell (2016) note, starting with the Greeks, have maintained a split between the political and natural world (pp.1–17). In Western political philosophies, there is a "deep ontological rift...between animal and human" (Dickinson, 2015b, p.173). Agamben (2004) expands on this, writing:

It is as if determining the border between human and animal were not just one question among many discussed by philosophers and theologians, scientists and politicians, but rather a fundamental metaphysico-political operation in which alone something like 'man' can be decided upon and produced. If animal life and human life could be superimposed perfectly, then neither man nor animal—and, perhaps, not even the divine—would any longer be thinkable.

(p.92)

This ongoing drive in the West to differentiate between human beings and animals, which is a project of philosophy, theology, and some of the sciences, leads to "a radical and total discontinuity between human and nonhuman" (Kompridis, 2020, p.252) and, consequently, the privileging of human beings over all other species. Put another way, nature remains split off from the "political" and this disavowal and alienation has and continues to contribute to instrumental violence toward other species (othered human beings as well) and nature. I claim that these political philosophers argue for the inclusion of nature in the "political," because nature is the material foundation of the polis, of political agency. As noted above, the earth "is the first condition of our existence" (Eagleton, 2016, p.228) and, therefore, a biodiverse earth is foundational for the polis and its spaces of speaking and acting together.

Of course, the inclusion of other species under the heading of "political" does not mean that they are given the status of citizen or that they possess political agency. Infants do not have political agency—only potentially—but they are necessarily included in the polis. They are "citizens" without the capacity for speech that undergirds the space of speaking and acting together. So, while we can consider other species to lack political agency and the capacity to speak and act together with other human beings, they are necessarily integral to the polis. If, as E. O. Wilson (2005) predicts, half of known species will be extinct by the end of this century, then human beings will face either extinction or a vastly degraded earth and a degraded earth undermines the well-being of human beings and other species. To restate, a biodiverse earth is necessary for the flourishing of political life.

This brief discussion of the political will provide background for the claim that this book is methodologically different in that it develops a psychoanalytic political philosophy, while also using psychoanalysis to critique political realities. I will return to and elaborate further on many of these ideas in the coming chapters.

## Coming Chapters

Now I want to turn to a brief outline of the remaining chapters of this book. Chapter 1 sets the stage for developing a psychoanalytic political philosophy by relying, in part, on psychoanalytic developmental perspectives in conversation with political philosophers. The following chapters of Part I build on this psychoanalytic political perspective. The premise here is that developmental theories are anthropological in nature and, as such, are linked, in part, to the polis. Put another way, psychoanalytic anthropologies can be utilized, with some caveats, in constructing a political philosophy for the Anthropocene Age. In placing developmental perspectives in conversation with political theories, I depict the development of political selves and identify several environmentally destructive illusions that have accompanied the development of political selves in the West.

The question of dwelling is central to human life, in general, and political philosophy in particular. This takes on particular existential significance in the Anthropocene Age, when human beings and millions of other species are displaced and threatened with extinction—with being unhoused from our only habitat. While the question of dwelling is of concern to all human beings (and other species), in Chapter 2, I build on the previous chapter by addressing this question from a psychoanalytic philosophical perspective. In so doing, I am, by implication, entering into the wider interdisciplinary discussions about what it means to dwell politically and economically, given the realities of climate change. An overview of dwelling and its attributes are illuminated, which includes brief discussions regarding some of the perennial existential and political challenges associated with dwelling that are framed in psychoanalytic terms. That is, a psychoanalytic lens can illuminate some of the unconscious or unstated aspects of human dwelling. Once this foundation has been constructed, I introduce a psychoanalytic, developmental political perspective vis-à-vis dwelling, which builds on the psychoanalytic political philosophy of Chapter 1. This section of the chapter portrays what is necessary for actualizing one's experience of dwelling, the transition from pre-political to political dwelling and, by contrast, what contributes to experiences of being displaced or psychosocially unhoused. In the last section, I depict the Anthropocene Age as a crisis of dwelling for human beings and other species, identifying several key systemic apparatuses that privilege human dwelling, while undermining the dwelling of other species (and Othered human beings) and, paradoxically and tragically, undermining the present and future dwelling of human beings.

The notion of sovereignty is a central concept in Western political philosophies and questions of dwelling. Thus, it is incumbent that a psychoanalytic political philosophy concerned about our climate emergency take it up. As in the previous chapters, my method in Chapter 3 is to offer psychoanalytic considerations as to the unconscious features of sovereignty and how it shapes subjectivity. In addition, I return to a psychoanalytic developmental perspective, arguing that human dwelling rests on anarchic foundations. Given this, it is important to begin by providing some background on the notion of sovereignty and identify its attributes. Included in this section is an explanation and discussion of the relation between sovereignty and political violence, which is a foundational aspect of ecological degradation. Once this foundation is proffered, I move to psychoanalytic considerations.

Chapter 4 identifies three interrelated systemic, global obstacles—obstacles to stemming the tragic trajectory of climate disaster. These obstacles, which are human artifices, are capitalism, nationalism, and new imperialism. While some people recognize these as barriers to working toward reducing or stopping greenhouse gas emissions, most people view them as necessary or inevitable for human dwelling. Other individuals may even believe they are not only not obstacles, but provide answers to climate change (e.g., Wagner & Weitzman, 2015). A possible, perhaps likely, tragedy is that the majority of human beings will not become conscious of this dangerous trinity until these obstacles kill us and numerous other species. The chapter begins with brief depictions of each obstacle, while also arguing that these obstacles are interconnected. I explain how these macro systems have contributed to climate change and how they impede getting any traction on effective climate action. This is followed by critiquing these obstacles using psychoanalytic concepts, which is the typical psychoanalytic approach to addressing social, political, and economic issues. Here I want to explain, relying on psychoanalytic concepts, how it is that many people are tragically unaware that these obstacles threaten human existence and the existence of millions of other species. In the last section of the chapter, I shift to a different psychoanalytic approach. I identify some of the key premises and principles of a psychoanalytic political philosophy, which become part of a hermeneutical framework for further critiques of capitalism, nationalism, and imperialism vis-à-vis climate emergency. Also included in this section is a discussion on how a psychoanalytic political philosophy provides ideas regarding how to respond to these (and other) obstacles.

Another key feature of political philosophies is the issue and methods of political change. Chapter 5 addresses the issue of political violence as a method of change from a psychoanalytic-phenomenological perspective, arguing that political violence, while understandable in some situations, is not justified, whether we are simply addressing interhuman political violence or the political violence directed toward more-than-human species. If political violence is not justifiable as a method for political change, then what methods are available? Here I turn to features of the psychoanalytic political philosophy developed in the previous chapters to argue that care, as a political concept, is a justifiable method for political change because it respects the singularities of all human beings, other species, and the earth. Political forms of care include aggression (e.g., civic transgressions, civil disobedience, and nonviolent protests), but not aggression associated with political violence. Since the issue of political change raises questions of hope, vis-à-vis the systemic obstacles to climate action and mass extinctions discussed in the previous chapter, the last section of the chapter discusses the relation between caring political methods and hope. Here I claim that, given the psychological complexity of human beings, political caring actions are not contingent on hope and, therefore, not necessarily obstructed by eco-despair. Stated differently, I consider climate hope to be a problem, which is resolved by focusing in the present on political care—care for Othered human beings, other species, and the earth.

Part II of this book moves to discussions regarding what a psychoanalytic political philosophy means for psychoanalytic vocation, education, and therapy. Chapter 6 considers psychoanalysis in relation to the public-political sphere, arguing that analytically informed therapists can integrate the vocation of therapy and the vocation of politics. To bridge these disciplines depends, in part, on developing a psychoanalytic political philosophy, which has been the focus of Part I of this book. I begin by claiming that from the earliest origins of the polis there have been critics, gadflies, and prophets who identified faulty social-political premises, railed against injustices, and sought to awaken the populace and leaders from soporific self-deceptions. The well-being of the polis depended and depends on, in part, those who took up this political vocation, sometimes at their own peril. This sets the stage for arguing that psychoanalytic therapies and institutes are, whether or not they are aware of it, inextricably tied to social, political, and economic realities. This implies an ethical demand to engage political realities—using just means—especially in situations where injustices are occurring and when societies are facing existential crises, such as the climate emergency. From here, using the psychoanalytic political philosophy of the previous chapters, I indicate that this political vocation of analytically informed therapists can take many forms. Included in this discussion is my depiction of some political virtues and analytic skills that attend this vocation.

The final chapter addresses the current status of psychoanalytic education in the United States, which I argue has inherent flaws when one considers the social, political, and economic realities of climate change. This discussion includes suggestions for making adjustments—adjustments that embrace a psychoanalytic political vocation and attending political philosophy that requires alterations in the training and education of analytic therapists. I then move to address how we might reimagine, *in part*, psychoanalytic therapy—at least for some patients. These last two chapters are not meant to be definitive, but rather invitations to engage in conversations about reimagining psychoanalytic organizations (belonging), education/training, and therapy, given a psychoanalytic philosophical perspective that is attuned to the realities of the Anthropocene Age.

Therapists and institutes of learning have roles to play. We need to engage the political-economic spheres, to explore and develop political philosophies, so we can more clearly participate in critical and constructive conversations with interlocutors from other disciplines, especially about issues and struggles linked to climate emergency. This necessarily includes engaging in conversations with diverse others in how we are to respond together toward the present and future political, economic, and social challenges human beings face and the sufferings of other species. This book is a small step in this direction.

## Notes

1  The scientific data regarding global warming is mountainous and easily attainable, which is why I have decided not to take it up here. I am presuming that readers are already acquainted with some of the research, since it is part of the news nearly every day. However, for those who may be interested in some of the research, I suggest the following websites: Sixth Assessment Report (ipcc.ch), https://www.ipcc.ch/report/ar6/wg1/, accessed 28 September 2021; NASA: Climate Change and Global Warming, https://climate.nasa.gov/, accessed 28 September 2021.

2  See also https://climateandsecurity.files.wordpress.com/2019/07/implications-of-climate-change-for-us-army_army-war-college_2019.pdf (wordpress.com), accessed 28 September 2021; GlobalTrends_2040.pdf (dni.gov), https://www.dni.gov/files/ODNI/documents/assessments/GlobalTrends_2040.pdf, accessed 28 September 2021.

3  Actually, there is an occult feature of the idea of adaptation to climate change. The question of adaptation does not concern all human beings. Instead, it implicitly entails elites and is, therefore, classist (and racist) in application. Consider Elon Musk's (in the TV series Mars) comment that we must become an interplanetary species if we are to survive. He and a couple of other billionaires are working to capitalize on space travel and the possibility of living on other moons or planets. It is not much of a leap to know that poor people and poor people of color will not be joining that elite class of human beings who may make it off earth. Add to this those people who have the financial resources to protect themselves from the effects of climate change (at least for now), while others face the brunt of rising temperatures, devastating storms, fires, and floods.

4  It is helpful to make a distinction between the notion of "public" and the notion of the "political." "Public" is broader than the concept "political." For Arendt (1958), the public sphere comprises the space of appearances or the space of political freedom, which I have associated with the political, and the *common world*—"a shared and public world of human artifacts, institutions, and settings" (p.76). The public square, this common space, is where people can raise and discuss issues and concerns, as well as participate in other shared activities. This common world certainly includes political realities, but it is broader, including cultural and religious artifacts and activities. There are many examples of the public realm. The mall, dining at restaurants, attending sports venues, going to movies and plays, camping, hiking, visiting the zoo, are just some examples.

To be sure, each of these has political tendrils in the sense that laws and regulations are associated with the market (mall), safe food, care of animals, etc., but these are not in the foreground of public engagements. In short, the ideas of public and political are distinct, though they overlap.

5  Researchers and scholars from other disciplines are also concerned about material and mental suffering linked to climate change (Adger, Barnett, Brown, Marshall, & O'Brien, 2013; Gasper, Blohm, & Ruth, 2011; Johansen, 2020; Keller, 2018; McCarroll, 2020, 2022; McKibben, 2010; O'Brien, Eriksen, Sygna, & Naess. 2006; Paavola, 2017).

6  For Giorgi Agamben (2009), the term "apparatus" refers to "a set of practices, bodies of knowledge, measures and institutions that aim to manage, govern, control, and orient—in a way that purports to be useful—the behaviors, gestures, and thoughts of human beings" (p.13). Referencing Foucault, Agamben writes that "in a disciplinary society, apparatuses aim to create—through a series of practices, discourses, and bodies of knowledge—docile, yet free, bodies that assume their identity and their 'freedom' as subjects" (p.19).

7  Franz Fanon (2008/1952) argued that therapy aims (a) "to *'consciousnessize'* [the patient's] unconscious, to no longer be tempted by a hallucinatory lactification," and (b) "to enable [the patient] to choose an action with respect to the *real source of the conflict*, i.e., the social structure" (p.80; emphasis mine). I will say more about this perspective in the last chapter.

8  There are all kinds of philosophical traditions (Europe, Mideast, Africa, Asia). Since my education and training has been in the United States, I am more informed by Western political philosophers. My point here is that I am not suggesting that Western political philosophies are better able to answer questions of dwelling, belonging, or political change. I am simply relying on the tradition with which I am most familiar.

9  Alfred Tauber (2010) argues that "Freud adopted…a philosophy that supported both his science and his therapy. For his psychology, he employed a form of naturalism (oriented by evolutionary theories) constructed around a dynamic psychic will; for his therapy, he accepted mind-body duality, which utilized a conception of reason independent of psychic forces" (pp.3–4). One aim that Tauber has is to shift away from Freud's epistemology and to psychoanalysis as a moral philosophy (p.4). Whether Tauber is correct in his formulations, he, like Peter Gay (1988), notes the philosophical underpinnings of Freud's psychoanalytic theories, such as Hobbes, Brentano, and Bentham (pleasure/pain). Psychoanalyst Donna Orange (2010) similarly appreciates, advocates, and makes use of philosophers in deepening psychoanalytic anthropologies. In this book, a psychoanalytic political philosophy is developed, which takes into account psychosocial development, therapy, and political realities.

10  Scientists Paul Crutzen and Eugene Stoermer (2000) coined the term "Anthropocene Age" to indicate that we are now out of the Holocene Age. This term refers to both the age of human beings and, for some (Klein, 2014; Kolbert, 2014), the age of a sixth extinction event—an event caused by human beings. There is considerable debate about this idea and when the putative date this era started. As Joni Adamson (2017) points out, this concept fails to account for the unequal accountability for climate change (p.160). See also Bilgrami (2020), Northcott (2017), and Nichols and Gogineni (2020). I should also mention that Jason Moore (2016) prefers the term "Capitalocene Era" because, he argues, capitalism is the primary culprit in global warming. While there is much to be said for this term, I will use the more common Anthropocene Era, in part because it is more inclusive of the many human factors causing climate change and species extinctions. I also recognize that Western imperialistic nations are largely accountable for both climate change and obstacles to climate action.

11  See also, R. D. Hinshelwood (2020), Dominiek Hoens (2020), and Christopher Turner (2020) for discussions on the political and Klein, Lacan, and Reich.

12 Readers may be aware of the work of Brazilian Paulo Freire (2018, 2021), who emphasized the importance of raising consciousness as a necessary step in moving toward the liberation of oppressed peoples. While not a psychoanalyst, Freire, like Frantz Fanon, believed that oppressed people (and their oppressors) are captive to what Layton calls the normative unconscious. For Freire, education in the public-political realm entails raising what is unconscious to consciousness.

13 President Clinton apologizes for 1893 overthrow of Hawaiian monarchy – Timeline – Native Voices (nih.gov), https://www.nlm.nih.gov/nativevoices/timeline/578.html, accessed 15 October 2021.

14 Germany Sets Aside an Additional $767 Million for Holocaust Survivors, Officials Say – The New York Times (nytimes.com), https://www.nytimes.com/2021/10/06/world/europe/holocaust-settlement-germany.html, accessed 15 October 2021.

15 I have relied on several scholars in arriving at this definition, namely, Maurice Hamington (2004), Daniel Engster (2007), and Joan Tronto (1993).

16 Philosopher Quentin Skinner (2009) provides an in-depth analysis of the meanings associated with the modern state, such as the difference between the notions of government and state. To delve into this, however, would take me far afield.

17 The notion of "nation" is relatively new in history, which some historians date back to 1648 and the Treaty of Westphalia. While "nation" is new, what can be seen throughout history is the idea of sovereignty, which includes geographical boundaries and attending identity associated with geography. In both cases, identity and citizenship are exclusive. I will take up the issue of sovereignty in Chapter 3.

# Part I

# Chapter 1

# Developing a Psychoanalytic Political Philosophy

## The Emergence of Political Selves and Environmentally Destructive Illusions

Frank Sulloway (1992) notes that in the late 19th century, it was commonly believed among evolutionary theorists that ontogeny recapitulates phylogeny, which means "the development from fetus to adulthood (ontogeny) provides a brief recapitulation of the entire history of the race (phylogeny)" (p.259). This view was adopted by Freud in a number of contexts, not the least of which is his depiction of the Oedipus complex in human development. For instance, Freud (1918) accepted the view of "phylogenetically inherited schemata" of which the Oedipus complex is "the best-known member of the class" (p.119). As noted in the Introduction, this view actually, under the guise of the authority of science, essentializes and universalizes a political patriarchal myth. Freud's method of using political myths[1] to explain human development is correct in that hegemonic political apparatuses will certainly shape human development. So, we can expect that a patriarchal political society might give rise to Oedipal complexes, but this pertains only to that particular society and not the history of humankind as seen in psychosocial development. But what if Freud had approached psychosocial development by observing parent-child interactions without relying on this belief and story of patriarchal ontogeny recapitulating phylogeny? Since parental care is shaped by a culture's dominant stories, which Erik Erikson (1952) noted among the Sioux and Yurok peoples, wouldn't observing infant-parent interactions simply end up recapitulating the themes of the group's dominant political myths? While I certainly hold to the idea that the political *shapes* parental care, dominant political realities do not determine care. There is always an excess when it comes to good-enough parental care of children—an excess that cannot be attributed to particular political, semantic visions of human belonging that parents consciously and unconsciously live out. If one accepts this premise, then it becomes possible to approach, from a psychoanalytic perspective, infant-parent interactions with an eye toward identifying political principles that form, in part, a basis of a political philosophy. Indeed, this method is not uncommon for political philosophers (e.g., Aristotle, Thomas Hobbes, John Locke, Alasdair MacIntyre,[2] John Macmurray, Maurice Merleau-Ponty, and Nel Noddings) who turn to childhood development to illustrate their points or to address philosophical questions and distinctions. It is also notable that political philosopher Martha Nussbaum (2019) argues that political philosophers and others engaged in thinking

DOI: 10.4324/9781003258827-3

about politics "need…to undertake a project the Stoics not only ignored, but also would likely have repudiated: the systematic study of infant attachments, as they unfold in constant interaction with cultural norms and perceptions. A kind of anthropological psychoanalysis" (pp.212–213). Nussbaum continues, arguing that "If we don't do this, our high-minded proposals will very likely prove fruitless, inasmuch as they will not be addressed to real people as they are" (p.213).

In this chapter, I set out to develop a psychoanalytic political philosophy by relying, in part, on psychoanalytic developmental perspectives and research, which the following chapters of Part I build on. The premise here is that developmental theories are also anthropological in nature and, as such, can be utilized, with some caveats, in constructing a political philosophy for the Anthropocene Age. This said, I will also avail myself of various political philosophers to deepen and expand upon a psychoanalytic political philosophy. That is, I intend to place developmental perspectives in conversation with political theories, which will help depict the development of political selves, as well as help understand several environmentally destructive illusions that have accompanied the development of political selves in the West. I begin by discussing the pre-political stage of psychosocial development, which is followed by depicting the transition from pre-political to political selves. Within this discussion, I identify central political principles, which are used in this and subsequent chapters to address the political, economic, and cultural aspects of climate emergency. The last section aims to illustrate the utility of this approach to political philosophy by identifying environmentally destructive political illusions that attend Western constructions of subjectivity.

Before beginning, I offer a clarification and a couple of caveats. Any political theory or, for that matter, psychosocial developmental theory runs into the issue of particularity versus universality. Since the rise of postcolonial theories, an understandable skepticism has arisen about discourse that uses universal principles or notions of a generalized Other, especially when this has served to eclipse the particularities of a culture and the needs and experiences of an oppressed group (McLaren, 2015). Yet, in my view, we should not abandon discourse that involves universal ideas, principles, responsibilities, rights, etc., not only because human beings, while diverse in language and culture, are alike in many ways, but also because we are all facing global challenges [though not equally] due to climate change—challenges that give rise to injustice, non-justice, carelessness, and non-care. Toward this end, I agree with Seyla Benhabib (1992), who argues for an interactive universalism that

> acknowledges the plurality of modes of being human, and differences among humans, without endorsing all the pluralities and differences as morally or politically valid…. Interactive universalism regards difference as a starting point for reflection and action. In this sense, 'universality' is a regulative ideal that does not deny embodied and embedded identity, but aims at developing moral attitudes and encouraging political transformation that can yield a point of view acceptable to all.
>
> (p.153)

She is careful to note that interactive universalism "is not the ideal of consensus of fictitiously defined selves, but a concrete *process* in politics and morals of the struggle of concrete, embodied selves" (p.153). I add to this Terry Eagleton's (1996) erudite and often humorous critique of postmodernism and its focus on particularity and rejection of universality. Eagleton argues that the idea of the universal does not, in and of itself, exclude the particular. So, in this chapter and those that follow, I make universal generalizations, which are aimed at identifying the contours of a political philosophy informed by psychoanalytic theories of development. Like Benhabib and Eagleton, my hope is to engage diverse others in their given particularities with the aim of moving toward a shared cosmovision that will promote care for all human beings, other species, and the earth.[3] Connected to this view of universalism is my admission, offered in this chapter and the book itself, that the psychoanalytic political philosophy constructed is not definitive, but rather heuristic.

With this caveat and clarification, let me add another. Readers may wonder why I begin with infancy when constructing a political philosophy. My first response is that while infants are subjects of and subject to the political, the very existence and survival of the polis depend on care of children (and let me add, care of a biodiverse earth). Political societies that undermine care of children undermine the well-being of the polis and, worse, the very existence of the polis. Another reason for beginning with infancy is the recognition—I think it is safe to say universal recognition—that infants are vulnerable and nearly absolutely dependent on the care of others for survival and flourishing. Indeed, the very existence of infants reveals the ethical or categorical demand to care. Yet, when we become adults, we often ignore or tacitly disavow our vulnerability and dependency, as well as the ethical demand to care.[4] Yes, adults may possess many capacities that enable them to be less dependent and less vulnerable, but the existential realities of illness and death remain, as does the demand to care. And in terms of the Anthropocene Age, the possible, if not likely, extinction of human beings should awaken us to our vulnerability and dependence on other human beings, other species, and the earth. In terms of a political philosophy, then, we should retain vulnerability and dependency as central to any anthropology or political philosophy (Butler, 2004), for the very existence of polis depends on care for all human beings, other species, and the earth. A third and related reason is that infants, like other species, cannot speak. In terms of the polis, good-enough parents and other adults listen to infants' communications and speak for infants in the polis, whether that refers to obtaining resources to meet their needs or to correcting injustices. A political philosophy for the Anthropocene Age will necessarily be concerned about listening to and speaking for those human beings and other species who are denied or incapable of speech. Fourth, parental caring recognition is the ground by which children obtain a sense of their own significance (over time) over and against the reality of vulnerability vis-à-vis existential insignificance and impermanence. All of this connects human beings to other species and their vulnerabilities. It seems to me, then, that psychoanalytic developmental perspectives entail accepting the reality of existential vulnerability all the while communicating to children their significance by way of innumerable acts of caring recognition, including repairs of relational disruptions.[5]

## Psychosocial Development and the Emergence of Political Selves

When Winnicott (1975) remarks that there is no such thing as an infant, he, like intersubjectivists who followed him, is claiming that infants can only be understood psychoanalytically or otherwise within the context of caring parents and the larger community/society. Given this, I begin by depicting the various aspects of good-enough parents, since infants are dependent and vulnerable, having been thrown into a particular family and polis. At the same time, I will be framing this in light of the political.

I think it is fair to say that psychoanalytic infant-parent researchers and theorists acknowledge that good-enough parents in any culture attune to their infants' assertions. Good-enough attunement is founded on parents' personal recognition of their infants. By personal recognition, I mean recognizing a child's uniqueness (singularity), inherent value, inviolableness (physical, psychological integrity), and responsiveness (nascent agency) (Macmurray, 1991).[6] Naturally, parents' recognitions include particular culturally inflected representations of their infants, which shape parents' perceptions and attuning actions. However, personal recognition is not determined by parents' particular representations and, therefore, personal recognition always exceeds these.

Another way to understand this excess is through feminist psychoanalyst Jessica Benjamin's (1995) use of Hegel's philosophy of recognition. Benjamin contends that personal recognition entails the dialectic of likeness in difference and difference in likeness. If this dialectical tension is lost toward one pole or the other, then there is an eclipse of personal recognition, resulting in the absence of excess. The child, in other words, is coerced to adopt and be determined by the parent's representation. When this excess or dialectical tension is present, parental personal recognition and attunement create spaces for infants to appear, to assert themselves such that extant representations no longer apply or are set aside so that infants appear in their singularities. So, we can say that parents' personalizing attunements, which are foundational to care (including repair, see below), foster a relational space for their children to assert their needs and desires, while, at the same time, internalize the representations/actions of their parents (Stern, 1985: Representations of Interactions that have been Generalized—RIGs).

Before continuing with this foundation of good-enough parental care, I want to connect this briefly with political philosophy. The importance of Emmanuel Kant to Western political philosophy is immense. His categorical imperative can be seen as the ground of a liberal political ethos in the West and clearly Kant's view seems to support the notion of personal recognition mentioned above, which neo-Kantian philosopher John Macmurray (1991) builds on and Hannah Arendt (2018, p.183) argues is necessary for the political space of speaking and acting together—the space of appearances. However, as philosopher Charles Mills (2017) notes, "Kant is also seen as one of the central figures in the birth of modern 'scientific' racism" (p.95),[7] which becomes painfully and disturbingly clear in Kant's lectures (pp.95–105). This means that, for Kant, "person" and personal recognition fall under the category of European males. Those Others who are not recognized as full persons are determined by negative representations, which accompanies a collapse of the dialectical tension between likeness and difference and difference in likeness and, correspondingly, accompanies a collapse of the relational space for Others to appear in and assert their singularities. There is, in other words, no excess in this type of exclusive "personal" recognition, which we note in other forms of political marginalization and oppression, namely, sexism, racism, classism, ageism, etc. In this, we see an inherent flaw and contradiction in Kant's political philosophy. The categorical imperative is meant to be universal, but if personal recognition is tacitly assigned to white European males, then the categorical imperative is particular, exclusive, and not universal. Put differently, when personal recognition is tied to white supremacist beliefs in white uniqueness, value, and inviolability, there is a collapse of the dialectical tension of likeness in difference and difference in likeness and a denial of excess, which means identity and agency are strictly determined. The white supremacist who believes he is superior, for instance, is dependent on this illusion of superiority which determines who he is in the present, past, and future, leading to a foreclosure of his potentiality, as well as the potentialities of so-called inferior persons. Being a person means being able to actualize one's potentiality without exhausting it, and depending on the illusion of superiority (and inferiority of the Other) is a disavowal of potentiality—more on this below.

This brief detour can bring out other features of parental personal recognition and treatment of their children. In reading psychoanalytic parent-infant research and theories, I never recall coming across the notion of parental attunement connected with parents' belief in the inferiority of their children or belief in parental superiority. This does not mean these beliefs are not unconsciously present, shaping parent-child interactions (Miller, 1998). For instance, Freud's notion of penis envy pertains, in my view, to parental recognitions connected to and supported by political apparatuses of patriarchy, which no doubt shape perceptions and treatment of female children as inferior to males. Nevertheless, when reading the works of Winnicott (1971), Stern (1985), Sroufe (1995), Schore (2003), Beebe and Lachmann (2002), and others, I have a sense that they would agree that beliefs in inferiority and superiority are not part of *good-enough* parental recognition and treatment of their children. To hold these beliefs, consciously or unconsciously, distorts and diminishes both recognition and care.[8]

Sadly, however, most of us are aware of how social, political, and economic apparatuses associated with racism, sexism, and classism distort personal recognition and can shape marginalized persons' care of their children, even as these good-enough parents seek to protect their children from social-political humiliation by communicating to their children that they are unique and valued. For instance,

Martin Luther King's (1998, p.3) parents (and religious community) worked to affirm his sense of "somebodiness" when young Martin discovered his white play-mate would no longer be allowed to play with him or when King experienced pub-lic humiliation. Similarly, activist Ruby Sales depicts how important her parents' reliable personal recognition and treatment of her was while growing up in a racist society. She writes:

> I grew up in the heart of Southern apartheid. And I'm not saying that I didn't realize that it existed, but our parents were spiritual geniuses who created a world and a language where the notion that I was inadequate or inferior or less-than never touched my consciousness. I grew up believing that I was a first-class human being and a first-class person, and our parents were spiritual geniuses who were able to shape a counterculture of black folk religion that raised us from disposability to being essential players in society.[9]

Similarly, Ta-Nehisi Coates (2015), recalling the racism of his youth and its impact on his family, writes, "It was a loving house even as it was besieged by its country, but it *was* hard" (p.126).

The point I want to stress here is that good-enough parental care entails a personal recognition of their children that is devoid of or sets aside beliefs in superiority and inferiority—beliefs that are produced and maintained by political, economic, and cultural apparatuses. When these beliefs are present, care is diminished and distorted, undermining the space for children to assert their needs and desires and experience a preverbal sense of singularity. Another point to stress is that parents' care for their children, even in situations of oppression and marginalization, is never completely controlled or determined by social, political, and economic apparatuses. There is a necessary excess to good-enough parental personal recognition and care, which is needed, in part, for children to appear, to assert their desires and needs.

Let me add to this. Philosopher John Macmurray (1991) writes that the infant "is, in fact, 'adapted', so to speak paradoxically, to being unadapted, 'adapted' to complete dependence…. He can only live through other people" (pp.48, 51). In infants' unadapted, dependent-vulnerable state, they possess an impulse or moti-vation to communicate—"the impulse to communicate is [their] sole adaptation to the world" (p.60). Of course, infants' side of the relational communication is by definition without speech ("infant" means without speech), but good-enough parents "dialogue" with their infants. Dialogue is in quotes because it is not really a dialogue between parents and infants, though both parties are communicating. It is more apt to call this a communicative space, wherein parents have proto conver-sations with their infants (Bonovitz & Harlem, 2018; Levin & Trevarthen, 2000; Trevarthen, 1993), which point to a *potential* for semantic dialogue that is present in their communicative interactions. This communicative space or space of speak-ing and acting together is pre-political in that infants, while possessing a nascent agency, lack the political agency associated with the polis' space of speaking and acting together, though political, agency is potential.

Erik Erikson (1982) also considers the first stage of psychosocial development in terms of a "dialogue" between parent and infant, wherein the parents' "almost unrestricted attentiveness and generosity" give rise to the child's basic trust (p.35). On the parents' side of the dialogue, unrestricted attentiveness and generosity represent consistent personal attunement to infants' assertions and this attunement includes repairs or "therapeutic adaptations" (Winnicott, 1990, p.127) to inevitable mismatches between parents and infants (see Safron & Muran, 1996, 2000; Tronick & Cohn, 1989). These mismatches can give rise to anxiety and mistrust, but when repaired, trust and communicative space of appearances are restored and deepened. It should be stressed that repair is a mutual effort in that infants signal distress—suggesting a nascent agency—and good-enough parents respond appropriately. A notable feature of this perspective, which is central to the discussion below, is that parents' reliable *care precedes and is foundational to infants' experiences of trust, which are necessary for their nascent agency in speaking and acting together*.

There is another feature of this communicative space of speaking and acting together. This dialogue or space of speaking and acting together between parents and infants is an early form of cooperation and rapport, which can be further understood in terms of a pre-political power. Philosopher Hannah Arendt (1958) differentiates between power and force vis-à-vis the political realm. While I will say more about power (versus force) in subsequent chapters, in general, power is, for Arendt, defined as people speaking and cooperating together, while force is a synonym for violence, which is characterized by its instrumental epistemology and relations (Arendt, 1970, pp.44–46). "Power and violence," she writes,

> are opposites; where one rules absolutely, the other is absent…This implies that it is not correct to think of the opposite of violence as nonviolence; to speak of nonviolent power is actually redundant. Violence can destroy power; it is utterly incapable of creating it.
>
> (p.56)

Power emerges from people speaking and acting together, which presupposes mutual-personal recognition and civic care/trust. This early form of power or pre-political power is the cooperative dialogue and rapport between good-enough parents and their infants.[10]

Allow me to focus more closely on infants. I mentioned above that infants have a potential for dialogue, suggesting that this potentiality becomes actual as a result of good-enough care and the emergence of the capacity for symbolization. Since this is a key point that I will return to in coming chapters, it is necessary to say a bit more. Philosopher Giorgio Agamben (1999) relies on, yet alters, Aristotle's depiction of potentiality and actuality vis-à-vis the polis. From Agamben's perspective, as human beings "of pure potentiality," we are not "reducible to biology, identity, or vocation" (Whyte, 2013, p.110). Sergei Prozorov (2014), in commenting on Agamben's view of potentiality, states, "there is an excess of living being that can never be subsumed under them" (e.g., apparatuses or disciplinary regimes and their representations) (p.24). As Adam Kotsko (2020) notes, for Agamben, "the human experience of potentiality (and impotentiality) is at the root of both politics and ethics" (p.60). What does this have to do with parents and children? Parents' personal caring attunements necessarily comprise particular representations vis-à-vis their children, but children, being wildly potential, are not reducible to these representations. As indicated above, this caring recognition creates a space for children to appear and experience embodied singularity—pre-representationally organized (Colman, 2022, p.128).[11] This embodied singularity emerges in relation to caring parents and is, in part, connected to semiotic experiences of rapport. Unfortunately, when parents' recognition of their children is determined by their representations of them, their children's potentiality is disavowed, which diminishes the space of speaking and acting together and undermines rapport. Children, then, are coerced to actualize their potentiality in relation to determinative representations, which, from a Winnicottian perspective, leads to the construction of false selves and senses of alienation. False selves, in other words, can be understood to disavow or deny their potentiality, because to actualize their potentiality is too risky.

There is another important point that Agamben highlights regarding potentiality. Agamben notes that the process of moving from potentiality to actuality means persons "must suffer an alteration," becoming other than or more than they were (Agamben, 1999, p.179). While he does not indicate what this process is, I suggest that a parent's idiom or logic of care (personalizing attunements and repair) establishes a process and space for children to surrender to and accept their vulnerability and dependency in order to receive care. This surrender is linked to preverbal experiences of trust, which makes possible a movement from potentiality to actuality— an actuality that does not exhaust a child's potentiality. Put differently, parents' personal recognition and care facilitate a space for infants to risk appearing, to risk actualizing their potentiality. This is reminiscent of a conference speaker who recalled the words of Dr. George Washington Carver: "If you love it enough, anything will talk to you." Love/care makes possible actualizing one's potentiality, and the "it" refers to children and other species.[12]

To surrender to parents' personalizing attunements implies agency and not mere passivity. Winnicott (1975), contra Freud, believed that infants possess a nascent ego/agency prior to birth. He writes, "(A)ctual birth can easily be felt by the infant, in the normal case, to be a successful outcome of personal effort owing to the more or less accurate timing" (p.186).[13] Whether prior to or after birth, nascent, pre-political agency is implicit in children's undergoing an alteration or moving from potentiality to actuality, which, I stress, does not exhaust children's (or adults') potentiality. The infant, then, is not passive with regard to receiving care, though the infant is vulnerable and mostly dependent.

So far, we see that the communicative space or space of speaking and acting together depends on parents' good-enough personal recognition attunements to infants' assertions, which provides necessary trust for infants to be vulnerable and dependent in actualizing their potentiality, but not exhausting it. This is quite abstract, so let me say more about infants' experiences that are emerging. Winnicott

(1971) distinguished between true and false selves. If all goes well enough, children develop a true self, while those who suffer parental impingement and deprivation survive by constructing a false self. Winnicott associates spontaneity and creativity with true selves, which to my mind includes Agamben's notion that potentiality is not exhausted by actuality. False selves, as noted above, as a result of parental failures in personal attunements, experience distrust and are overly anxious about vulnerability and dependency. This means they avoid the risk of appearing, of act-ing on their potentiality. We can take this further and wonder what organizations of experiences are associated with the notions of true and false selves. Early "true" selves, I contend, comprise embodied-relational, pre-representational, or pre-symbolic experiences and organizations of singularity and rapport that result from risking and then actualizing their potentiality. Embodied singularity can be further understood as self-esteem, self-confidence, and self-respect—pre-representational organizations of experiences of being significant.[14] These senses of self are integral to a nascent agency that is needed to engage in communicative spaces with parents and to actualize potentiality. By contrast, "false" selves are understood as lacking esteem, respect, and confidence, which accompanies diminished agency and, like-wise, actualization of potentiality.

There is another key factor regarding potentiality and agency in psychosocial development, namely, impotentiality. Agamben (1999) writes:

> *Other living beings are capable only of their specific potentiality; they can only do this or that. But human beings are the animals who are capable of their own impotentiality. The greatness of human potentiality is measured by the abyss of human impotentiality.* Here it is possible to see how the root of freedom is to be found in the abyss of potentiality. To be free is not simply to have the power to do this or that thing, nor is it simply to have the power to refuse to do this or that thing. To be free is…*to be capable of one's own impotentiality.*
>
> (pp.182–183)

To illustrate this complex discussion, Agamben turns to Herman Melville's *Bartleby, The Scrivener*. When Bartleby is told by his boss to do something, Bartleby replies, "I prefer not to." For Agamben, impotentiality is key with regard to agency, human freedom, and ungovernable selves (LaMothe, 2021b), which I will say more about in Chapter 3. For now, in terms of psychosocial development and parental care, it is important to say that Winnicott (1965) held a similar idea when he claimed that children had a "right not to communicate" (p.179)—to prefer not to communicate. I would suggest, then, that parental care creates spaces for children to actualize their capacity to prefer not to, which I contend is part of their experience of sin-gularity/significance, belonging, and rapport, as well as their developing agency. Indeed, impotentiality will become increasingly important and more noticeable as children make use of more complex cultural symbol systems.

Now I want to turn to the transition from these preverbal agency and semiotic organizations of embodied-relational trust and rapport, and senses of self-esteem, self-respect, and self-confidence to children's entry into and use of the symbol systems of the cultures in which they are thrown. An emended version of Winnicott's notion of transitional objects (TOs) will be helpful here. This said, let me stress at the outset that this transition is not yet a transition to public-political spaces of speaking and acting together, which will be discussed below. Winnicott (1971) famously coined the term "transitional objects/phenomena" to refer to the infant's movement from near-absolute dependency to interdependency. The first TO[15] (e.g., blanket), during times of anxiety and separation from the parent, represents parent-child interactions that are projected onto the object, enabling "him (the child) to hold himself, to carry along with himself a part of his intimate and pleasing sensory experience; to *keep all parts of himself together* as it were" (Brody, 1980, pp.580–581; emphasis added). This object is under the child's "omnipotent control"—the experience of and belief (illusion) in omnipotence. The experience of and belief in omnipotence, which is an early feature of nascent agency, is facilitated by the parent's care—maternal/paternal preoccupation—and in time, as the child develops and actualizes greater agency, there is a gradual, non-traumatic disillusionment vis-à-vis the belief in omnipotence.[16] This said, it is important to point out that this first object is not necessarily a cultural object. It can be any soft object, like a blanket, that, for the infant, represents experiences of parent-infant "dialogues," rapport, as well as preverbal embodied experiences of singularity—self-esteem, self-confidence, and self-respect.

This first or primary TO (PTO) provides a resting place and soothes infants during periods of anxiety or separation from the caring parent (Winnicott, 1971, pp.2–4). Winnicott also claims that, while infants possess the illusion of omnipotent control, the PTO is the first not-me object—an object that is independent of the infant. "[I]t must seem to the infant," Winnicott writes, "to give warmth, or to move, or to have texture, or to do something that seems to show it has vitality or reality of its own" (p.5). For Winnicott, the transition is primarily concerned with infants' work of establishing distinctions between inner reality and external reality. Here, we see the seed for the dialectical tension between likeness in difference and difference in likeness vis-à-vis important objects, though naturally preverbal infants, while potential, are completely incapable of recognizing their parents as persons or the TO as inherently distinct from the self.

I add that this initial transition includes exercising nascent agency to actualize potentiality and impotentiality in relation to an object that is not the parent—an object under the infant's omnipotent control. Here is a space, in other words, where an infant can undergo an alteration while retaining and affirming pre-representational, embodied, and relational experiences of singularity. The PTO, in other words, represents a space of "speaking" and acting together (RIGs—representations of interactions generalized, Stern, 1985), wherein infants exercise nascent agency and experience rapport with an object that is independent of the parent.

The secondary TO (STO) is of particular importance with regard to moving from pre-political spaces to public-political spaces of speaking and acting together.[17]

Younger children, who are developing their capacity for symbolization, select and use objects from the cultural-symbolic field that serve as STOs. A child, for instance, plays with a doll or stuffed toy. Playing includes dialogue—speaking and acting together—albeit in children's imaginations and under their omnipotent control. Like the first TO, this STO represents parent-child caring (including repair) interactions, which includes the child's recognition of the object as an independent self that is, in the child's imagination, capable of engaging in varied forms of dialogue (e.g., play, conflict, and repair).

A question might emerge regarding what other experiences in particular accompany "forms of dialogue." Above I indicated that parents' idioms of care entail forms of attunement or forms of personal recognition and treatment of their children. With regard to the STO, children *begin* to actualize their capacity for personal recognition[18] by recognizing that the object is independent, unique, and valued. Since the STO has an imaginary vitality of its own, we might imagine that children engage the STO as if possessing its own agency, which includes a rudimentary recognition and treatment of the STO as singular. This means that the STO consolidates and confirms children's sense of their singularity (self-esteem, self-confidence, and self-respect) and experiences of rapport. Sara Beardsworth (2019) calls this an affective, representational experience of one's dignity and significance (p.242), but also the dignity of the Other (STO).[19] I add here that these "dialogues" include actualizing children's (and STOs) potentiality, as well as exercising impotentiality. When children forget or set aside the STO, they are preferring not to communicate, which is exercising their capacity for impotentiality.

Another question may arise as to why Winnicott contends that children possess a belief in and experience of omnipotence vis-à-vis TOs/phenomena. Children are vulnerable and dependent on parents for care, protection, etc. To undergo change, to move from potentiality to actuality, children, from my perspective, rely on a belief in omnipotence to handle emotions associated with vulnerability and dependency, as well as existential insignificance and impermanence. In terms of the STO, children risk dialogue with the STO, which includes risking surrendering to the imagined ministrations and recognitions of the STO—under children's omnipotent control. When there are imaginary failures, children's dialogue with STOs can include repairs—repairs that are linked to their experiences of repair with parents. All of this indicates that relational care and trust vis-à-vis the STO are under a child's omnipotent control. That is, a child can risk surrendering—being vulnerable—to the cherished STO because of trust and the belief that the STO cares for the child. In addition, the STO provides a space for children to make use of and obtain confidence in using cultural symbol systems to organize experience.

Before moving to children's transition to public-political spaces and the emergence of political selves, I want to summarize key points and indicate the political principles that can be gleaned from this analytic view of development, as well as highlight two key contributions psychoanalytic developmental perspectives offer political philosophy. First of all, care is constitutive to parents-infants' speaking and acting together. This care is founded in parents' personal recognition that founds relational trust and retains the dialectical tension between likeness in difference and difference in likeness. This creates a space for children to use their nascent agency to appear and experience (actualize, but not exhaust their potentiality) their singularity (pre-representational embodied senses of esteem, confidence, and respect) and rapport. It was also mentioned that parental care and personal recognition are shaped by their cultural narratives and rituals, though care is not completely determined by the culture's symbol systems. When it comes to good-enough parental care, there is always an excess. All of this gives rise to trust that enables infants to surrender to care (nascent agency), to move from potentiality to actuality without exhausting their potentiality. While all of this is pre-political, we can begin to derive foundational principles for a psychoanalytic political philosophy, namely, the necessity of care, trust, relational repair, and mutual-personal recognition for viable spaces of speaking and acting together—spaces that foster agency, relational rapport, and the exercise of the capacities for actualizing potentiality and impotentiality/inoperativity.

Let me rush to state that these principles are not exclusive to a psychoanalytic political philosophy. Indeed, these principles are represented within the Western political philosophical tradition. For instance, as noted in the Introduction, in the last 40 years, numerous political theorists (Bubeck, 1995; Engster, 2007; Engster & Hamington, 2015; Gilligan, 1982; Hamington, 2004; Held, 1995, 2006; Koggel & Orme, 2015; Løgstrup, 1997; Noddings, 1984; Oliner & Oliner, 1995; Robinson, 1999, 2011; Sevenhuijsen, 1998; Tronto, 1993, 2013) have argued that personal recognition and care are foundational to a well-functioning polis. Moreover, a critical hermeneutic toward societal structures is seen as a necessary act of care aimed at justice and the possibility of societal transformation (Conradi, 2015). Recall Shawn Fraisart's (2021) analysis of Plato, Rousseau, and Godwin, wherein he argues that care has been a key concept in Western political philosophies. His view is contested, but it is nevertheless a needed perspective in philosophical renderings of the political. In terms of the importance of mutual-personal recognition, Hannah Arendt (2018) quotes John Adams regarding recognition in the polis:

> Whenever men, women, or children are to be found, whether they be old or young, rich or poor, high or low...ignorant or learned, every individual is seen to be strongly actualized by a desire to be seen, heard, and talked of, approved and respected by people about him and with his knowledge.
>
> (p.375)

Neo-Hegelian political philosopher, Axel Honneth (1995, 2021), echoes this view, as does neo-Kantian political philosopher John Macmurray (1991). In terms of the importance of reparative actions, philosopher Hannah Arendt believes that reparative actions are crucial for a viable polis. She (2018) argues, for instance, that "we have no possibility ever to undo what we have done" (p.306), though the "possible redemption from the predicament of irreversibility is the faculty of forgiving" (p.306). In another work, Arendt (2005), in referring to the polis, writes, "It is rather that forgiving attempts the seemingly impossible, to undo what has been done, and that it succeeds in making a new beginning where beginnings seemed to have become no longer possible" (p.58). The point I want to emphasize is that a psychoanalytic developmental view of care and personal recognition is not divorced from political philosophies and that it can be used to engage in philosophical discourses, especially when we consider the realities of climate change.

Given this, one may wonder what a developmental psychoanalytic perspective contributes to political philosophies. There are three interrelated answers. First, the pre-political features discussed above represent organizations of experience that are semiotic or pre-representational. For psychoanalysts, these semiotic organizations are mostly, but not entirely, enfolded into later symbolic organizations of experience. Christopher Bollas (1987), for example, uses a term "unthought knowns" to refer to adult experiences of rapport that are rooted in early developmental experiences. From a negative analytic perspective, we could turn to Melanie Klein (1949) or Thomas Ogden (1986) to point to unconscious organizations of experience connected to adults' schizoid or paranoid styles of relating, which, in terms of politics, is best noted in Richard Hofstadter's (1963) classic book, *The Paranoid Style of American Politics*. In terms of the political, this means that early organizations of experience are present in our political discourses, though we are unlikely to be aware of this. Second and relatedly, psychoanalytic theories challenge much of Western political philosophy's idolizing of and preoccupation with reason (and negatively tainted views of emotions). For psychoanalysts, the capacity for reason is never divorced from unconscious affective processes (McAfee, 2008; Mitchell, 2000), which indicates that reasoned actions are overdetermined and shaped by unconscious processes. Terms like historical unconscious (Zeddies, 2002; or Arendt's de-historicization) or normative unconscious (Layton, 2020) can help explain the persistence of epistemic apparatuses that produce varied forms of oppression and marginalization that are unquestioned and unquestionable, all the while distorting recognition, eschewing civic care, fostering alienation, and impeding actualization of embodied political agency—undermining the development of an ungovernable self (a self exercising impotentiality).[20] This perspective becomes particularly relevant when psychoanalysts concerned about climate change seek to explicate climate-denial, eco-anxiety, eco-disavowal, etc. (Weintrobe, 2013, 2021; Westcott, 2019), as well as cultural-political resistance to the inclusion of other-than-human species and the earth in our political conversations (Kassouf, 2017). I add that an appreciation and understanding of unconscious processes and organizations of experience in political life can help grasp the complexity of human behaviors and communication, especially when considering human beings' tragic trajectory toward extinction. Third, the two points already mentioned further indicate that a psychoanalytic perspective will not separate or divorce parent-child interactions from political theorizing, as much of Western philosophy does. The political is in the background of parental care, shaping but not determining care. This might shift the conversation about how the political realities (e.g., conflicts and inaction) associated with climate change are impacting parents' care for children and children's subjectivities.

Now I turn to a depiction of children's transitions to the public-political spaces of speaking and acting together and the development of political selves (see also Samuels, 1993, 2001, 2004, 2015). The STO is part of the cultural semantic field. It provides children the space and time to use the culture's symbols for organizing experience in relation to an important, though imaginary, other. Eventually, children let go of the STO as they transition to public-political spheres. Winnicott (1971) writes that TOs are not mourned, because children ideally possess the confidence to participate in and make use of the wider cultural field. I would alter this slightly and say that the STO (e.g., a stuffed toy) is not mourned because the child continues to develop the capacity to use shared objects (as well as narratives and rituals) that confirm and affirm their unconscious and emerging conscious experiences of and beliefs in their singularity (senses of esteem, confidence, and respect—significance), as well as agency and rapport. Put differently, children transition to public spaces of speaking and acting together, wherein they risk appearing because they possess social confidence and trust that results from personal recognition and civic care. For many, the transition to public-political spaces of speaking and acting together—space of appearances—is entirely unnoticeable. However, by observing problems that arise in this transition, we gain a better picture of how important this transition is psychosocially and politically. Toward this end, I offer several brief illustrations of this transition taken from the public realm.

Martin Luther King Jr. remembers a painful event that occurred when he was five or six years old. At that time, he discovered that his white playmate would no longer be allowed to play with him and that King would be going to an all-black school—an initial experience of the restriction of the space of appearances. Martin was understandably confused and hurt, turning to his parents for comfort and explanation. Decades later, toward the end of his short life, King recalls expressing his pain to his parents. King (1998) wrote,

> My mother confronted the age-old problem of the Negro parent in America: how to explain discrimination and segregation to a small child. She taught me that I should feel a sense of "somebodiness" but that on the other hand I had to go out and face a system that stared men in the face every day saying you are "less than," you are "not equal to."
>
> (p.3)

Two points are to be made here. First, "somebodiness" can be understood as experiences of singularity (self-esteem, self-respect, and self-confidence) that emerge from good-enough parent-child dialogue/play (speaking and acting together) and, in this case, the respect that came from his church community. "Somebodiness" can be further understood as emerging from idioms of parental care joined to a deep sense of trust and rapport, which was present in his playing with his white friend and abruptly shattered when their friendship/rapport was terminated. Second, the shock and pain King felt as a child reveals how embedded these senses of self were. Not being allowed to play was a transgression that violated these early experiences that Martin unconsciously took for granted (his assumptive world), largely because his parents (and the parents' religious community) provided spaces to not only protect him, but also to equip him with a resilient sense of esteem, confidence, and respect by virtue of their consistent caring actions.

King, as a child, would have unconsciously anticipated that the transition to public-political spaces, like school, would be without disruptions or pain, because he had obtained sufficient experiences of care and trust in his family and religious community. This first conscious memory of rejection and humiliation was followed by many more, because almost anytime he entered into the public-political spaces of southern apartheid, he would not receive political personal recognition, care, and trust. Put differently, apparatuses of racism, then and now, deny the potentiality and singularity of African Americans, like Martin Luther King. What exists is the racist production of alienation and insignificance, not rapport, dignity, and cooperation. Like other African Americans, King was coerced by white supremacists (and their apparatuses) to actualize subordination and inferiority (lack of self-esteem, self-confidence, and self-respect), pushing him to the fringe of political spaces of speaking and acting together.[21] Children, like King, would painfully transition to this political reality. Ruby Sales' previously mentioned experience confirms this, though she and King had a psychosocial shock absorber of parental care that helped their political resistance (impotentiality—rendering racist apparatuses inoperable) and resiliency in the face of marginalization and oppression.

Malcolm X, a contemporary of King, also experienced deep psychological pain when he became conscious of the hegemony of white racism. Like King, Malcolm X (Haley, 1964) recalled the first time he became painfully aware of the perfidy and social-political carelessness of racism, which occurred when he was in eighth grade. His teacher, Mr. Ostrowski,[22] asked Malcolm if he had considered a career. "The truth is I hadn't. I never have figured out why I told him, 'Well, yes sir, I've been thinking I'd like to be a lawyer,'" Malcolm replied (p. 38). Here, we see a young boy aspiring to reach for a socially esteemed profession. His teacher responded,

> Malcolm, one of life's first needs is for us to be realistic. Don't misunderstand me, now. We all here like you, you know that. But you've got to be realistic about being a nigger. A lawyer—that's no realistic goal for a nigger. You need to think about something you can be. You're good with your hands—making things. Everyone admires your carpentry shop work. Why don't you plan on carpentry?
>
> (p.38)

From this point, Malcolm withdrew from white people (preferring not to communicate) and no longer would let the term "nigger" slide off his back. This painful, jarring epiphany involved the realization that despite how hard he worked to be accepted (recognized and appreciated) by white people, he would be forever excluded from privileged social-economic and political spaces—denied singularity and rapport. No matter how bright or gifted Malcolm was, no matter how much potentiality he possessed, he knew that the only options available to him were on the lowest rung of the economic, cultural, and political ladder—a restriction of the space of appearances.

James Baldwin and Ta-Nehisi Coates can deepen our understanding of this transition to the public-political realm. Baldwin (1984) writes, "Long before the Negro child perceives this difference [white superiority], and even longer before he understands it, he has begun to react to it, he has begun to be controlled by it" (p.26). Baldwin (1990) also notes that,

> Negroes in this country—and Negroes do not, strictly or legally speaking exist in any other—are really taught to despise themselves from the moment their eyes open on the world. This world is white and they are black. White people hold power, which means they are superior to blacks...and the world has innumerable ways of making this difference known and felt and feared.
>
> (pp.25–26)

The *illusions* of white supremacy and black inferiority and the apparatuses that produce and enforce them determine public-political recognition and participation in spaces of speaking and acting together, though for Baldwin much of this is unconscious, until it is not. Baldwin, like King and Malcolm X, reveals how, even prior to the transition to public-political spaces and prior to consciousness of this transition, racism is shaping (not determining) African American subjectivity and preparing and forcing African Americans to exist on the margins of the political spaces of appearance. As mentioned in the Introduction, Orlando Patterson (1982) uses the term "social death" [see also Frantz Fanon's (2008) "zone of nonbeing" (p.xii)] to refer to how Africans and African Americans are treated. At worse, social death or political death refers to the ultimate exclusion from the spaces of speaking and acting together, the complete disavowal of singularity, and concomitantly the absence of civic care and cooperation. Political death can also refer to political apparatuses that produce forms of misrecognition or non-recognition that lead to maldistribution of social and economic resources to African Americans (Fraser & Honneth, 2003), as well as restrictions on their participation in the political-public spaces of speaking and acting together.

In writing to his son, Ta-Nehisi Coates (2015) states, "racism is a visceral experience, that it dislodges brains, blocks airways, rips muscle, extracts organs, cracks bones, breaks teeth" (p.10). This obviously refers to myriad experiences of violence perpetrated on African Americans by people who believe themselves to be white. For Coates, the reality of racism evokes "the sheer terror of disembodiment" (p.12), which has its roots in the violent commodification of black bodies—"they transfigured our very bodies into sugar, tobacco, cotton, and gold" (p.71). "Disembodiment," he writes, "is a kind of terrorism, and the threat of it alters the orbit of all our lives and, like terrorism, this distortion is intentional" (p.114).[23] For Coates, the presence of violence raises "the question of how one should live within a black body, within a country lost in the Dream.... how do I live free in this black body?" (p.12). Nakedness, disembodiment, body, and blood are terms used throughout the book.

There are two aspects of this to draw out. First, the fear of disembodiment is akin to Orlando Patterson's (1982) notion of social death, wherein enslaved persons were violently excluded from social-political spaces of speaking and acting together (non or misrecognition and the denial of political agency), which could very well include the ultimate exclusion—death. I am suggesting that Coates' use of this term signals that the transition to public-political spaces comes with a threat to persons' embodied experiences of singularity, which can be understood as comprising embodied pre-representational and representational self-integrity, self-esteem, self-respect, and self-confidence. That is, at home, Coates could experience sufficient care and trust to possess self-esteem, self-respect, and self-confidence—to live in his black body—an embodied sense of agency. However, public-political spaces represent danger. As an adult, Coates experienced this violation when he was enjoying time with his son. After a movie, a white woman shoved his young son out of her way and Coates angrily responded, as any protective parent would. A crowd of white people quickly formed and a white man came up, saying "I could have you arrested!" Coates heard this as "I could take your body" (p.95). The transition to political spaces of appearances, then, is not only fraught for children who are making that transition, but also for African American adults who have to navigate hegemonic apparatuses that produce the illusions of white supremacy and black inferiority.

The focus above has been on psychosocial development and the reader will observe that there is no mention of the natural world, whether in terms of the political or development. In a prescient, if not Cassandra type work, Howard Searles (1960) argued that the first phase of psychiatric theories and research focused entirely on human beings. "It would seem then," he went on to suggest, "that a natural next phase would consist in our broadening our focus still further, to include the investigation of man's relationships with his nonhuman environment" (p.23). Of course, as Susan Kassouf (2017) points out, there has been little done in psychoanalytic theory and research regarding the importance of other-than-human species and the earth in psychosocial development. It is unfair to single out psychoanalysis or other psychologies for this lacuna. As noted in the Introduction, Giorgio Agamben points out, a central theme in Western philosophies is a "deep ontological rift...between animal and human" (Dickinson, 2015b, p.173).[24] This rift, as Agamben notes, has roots in ancient Greek philosophy (and theology).[25] Aristotle informed us that human beings are political animals. As political animals, human beings exercise political agency and freedom[26] (and now eco-agency), which other species lack. This means that other species (and the earth) have been rendered included-excluded Others and politically irrelevant. Aristotle, in other words, does not include other species in his political theorizing because other species are not deemed to have the faculties needed for political involvement—hence inferior. This seems, at first glance, quite logical or reasonable. Other species do not exercise political agency, so it would be a category mistake to include them. However, the looming disasters of the current climate emergency reveal that, while other species and the earth do not possess political agency, they are nevertheless critical for human existence and for the very existence of the polis. Recall that a biodiverse earth "is the first condition of our existence" (Eagleton, 2016, p.228), which, therefore, means psychosocial development is similarly dependent on other-than-human species, even as we disavow this truth.

So, it is not surprising that this ontological rift is likewise manifested in the natural and physical sciences. For example, Francis Bacon (1561–1626) claimed that "the practical aim of improving humanity's lot [depended on] increased understanding and *control* of nature" (Grayling, 2019, p.197). If we leap to the 20th century, Sigmund Freud (1927) argued that the aim of civilization is "to defend us against nature," as if nature is our enemy and we somehow exist apart from it (p.15). In terms of climate crisis, scientist Paul Crutzen, who was one of the scientists to coin the term "Anthropocene Age," was a strong advocate of geoengineering, which, in my view, is connected to the anthropocentric illusions that human beings have dominion over and are superior to the earth, which was created for the sake of human beings. This provides legitimacy for the instrumental use of other species and the earth solely for human benefit. Michael Northcott (2017) writes,

Crutzen does not call for a moral and spiritual renewal to reduce humanity's impacts and tread more gently on the earth. Instead, his call is for a new intentionality in the human management of the Earth System, and for a significant ramping up of research and development by scientists and technologists of the technical means for intentional intervention in the Earth System, including active geoengineering of the atmosphere.

(p.24)

This ontological rift is evident in the techno-scientific domination of nature, observed by critical theorists such as Adorno and Horkheimer (Rigby, 2017, p.278). The problem, then, is not simply differentiating between human beings, other species, and the earth, but holding to and acting on beliefs that human beings are separate and independent from nature, are superior to nature, and, as result, have dominion or control over nature. This leads to "a radical and total discontinuity between human and nonhuman" (Kompridis, 2020, p.252), which is fueled by the privileging of human beings over all other species.[27]

While I will say more about the ontological rift and our response to it in subsequent chapters, for now a theory of psychosocial development can render this rift inoperative by considering other-species and the earth in the formation of subjectivity and its relation to the political. To do so fully would take another book. I can, however, acknowledge the lacuna, while also claiming that a psychoanalytic political philosophy and, for that matter, any political philosophy will need to find ways to be inclusive of other-than-human species and the earth. For this reason, I return to this topic in later chapters with the aim of beginning to explore what this would mean for psychoanalysis and political philosophy. I also mention that, while the lacuna is evident in psychoanalysis and Western political philosophies, there is the reality of other-than-human beings playfully represented in a great deal of children's literature, which I return to in Chapter 3. While it is not my intention to explore this literature from a psychoanalytic developmental perspective, it is important to note that even though much of Western thought constructs animals instrumentally, children's literature, more often than not, anthropocentrically and playfully constructs other-than-human animals as engaged in the public spaces of appearances.[28]

Let me summarize some of the key features regarding a psychoanalytic political philosophy and the development of political selves. First, the existence of infants and their vulnerability reveals the existential ethical demand to care. This extends to the realities of the polis and the polis' dependence on a biodiverse earth. Second, care, in terms of psychosocial development, includes repairs of relational disruptions, which, in turn, is necessary for fostering trust and a cooperative space of speaking and acting together—semiotically organized experiences of rapport and pre-political power of cooperation. This care is ideally free of the illusions of superiority and inferiority, as well as the concomitant relations of subordination and subjugation—relations which undermine trust and reduce the spaces of speaking and acting together. Third, personalizing attunements are shaped by but not determined by cultural symbol systems. Ideally, the culture's symbol systems reflect equality in dignity vis-à-vis speaking and acting together and provide for the emergence of experiences of singularity that undergird pre-representational and representational embodied senses of self-esteem, self-respect, and self-confidence associated with personal-political agency. Early pre-representational experiences and organizations of singularity, while tied to representational symbol systems, exceed these. That is, the experience of singularity also means actualizing one's agency and identity, both of which are not exhausted (excess) by parental representations of their children. Fourth, good-enough parental care is necessary not only for children undergoing an alteration from potentiality to actuality, but also for children's preferring not to communicate or impotentiality. Fifth, developmentally all of this initially takes place outside of awareness as children transition to making use of the cultural symbol systems at hand. This pre-political self transitions to a political self as children begin to engage in public-political spaces of cooperation, of speaking and acting together. In a good-enough or decent society (Margalit, 1996), there is sufficient civic care/recognition and civic trust for children, and later adults, to confirm and have affirmed their singularity and agency (senses of self-esteem, respect, and confidence), which are necessary for risking vulnerability and dependency that attends their speaking and acting with others.

Someone might observe that the discussion above sneaks in political values associated with liberalism and liberative political philosophies (e.g., feminism and postcolonialism). If this is the case, it would suggest that the psychoanalytic developmental perspective offered above is simply my way of furthering a liberal or liberative political philosophy. I have two responses. First, it is highly likely that my conscious and unconscious political biases or values are in the background, shaping my approach. This is neither a serious problem nor a disqualification of this developmental perspective. Any discussion of human development, which entails anthropologies, necessarily includes the values of the culture (ethos and polis) in which it arises. Recognizing this means we can engage in diverse political discourses, acknowledging plurality, while also seeking ways of connection and cooperation. I can also stress here that while the discussion above uses language suggesting universality, it also recognizes the particularities of political cultures. As we engage in political spaces of speaking and acting together vis-à-vis climate change, we need to hold in tension plurality and universality to avoid the Charybdis of inaction and the Scylla of political violence. It is also not a problem because this developmental perspective questions neoliberalism's tendency to idolize the independent individual by locating the emergence of the political self in caring relations, wherein the individual is vulnerable and dependent. Moreover, as I will elaborate in greater detail in Chapter 3, this perspective undermines neoliberalism's focus on individual political agency vis-à-vis democracy. Democracy is yet another form of sovereignty (sovereign selves) that retains relations of subordination and subjugation, as well as illusions of inferiority and superiority evidenced in excluded Others (non-citizens) and other-than-human species—other-than-human species that are constructed largely as existing for the sake of the political dwelling of human beings.

## Western Political Selves and Dangerous Illusions of the Anthropocene

I have already mentioned that the particularity of a culture's symbol systems and apparatuses shapes the political subjectivities of its members. While there is a rich diversity of cultures and, therefore, political subjectivities, I contend there is some overlap at least with regard to Western political philosophies and theologies.[29] Indeed, these political philosophies and theologies serve as apparatuses that produce and maintain interrelated illusions, which masquerade as ontological facts, and I contend that these illusions facilitate exploitative, destructive relations toward Othered human beings, other species, and the earth. In other words, these illusions tragically undermine the very existence of the polis. By becoming conscious of these illusions and their accompanying political, economic, and cultural apparatuses, we are invited to alter our ways of *perceiving and being* in relation to each other,[30] to other-than-human species, and the earth. Put differently, a post-anthropocentric (psychoanalytic) political philosophy encourages eco-epistemologies, behaviors, and relations that set aside these destructive illusions, creating spaces and relations to "attend to animal, water, stone, forest, and world—and not to deny force, thought, agency, emergence or thriving to any of these entities" (Cohen, 2017, p.29).

The first illusion of Western political philosophies and theologies falls under the heading of anthropocentrism. Many Western traditions of political philosophy over the last two millennia have largely depended on Judeo-Christian scriptures, which place human beings (often one group) at the center of the cosmos and God's attention. The very creation of the earth is central in the Judeo-Christian religious drama of creation,[31] and it is the earth that human beings, as exceptional creatures, are given dominion over. This includes dominion over all species. Since the Enlightenment, Western political philosophers have tended to move away from theology, but have retained this anthropocentric illusion, which shapes and supports instrumental epistemologies and exploitative behaviors toward Othered human beings, other-than-human species, and the earth. In practice, then, the illusion that human beings are the center of the universe or of central ontological significance means that other-than-human species and the earth are, at best, of secondary importance—they are impermanent, insignificant, and vulnerable. More bluntly stated, the existence of the earth and other-than-human species is perceived to be for the sake of serving the needs and desires of human beings. As Lynn White (1967) presciently noted decades ago, "Man's monopoly on spirit in this world…made it possible to exploit nature in a mood of indifference to the feelings of natural objects" (p.1205).

The psychoanalytic political perspective I propose is not necessarily a cure for anthropocentrism. Indeed, psychoanalytic traditions tacitly confirm an anthropological view of human narcissism, which is but one step away from the illusory belief that human beings are the center of the cosmos. To contend that narcissism is a feature of psychosocial development does not necessarily mean human beings are determined to adopt the illusion of anthropocentrism. Psychoanalytic developmental theories, for instance, also claim that good-enough parental care enables children to eventually set aside their narcissism in order to welcome people who are different and to cooperate with them. Indeed, not setting this narcissism aside leads to a diminished ability to recognize others in their singularities, which accompanies attenuated or distorted care for others and a corresponding eclipse of space of appearances, rapport, and political agency. This said, I suggest Western cultural and political apparatuses are more likely to produce the illusion of anthropocentrism, which implies that a psychoanalytic political philosophy will operate to identify and critique these apparatuses, as well as promote apparatuses that eschew anthropocentrism with the aim of inclusive political care of all human beings, other-than-human species, and the earth.

Anthropocentrism is, then, closely linked to the belief (illusion) in exceptionalism and its myriad forms (see Weintrobe, 2021, pp.33–40, 264–267). I have already commented on Abrahamic scriptures, which are also a source of beliefs in ontological exceptionalism (e.g., chosen people). But sources for the illusion of exceptionalism have secular sources as well. Varied iterations of nationalism manifest exceptionalistic beliefs that exclude or marginalize those who are constructed as not belonging (which includes other species). More particularly, there is an inherent exceptionalism in state imperialistic adventures. Every empire is founded on the illusion of exceptionalism, until that imperial nation falls, usually leaving a long trail of violence and environmental destruction. There is an exceptionalism to capitalistic exploitation of the earth and other-than-human species. Mountain Top Removal, industrial or factory farms, and deforestation are just some of the environmental disasters that emerge, in part, from the belief that human beings, in general, and, in this case, capitalists in particular are exceptional and, therefore, entitled to exploit nature. Of course, it is not simply other species who suffer as a result of beliefs in exceptionalism; it is also Othered human beings. The exploitation of workers (Mander, 2012; Valencia, 2018), the use of enslaved persons for profit (Baptist, 2014; Kendi, 2017), and the capitalistic colonization of other states (Klein, 2007) are examples of one group of people believing they are exceptional while Othered human beings are not exceptional and thus open for instrumental use or worse neglect. This exceptionalism is also evident in how the impacts of climate change are not equally shared by all human beings. Poor nations and their peoples are bearing the brunt of climate disasters, as are people of color and poor white persons in the United States.

I argue that the psychoanalytic political philosophy offered in this chapter and in subsequent chapters cannot support the belief in human exceptionalism. Above I discussed the importance of parents' recognition of and care for their children's experiences of singularity. Singularity by definition implies diversity, not identity or sameness. Moreover, singularity does not necessarily accompany a belief in exceptionalism. In my view, if children have a relatively secure sense of singularity, they are able to acknowledge and accept the singularities of others. By contrast, to be exceptional necessarily means that some other individuals or species are not. The belief that one is exceptional, in other words, interferes with recognition of and care for those constructed as unexceptional, which includes Othered human beings and other-than-human species. I suggest that a psychoanalytic perspective that embraces the importance and singularity of nature vis-à-vis human development, as Howard Searles hoped, can facilitate our recognition and treatment of all other species in terms of their singularity. Other species may not "experience" singularity, but by recognizing their varied singularities, human beings are challenged to treat or care for them as such.

Anthropocentrism and exceptionalism are buttressed by the illusions of superiority and Others' inferiority. I have already discussed how these illusions are destructive psychologically and physically,[32] evident in political situations where racism, sexism, classism, and other apparatuses of marginalization and exploitation are at work. But these illusions, which are embedded in Western political philosophies, also pertain to how we recognize or construct other species. For instance, Aristotle's political explorations and his scientific taxonomies (and experiments) contain a hierarchic schema with women, slaves, and barbarians occupying the bottom rungs. In terms of nature and all other species, human beings reside at the top and believed to be superior. These illusions accompany instrumental epistemologies that facilitate not only exploitation (absence of care), but also a disavowal of the singularity and suffering of those who are constructed as inferior.

Accompanying these illusions (anthropocentrism, exceptionalism, superiority-inferiority) is the illusion that human beings are not animals. If people can bring themselves to acknowledge that they are animals, they usually retain the illusions above, which serves to place human beings at the pinnacle of the animal "kingdom."

An illustration of this is a phrase sometimes used to refer to egregious treatment of human beings. Recently in the news, there was an article about a Sri Lankan woman who died while in the custody of Japanese authorities. One Sri Lankan person said the Japanese had treated this woman like an animal. What is interesting in this statement is not only the disavowal that human beings are animals, but also the seeming acceptance of the exploitation of "animals," but not human beings. As noted above, a central theme in Western philosophies (and theologies) is the "deep ontological rift…between animal and human" (Dickinson, 2015b, p.173), which is the foundation for the subsequent non-empathic, instrumental use of "animals."

There are three more points to stress before concluding. First, in the initial sketching out of a psychoanalytic political philosophy, I have sought to exclude the illusions of exceptionalism and superior/inferiority in terms of parents good-enough care. While good-enough parents recognize their children as unique, it does not necessarily follow that they view them as exceptional or superior. That is, from a phenomenological perspective, parental care (or care in general) *qua* care does not depend on these illusions. I contend that parental care is optimal when it is not tied to these illusions. Of course, as indicated above, good-enough parental care is shaped by society's apparatuses and, therefore, these illusions may surreptitiously make their way into the parents' care. When this occurs, however, varied forms of exclusion and disavowal occur. When Harold Searles (1960), for instance, called upon psychoanalysts to explore the relation between human development and the "nonhuman" world, he was, in my view, pointing to the exclusion that comes from the unwitting acceptance by psychoanalytic theorists of the illusions identified above.

A second point: I contend that these illusions function psychologically to protect human beings from the reality of our existential vulnerability and dependency, as well as human insignificance and impermanence. Religious narratives that promise life after death or nationalistic stories that provide citizens with a sense of continuity or going on being tend to promulgate these illusions, providing psychological protection from the harsh realities of life, inescapable death, and the overwhelming evidence of the universe's "indifference" to humanity.[33] Even though Freud relied on his beliefs in science and progress, he was, in my view, mostly correct in his view that if human beings are to "progress" or, better, change our relationships with nature, we need to face and let go of our illusions (for Freud, religious illusions). In so doing, it means accepting our vulnerability and dependency, our existential impermanence and insignificance,[34] which unites us to all living beings. A psychoanalytic political philosophy accepts that caring recognition communicates significance, which children organize into experiences of self-esteem, self-confidence, and self-respect. To take this a step further, a political philosophy vis-à-vis the Anthropocene Age accepts the reality of existential insignificance and impermanence as a feature of all life. This is not a counsel of despair, but one of humility and the acknowledgment that our acts of care for each other and for other species means creating significance while accepting existential insignificance and impermanence.

But disillusionment is very difficult. Freud argued that there were three narcissistic blows to humanity—blows to our cosmic and earthly significance and impermanence. The first shock was from Copernicus, when human beings learned that we are not the center of the universe. The second jolt from Darwin is when we learned that human beings were part of evolution, like all other living creatures. Freud (1917) contended that human "megalomania will have suffered its third and most wounding blow from psychological research of the present time which seeks to prove to the ego that it is not even master in its own house" (p.285). Of course, Freud did not account for the collective resistance to these shocks and the persistent power of these and other illusions to shield human beings from the stark realities of existential vulnerability, dependency, impermanence, and insignificance. Maybe the ongoing revelations of climate change will finally puncture our collective psyches, though it may not be in time. Nevertheless, I am convinced that if we do not face and let go of these illusions (and others, identified in subsequent chapters), we will continue toward the extinction of millions of species, including ourselves.

The third point concerns why I argue these beliefs are illusions. First of all, these beliefs are constructions of human beings and the evidence human beings use to confirm these false beliefs is also constructed. As Clifford Geertz (1973) notes, a human being is "an animal suspended in webs of significance he himself has spun" (p.5). We are exceptional, superior, the center, or apex of the cosmos, because our stories tell us so. There is, in short, nothing in nature itself that confirms human beings are the center of the cosmos or superior or exceptional. Indeed, the reality that there are billions of galaxies, trillions of stars and planets, would seem to belie any claim to humans being the center or apex of the created order. Moreover, that human beings are destroying the habitat we depend on and in the process of killing off millions of species does not provide evidence of our superiority, only that we are deeply tragic creatures. Add to this that the "lowly" cockroaches are likely to survive us and would it then suggest that they are "superior"? More to the point, the facts of the Anthropocene Age reveal in a stark way that we are not of central importance to the earth, not superior, not exceptional, and not separated, even though we may continue to cling to these political-economic illusions.

## Conclusion

This chapter is the first step toward elucidating a psychoanalytic political philosophy, which I expand on in subsequent chapters of Part I. I have tacked back and forth between psychoanalytic developmental perspectives and political philosophies, identifying what I consider to be key principles for a political philosophy, not the least of which is care. Care is a concept central to both psychosocial development and life in the polis. In terms of psychosocial development, care refers to parents' personal attunements, which facilitate a space of speaking and acting together such that children begin to actualize their potentialities. As a political concept, care refers to relations and actions that make possible a habitat (earth and polis) wherein human beings and other-than-human beings are able to actualize their potentialities. The very material existence of the polis, in other words, depends on a viable, biodiverse habitat. At the same time, a polis cannot continue to exist in the absence of caring relations, whether that refers to care of children or, more generally, civic care. I also argued that a psychoanalytic philosophy for the Anthropocene Age needs to identify and raise to consciousness those collective political illusions (and the apparatuses that produce and sustain them) that are environmentally destructive—harming Othered human beings, other-than-human beings, and the earth. In short, the psychoanalytic political philosophy initiated here is a kind of cosmopolitics (not cosmopolitanism) in the sense of what Bruno Latour (2004, p.453) called for, wherein human beings and other-than-human beings live in mutual cooperation and peace.[35]

## Notes

1  Another political myth is noted in *Totem and Taboo* (Freud, 1950).
2  Interestingly, communitarian philosopher Alasdair MacIntyre (1983, 2016) and political philosopher Axel Honneth (1995) make use of the work of Donald Winnicott in their political philosophies. See also Bowker and Buzby (2017) for the use of Winnicott in political theory.
3  I recognize that nature entails contestations between species as all species seek to survive. Caring for other species may result in learning to adapt to conditions that negatively effect human beings. In other words, care may mean finding ways to live with other species that are dangerous to human beings, instead of trying to find ways to eliminate them. For instance, mosquito born illnesses and deaths are in the millions every year. There are researchers that hope to find ways to eliminate mosquitoes, thus saving millions of human beings. Yet, to eradicate mosquitoes will undermine those species that depend on mosquitoes for food. A better approach is to find drug regimes that reduce if not eliminate deaths.
4  Philosopher Knud Løgstrup (1997) argues that there is an ethical demand to care embedded in human existence. It seems to me that Levinas (1969, 1998) makes a similar case when he uses the metaphor "face" to refer to our existential obligations to care for and to show hospitality to the Other.
5  While I will return to this, part of the humanity's problem is believing in their ontological significance, while relegating other species and the earth to insignificance—creating an ontological rift, which is an illusion.
6  Recognition is a key concept in Western political theorizing. John Macmurray (1991), Axel Honneth (1995, 2021), Judith Butler (2005), and Charles Taylor (1992) are some of the prominent philosophers who address the complexities of recognition, which locate in psychosocial development.
7  Mills would likely include Georg Hegel in this critique. This said, Western political philosophy is rife with misrecognitions of Othered people, including women. We need only recall Plato and Aristotle's philosophies to note not simply how influential they were to Western political philosophies and theologies, but their negative biases toward so-called barbarians, women, etc., which often accompanied instrumental and depersonalizing forms of knowing. This is not a counsel to reject Western philosophers, but rather to acknowledge their political shortcomings.
8  Adam Phillips (2021b) points out that Winnicott's good-enough care is foundational to psychoanalytic therapy and not "cure" or remedy. Care, he writes, "can be less purposive, have less of a palpable design than cure" (p.27). Indeed, he goes on to say that good-enough parents prefigure the psychoanalyst-patient couple, though with important distinctions.

 9  Ruby Sales—Where Does It Hurt?|The On Being Project – The On Being Project, https://onbeing.org/programs/ruby-sales-where-does-it-hurt/#transcript,        accessed 16 November 2021.

10  There may be times when good-enough parents use force to protect their children from some harm, which means there is an absence of cooperation or space of speaking and acting together. This said, acts of parental impingement and deprivation vis-à-vis their children represent force, which eclipses the space of speaking and acting together. Put another way, whether in childhood or adulthood, trauma is use of violence and the complete collapse of a space of speaking and acting together. Children, in other words, are forced to cooperate to survive.

11  Philosophers Mark Johnson (1987) and George Lakoff (Lakoff & Johnson, 1999) make clear that embodied semiotic organizations of experience make their way into complex philosophical perspectives.

12  In an analogous way, therapists' care for their patients is a key ingredient in patients actualizing their potentiality. I add that, in terms of climate change and other-than-human species, there are innumerable examples of how the care of human beings toward other species facilitates the actualization of the capacities or potentialities of other-than-human beings.

13  Jeremy Elkins (2017) notes the strong correlation between Winnicott's view of motility and agency, which are together located in the social.

14  Political philosopher Axel Honneth (1995) uses these senses of self when addressing political agency and freedom. I am adapting these to show a relationship between a pre-political selves and political selves.

15  The earliest selection of a TO is in "accordance with its consistency, texture, size, volume, shape, and odor" (Kestenberg & Weinstein, 1978, p.89), as well as the parent's "technique of mothering"—the caregiver's handling, holding, comforting, and consoling of the infant (Winnicott, 1971, p.11). That is, the child unconsciously chooses a TO that represents the parent's care for the child and the earliest selection is, as Kestenberg and Weinstein suggest, an object that is not a cultural object—for example, a blanket or soft toy.

16  This does not mean that the belief in omnipotence is no longer present. Winnicott knew well that transitional phenomena are also associated with adulthood, and we can see numerous cultural examples of the belief in omnipotence in religions, science, and the arts.

17  There are two difficulties with Winnicott's use of the term "transitional objects" in referring to cultural objects (in particular religious objects). First, on its face, Winnicott's assumption that transitional objects are present in adult life (e.g., religion, art, and science), vis-à-vis illusion and reality, seems correct. However, the psychosocial achievements of adulthood clearly indicate that adult object usage and the infant's use of objects are not identical (Brody, 1980; Busch, Nagera, McKnight, & Pezzarossi, 1973). For instance, Winnicott states that the TOs in infancy and childhood are idiosyncratic and not shared. There is a solipsistic aspect to the child's use of the TO, even in the presence of caregivers. The "TOs" of adulthood, on the other hand, are often shared. Second, Winnicott contends that the TO of infancy represents the "technique of mothering," which does not necessarily fit well with adult cultural activities. When, for example, we consider religious objects, we find that they are much more complex with regard to use, function, and representation than the transitional objects associated with infancy and childhood. Nevertheless, I would argue that transitional objects in adulthood represent, in part, unthought knowns.

18  Macmurray (1991) argues that personal recognition is both a matter of fact and a matter of intention. He wishes to locate the personal as an existential or ontological fact, while also saying it is something human beings can intend. All human beings, for Macmurray, are persons—potentially. To actualize this potentiality requires the Other's intention to

recognize and treat individuals as persons. Infants are potentially persons and depend on parents' consistent caring intention to recognize and treat them as persons to actualize personhood. The secondary transitional object is the beginning of the child's capacity to intend personal recognition of the object. I add that this is true as well in the political sphere, where civic care entails personal recognition and treatment of others as persons, which facilitates civic trust necessary for people to appear in their singularity.

19 Martha Nussbaum (2019), in reflecting on the relevance and limitations of Stoic philosophy vis-à-vis cosmopolitanism, highlights Cicero's core political principle of equal dignity that undergirds reciprocity (pp.146–147).

20 Gayle Salamon (2022) brings together and uses the works of Merleau-Ponty and Frantz Fanon to argue that systemic apparatuses can undermine the embodied agency of oppressed and marginalized persons. Ta-Nehisi Coates (2015) similarly depicts this dynamic when discussing his experiences of growing up in a racist society.

21 Historian Carol Anderson (2016) and legal scholar Michelle Alexander detail the backlash by white society whenever African Americans assert and live out their self-esteem, self-respect, and self-confidence in white-dominated political-economic spaces. The political courage and resiliency of many African Americans indicate that the development of their political selves occurs within African American families and communities that nurture their self-esteem, self-respect, and self-confidence. I will say more about this in later chapters, but these are inoperative communities, rendering the racist apparatuses inoperative with regard to their political communities. For Agamben, "inoperativity" means to deactivate the functioning of apparatuses, which does not mean that these apparatuses cease operating or do not continue to have effects (Prozorov, 2014, pp.31–34).

22 Biographer Manning Marable (2011) indicates that the teacher's name was Richard Kaminska. Malcolm may have misremembered or altered the name, possibly for legal reasons. Since the autobiography uses a different name, I have decided to retain Malcolm's version.

23 See also Jean Khalfa (2022) discussion of the impact of racism and colonialism on embodied agency.

24 Agamben is not the first person to notice this. Psychoanalyst Erich Fromm's reading of Marx believed that capitalism alienates human beings from nature by way of instrumental epistemologies. Socialism, for Fromm, promoted an unalienated individual—an individual "who does not 'dominate' nature, but who becomes one with it, who is alive and responsive toward objects, so that objects come to life for him" (in Thompson, 2020, p.26).

25 Other philosophers have been concerned about the ontological rift. Philosophers Deleuze and Guattari (2003) agree with Agamben's claim, arguing that "We make no distinction between man and nature…man and nature are not like two opposite terms confronting each other…rather they are one and the same essential reality" (pp.4–5). These philosophers argue that the ontological rift is a human construction and one that is, in the end, deadly for human beings and other species. Interestingly, earlier echoes of this are evident in Ralph Waldo Emerson's (1849) writings about nature and more recently in the works of philosopher Peter Singer (1975, 2016).

26 While the philosophical notion of freedom is complicated, let me note that in relation to the ontological rift scholars recognize that freedom is actually connected to the rift. Erich Fromm viewed this as negative freedom, because it represents separation and alienation with regard to nature. Positive freedom aims to overcome this alienation into a union with nature (see, Thorpe, 2020, p.170). Reading Marx, David Harvey (2016) also remarks that estrangement from nature gave rise to "emancipatory forms of knowledge (such as science); but it also poses the problem of how to return to that which consciousness alienates us from" (p.205). In my view, the ontological rift is part of Western thought and we may find that other cultures do not rely on alienation from

nature vis-à-vis consciousness and freedom. In other words, Marx, Fromm, and Harvey seem to think that estrangement from nature is universally necessary for consciousness when it is more a factor of Western philosophies and theologies.

27  Philosophers Deleuze and Guattari (2003) agree with Agamben's claim, arguing that "We make no distinction between man and nature…man and nature are not like two opposite terms confronting each other…rather they are one and the same essential reality" (pp.4–5). They argue that Western epistemologies are hierarchal, privileging human beings over other species. They use the metaphor of rhizome as a way to conceptual knowledge. A rhizome grows horizontally with underground stems which put out lateral shoots. This differs from the metaphor of tree that dominates Western conceptualizations of knowledge. John Gray (2013, p.76) makes a similar point indicating the superiority of human beings over nature is an illusion that Montagne affirmed centuries ago. I need to point out that so-called primitive cultures, past and present, possess narratives and rituals that are inclusive of nature. Their philosophies are in contrast to most Western philosophical theories that not only separate human beings from animals, but place human beings on top of the taxonomic hierarchy such that other-than-human species and the earth exist solely to serve humanity (and, more often than not, a particular class of humanity).

28  Over the years I have read hundreds of Native American stories that do not produce the ontological rift, but rather include other species as key figures in the lives of native peoples. See Kerven, *Native American Myths: Collected 1636–1919*; Erdoes and Ortiz, *American Indian Myths and Legends*.

29  There are three points I wish to make here. First, granted, I am making sweeping generalizations regarding Western philosophy, but I am doing so for heuristic purposes. Second, it should also be pointed out that in the colonized and colonizing West, there were and are native peoples whose political philosophies are more amendable to viewing "nature" as a central value in itself and seeking to cooperate with nature. I am not as familiar with these traditions. My emphasis and concern is with the hegemony of Western political thought, especially as it pertains to imperialism, capitalism, and nationalism. Third, there is a tendency of political philosophers after the Renaissance to disavow theology in their theorizing. Carl Schmitt, however, claimed that "all significant concepts of the modern theory of the state are secularized theological concepts" (in Brown, 2010, p.59). For those in the psychological sciences who are interested in political philosophies, Schmitt's view is to be taken seriously, especially for those of us the West.

30  My perspective regarding consciousness raising and action, whether that is in therapy or the larger culture, is derived from postcolonial philosophy and psychology, which I will address in greater in Chapters 6 and 7. For now, let me briefly mention psychiatrist Frantz Fanon's (2008/1952) view of therapy. He argued that therapy aims (a) "to *consciousnessize*' [the patient's] unconscious, to no longer be tempted by a hallucinatory lactification," and (b) "to enable [the patient] to choose an action with respect to the *real source of the conflict*, i.e., the social structure" (p.80; emphasis mine). An ocean away and around the same time, Ralph Ellison (1995/1953), commented about the psychiatric clinic in Harlem. He wrote, "As such, and in spite of the very fine work it is doing, a thousand Lafargue (psychiatric) clinics could not dispel the sense of unreality that haunts Harlem. Knowing this, Dr. Wertham and his interracial staff seek a modest achievement: to give each bewildered patient an insight into the relation between his problems and his environment, and out of this understanding to reforge the will" (p.302). From a different but related field, scholar and activist Paolo Freire (2018, 2021) used the concept "conscientization" to refer to the awakening of people to the political, cultural, and economic sources of their oppression and marginalization. I add here that raising consciousness necessarily includes awareness of the sources of suffering and exploitation of other-than-human species and the earth.

31  Similarly, Christian views of the afterlife (kingdom of God) are devoid of the earth and other species. Moreover, Christian beliefs about other species possessing no souls means they are excluded from the kingdom of God, because they lack, most Christians believe, ontological significance. This is in contrast to some native peoples' stories where humans and other-than-human animals populate the afterlife (Varner, 2010). Many indigenous philosophies claim hold that land, water, and animals have spiritual essences, which suggests they are included in the polis (see Plumwood, 2008). While there are strands of Christian thought that are similar, political Christian views, including views of the afterlife, parallel Western political theologies that exclude other-than-human animals from the political (and the spiritual).

32  It is important to qualify this. A group's belief in their superiority may provide resilience in the face of oppression. Malcolm X (Haley, 1964) initially adopted the Nation of Islam's origin myth that depicted Africans as superior and whites as inferior. This provided Malcolm X with a sense of self-esteem. This said, the illusion of superiority leads to exclusion (sometimes violent) of those constructed as inferior and, in worse cases, leads to the exploitation or annihilation of "inferior" others.

33  I use quotes to indicate that the universe cannot be indifferent or caring or interested. To suggest as such is to succumb to the human tendency to anthropomorphize the universe.

34  To claim that human beings are existentially insignificant does not mean they, like other species, are in and of themselves insignificant. Human beings create significance by recognizing the existential singularities of other human beings (and other species). We construct significance diachronically and synchronically, which ultimately is existentially impermanent. Existential insignificance means that human beings, like all other species, are not significant vis-à-vis the cosmos. The fact that human beings have emerged on this earth, does not mean we have any more significance existentially than those species that have gone on before us or who will come after us. The cosmos is not a signifying entity.

35  Joni Adamson (2017) discusses the 2010 World People's Conference on the Rights of Mother Earth and Climate Change (UDRME). The document produced by this conference challenges participants and others to "gather up philosophies that summon 'natural entities' as allies into the organization of a 'livable' political 'cosmos' (p.167). The document also challenges "fellow humanists to think in terms of what it might mean to support intergenerational justice for 'multispecies aggregates' or the most vulnerable humans and nonhumans" (p.167). My hope is that this and remaining chapters take up, in part, these challenges from a psychoanalytic political perspective.

# Chapter 2

# A Psychoanalytic Political Philosophy of Dwelling

Throughout human existence, Stephen Larsen (1990) contends, myths provide people

> several vital purposes. They explained the workings of the world to those bewildered by natural phenomena. They assisted people's transitions through life's developmental stages. They helped members of a society find meaning in their social position, economic status, and ethical constraints. They enabled human beings to participate in the mysteries of the cosmos and to worship an entity or process deemed worthy of supreme importance.
>
> (p.xv)

To be sure, myths have many functions, as various anthropologists have observed (Frye, 1982; Geertz, 1973; Levi-Strauss, 1995), but I suggest that religious and cultural myths, generally speaking, offer answers to questions about how a people came to be and what is their place in the world/cosmos. It is the latter that includes the group's ethos, and ethos is founded on the question: How are we to dwell in this particular place, in this polis, in this world (van Dooren & Rose, 2017, p.256)? The Jewish origin myths, for example, detail not simply how humans came to be, but also how they came to live in this place and how they were and are to live together—polis and ethos.

It is not simply religion that has its myths that deal with the questions of dwelling. We glimpse the intersection of mythic imagination and philosophy in the works of Plato and Aristotle, as well as in the works of Thomas Hobbes, Jean-Jacques Rousseau, and other political philosophers. If myth, as Bruce Lincoln (2000) noted, is "an ideology in narrative form" (p.36), political philosophical ideologies often have roots in mythic imagination (Boer, 2009). This is particularly evident in Carl Schmitt's claim that "all significant concepts of the modern theory of the state are secularized theological concepts" (Brown, 2010, p.59), and these theological/philosophical concepts are rooted in religious mythologies.[1] Hobbes and Rousseau (as did Freud), for instance, each had myths regarding the origins of civilization, which, from Schmitt's perspective, were linked to religious concepts that shaped their political philosophies. In brief, political philosophies and their often-unstated

DOI: 10.4324/9781003258827-4

myths have to do with answering questions regarding how are we to dwell together in this place.[2]

If we shift to the quotidian realities of individuals and families, we find family stories or myths about how their children came to be, came to dwell with them. Family stories, like cultural and religious myths, have many purposes, but they reveal how a family is to dwell together. We observe this in memoirs and autobiographies, as well as when listening to patients' stories. Malcolm X's (Haley, 1964) autobiography begins with a mythic tale of the birth of a hero. Malcolm X relates the story of his mother who, pregnant with Malcolm, was threatened by the Klan. To dwell as a Black man or woman in this society meant being imperiled, oftentimes from birth. Malcolm's story reveals the challenges he and his family faced in a racist culture that displaces and unhouses African Americans, in numerous ways. To shift to therapy, listening to patients' stories/myths exposes how they have come to dwell in the world and often how this way of dwelling is no longer satisfactory. Transference, in one sense, is the patient's lived story, which is the communicative attempt to get the therapist to dwell with the patient in a particular way.

The question of dwelling is central to human life, in general, and political philosophy in particular. This question is lived before it is thought or answered, which can be understood in a couple of ways. Long before philosophers put stylus to tablet addressing political questions, people for millennia shared stories and myths about their dwelling together in this particular place. In one sense, their myths were political philosophies regarding the collective meaning and purpose of their lives together in this specific place and time.[3] There is also another sense of the question of dwelling being lived before being enunciated. Even if we think carefully about what it means for "us" to dwell together, a great deal of how we dwell remains outside of consciousness. The ethos we inhabit comprises conscious and unconscious processes, insuring the reality of both normative and historical unconscious factors in our dwelling with others. Put another way, the ethos we inhabit also inhabits us. Even the most erudite, rational political philosophy, which has ties to mythic imagination, leaves as much unconscious as there is conscious. As philosopher Iris Murdoch (2001) acknowledges regarding ethos and dwelling, human beings "are anxiety-ridden animals. Our minds are continually active, fabricating an anxious, usually self-preoccupied, often falsifying veil which partially conceals the world" (p.82). This said, whether we attend to myths, philosophy, or family stories, this inevitable existential fact becomes clear: human beings anxiously endeavor to answer and live out, consciously and unconsciously, the question of dwelling by relying on their mythic imagination or what Cornelius Castoriadis (1998) calls our social imaginary.

This takes on particular existential significance in the Anthropocene Age, when human beings and millions of other species are displaced and threatened with extinction—with being unhoused from our only habitat. While the question of dwelling is of concern to all human beings (and other species), in this chapter I build on the previous chapter by addressing this question from a psychoanalytic philosophical perspective. In so doing, I am, by implication, entering into the wider interdisciplinary discussions about what it means to dwell politically given the realities of climate change. I begin by offering an overview of dwelling, depicting its attributes, and locating the notion of dwelling in philosophical anthropologies. This section includes brief discussions regarding some of the perennial existential and political challenges associated with dwelling, which are framed in psycho-analytic terms. A psychoanalytic lens can illuminate some of the unconscious or unstated aspects of human dwelling. Once this foundation has been constructed, I introduce a psychoanalytic, developmental political perspective vis-à-vis dwell-ing, which builds on the psychoanalytic political philosophy of Chapter 1. This section portrays what is necessary for actualizing one's experience of dwelling, the transition from pre-political to political dwelling, and, by contrast, what con-tributes to experiences of being displaced or psychosocially unhoused. In the last section, I depict the Anthropocene Age as a crisis of dwelling for human beings and other species, identifying several key systemic apparatuses that privilege human dwelling, while undermining the dwelling of other species (and Othered human beings) and, paradoxically and tragically, undermining present and future dwelling of human beings.

A few clarifications are to be made before beginning. First, a psychoanalytic political perspective on dwelling is not intended to be comprehensive or exhaus-tive. It is doubtful that a single chapter can do justice to the notion of dwelling, especially given that it touches on all aspects of human and other-than-human life. This said, my aim, in part, is to begin the conversation regarding psychoanaly-sis' contribution to political philosophical discourses that address dwelling in the Anthropocene Age. Second, I intend to make clear in this and other chapters that the issue and question of dwelling bridge the consulting room, politics, and ecol-ogy. This may not be obvious with some patients and their struggles, but I contend it is tacitly present and, if ignored, can result in colluding with systemic forces that are implicated in human and more-than-human suffering. Relatedly, since the issue and question of dwelling are existentially foundational, I have placed it before sub-sequent chapters that deal with sovereignty, systemic obstacles, political change, etc. Fourth, the varied schools of psychoanalysis and their anthropological theories can be understood as answers to the questions of dwelling—ethos and polis. If one agrees with this claim, then it is another step to recognize that psychoanalysis can contribute to political philosophical discourse regarding what it means to dwell in an era of climate emergency.

## Dwelling: An Overview

Interestingly, the Old English verb "dwellen" meant to lead astray, hinder, or delay. These meanings receded in time, leaving the verb "dwell" to mean to live or reside in a specified place. The specific place where one resides is the noun "dwelling," which denotes a place of habitation, home, abode, residence, apartment, etc. Of course, there are people who do not dwell in a specific place, such as nomadic peoples or those who are constructed as houseless. Regardless, whether nomadic, peripatetic, or houseless, all human beings dwell in some place and all life dwells on this one earth.

Dwelling is a theme throughout Western literature, religion, and philosophy. In Greek literature, for instance, Odysseus leaves home to embark on his adventures. Departing accompanies a longing to be home with his wife, Penelope. Home is where Odysseus starts from and returns to. In Judeo-Christian scriptures, the Hebrew word for God is *Makom*, which means place (Casey, 2009, p.17). God may mean place, but there are many stories of homelessness, homesickness, dwelling, belonging, and the ambiguities of finding a home in Judeo-Christian scriptures. Abraham is called a wandering Aramean (Deut. 26:5), Joseph is unhoused by being sold into slavery by his brothers (Gen. 37:25–28), Israelites are aliens in Egypt and Babylon, and they come to dwell in the promised land by violently unhousing its residents (Joshua). In Christian scripture, Jesus leaves home, gathering his disciples, to do the work of God. Jesus claims, "The foxes have holes and the birds of the air have nests, but the Son of Man has nowhere to lay his head" (Lk. 9:58). And he remarks that in his Father's house there are many dwellings, indicating to his disciples that while they have left their homes, their real home is with God (John 14:2). The Koran has numerous references to dwelling and homes. In Buddhism, it is believed that Siddhartha Gautama left home in his quest to understand and find the cause of human suffering. Whether he was ever homesick is another question. History is replete with stories of people leaving home to embark on a quest, people being displaced from their homes and migrating to find new places to dwell, and fantasies of an eternal dwelling place.

The theme of dwelling is evident in philosophy as well. Plato's dialogues portray Socrates dwelling in Athens until he is charged with corrupting the youth and sentenced to death—the ultimate political act of unhousing someone. Instead of heeding the call of his friends to escape, Socrates chooses death over exile, confident that the judges of the dead would deem him to have lived piously and well (Rouse, 1956, p.517), implying a place after death where he would abide with other pious people that sounds to me more like one of the circles of hell, which is also a place of dwelling. The Phaedo's dialogues are rife with the language of traveling, embarking, home as the earth, and the more perfect world of forms. It is as if Plato's Socrates viewed life as moving from this inadequate world to an Edenic dwelling after death—at least for those who had lived well and piously. For those who were not pious or virtuous, the afterlife entailed just torment for their failings—hell is a dwelling of eternal suffering.

Plato's Republic (Rouse, 1956) is another example of a philosophical depiction of dwelling, albeit dwelling as it refers to the polis and how to organize it so that citizens can dwell together, though one would not want to be either a barbarian or a woman dwelling in this city-state. Aristotle argued that place is prior to all things (Casey, 2009, p.14). To be, whether a rock or living being, is to have a place. Referring to the Greek philosopher Archytas, Edward Casey (2009) claims "there is no being except being in place" (p.313). In other words, "To be," Todd Mei (2017) writes, "means to carry out a manner of dwelling…on this land" (p.145). Add to this, Aristotle wrote his *Nicomachean Ethics* (Irwin, 2019) before his *Politics* (Barker, 1971), which suggests that the question of ethos, which is equivalent to the question of how shall we dwell together, precedes questions regarding the structuring of the polis. Philosopher Melissa Lane (2014) points out that the polis, in Greek thought, was understood primarily to be "a community in which citizens share; it is a community of common activities" for the "sake of life" (pp.206–207). In Aristotle's view, for instance, the polis is a "sphere of conscious creation," which is allied with humankind's natural inclination to dwell together—to live life in common (Barker, 1971, p.xlix). Other philosophers commenting on Aristotle argue that the polis is necessary for human beings to "attain their full humanity, not only because they are (as in the privacy of the household) but also because they appear" (Arendt, 2005, p.21). Put differently, for Aristotle, the polis is humankind's "most proper dimension" (Agamben, 2011, p.xiii), because it is the medium through which human potentiality is actualized, and this actualization necessarily takes place in a particular place of human dwelling where there is civic care and trust. Ethos and polis, in short, are interrelated, both answering and living out the questions: How are we to dwell together? How are we to facilitate the flourishing of members of the polis? In brief, place, vis-à-vis human beings, means to dwell and dwelling is inhabiting a place.

Nearly a millennia later, philosopher and theologian St. Augustine (1972) wrote about the City of God, which is, for Augustine, our true home versus our earthly temporary home/city. In Augustine's theology, Adam and Eve were expelled from their perfect home because of disobedience, which left subsequent descendants to live lives of restlessness—a restlessness or homesickness that is unresolved until one resides in God (1963, p.333). This tension between home and homelessness, not dissimilar from Plato's rendition of Socrates, is reflected when Augustine, in the very opening lines of his Confessions, states, "you have made us for yourself, and our hearts are restless until they can find peace in you" (p.17). Much of subsequent Christian political theology reflects the tension between our material dwelling on the earth and spiritual dwelling with God.

If we leap over the centuries to the European Enlightenment, we note Immanuel Kant's (1963/1784) recognition of the problem of dwelling in a complex and diverse political world. He argues for cosmopolitanism—the etymological root means a world polis.[4] Soon after Kant, Georg Hegel had a Platonic take on homelessness, arguing that Socrates gave birth to the homeless spirit by liberating subjectivity (independence of an individual's thought) through the Socratic method of questioning (Gauthier, 2011, pp.3–5). It is not that human beings are ontologically homeless, as Augustine and other theologians claimed. Rather, human beings are existentially homebound or in chains until partially liberated by the Socratic method. Over a century after Hegel, three prominent philosophers, Helmut Plessner, Martin Heidegger, and Emmanuel Levinas, agreed about existential homelessness, but disagreed on its causes and implications. Plessner (2018/1931) viewed dwelling as "belonging to a people [and] is an essential trait of the human, like being able to say I and You." His more famous contemporary, Martin Heidegger, agreed but had a more abstract rendering of dwelling. Heidegger said, "Upon the earth and in it, the historical man grounds his dwelling, in the world" (in Gauthier, 2011, p.60). Regarding Heidegger's view, Todd Mei (2017) points out that the earth "is not just a material precondition of our being-in-the-world, but one that figures into every aspect of our being" (p.121). Stated differently, Heidegger "wants to elucidate how the status of the earth is the material precondition that governs our dwelling" (p.122). Heidegger's philosophical view, according to Norberg-Schultz, is a "new way to speak about and care for our human nature and environment...so that love of place and the earth are scarcely sentimental extras to be indulged only when all technological and material problems have been resolved" (in Harvey, 2016, p.177).

And yet human dwelling, for Plessner and Heidegger, is entwined with existential homelessness. David Gauthier (2011) argues that Heidegger "interprets homelessness as a symptom of the abandonment [or forgetfulness] of Being by beings" (p.129). He therefore understood that while dwelling is an existential need (Vogt, 2017, p.243) and the ground of ethics (Wood, 2019, p.56), it nevertheless is accompanied by a sense of homelessness. Phillip Tonner (2018) adds to this discussion, arguing that, for Heidegger, "Dwelling is the constitutive state of a manner of existing that is at once engaged, embedded and bodily" (p.8). As part of this engaged, embedded, and embodied aspect of dwelling is the importance, for Heidegger, of place,[5] identity, and tradition, which together mitigate our estrangement or sense of homelessness. Heidegger believed, Gauthier (2011) contends, that the challenge "is to create a philosophy that will facilitate a return to rootedness to help man to become at home in the world" (p.9).[6] "I know that everything essential and everything great," Heidegger writes, "originated from the fact that man had a home and was rooted in tradition" (Gauthier, 2011, p.92). Todd Mei (2017) notes further that "Heidegger draws on the ancient notion of *phusis* to indicate" that the earth is the "primordial source constituting the being of things" (120). As such, "the earth as the material precondition governs our dwelling" (p.122). Echoing Heidegger, Simone Weil (1952) believed that dwelling or "To be rooted is perhaps the most important and least recognized need of the human soul" (p.43), which necessarily depends on place. Critics of Heidegger, like Levinas, argue that his obdurate focus on place, identity, and tradition vis-à-vis existential homelessness fits well with the Nazis' racism, antisemitism, and German exceptionalism (Guess, 2017, pp.226–249). Phillip Tonner (2018) also criticizes the Heideggerian philosophical view that "only anatomically fully modern humans dwell" (p.9), which disavows the dwelling of early humans, as well as all other species.

Emmanuel Levinas' philosophy is, in one sense, his corrective response to Heidegger's philosophy of dwelling. Levinas contends that Heidegger "effectively subordinates ethics to ontology" (in Gauthier, 2011, p.104), and it is ontology that tends to eliminate "the alterity, or otherness, of the comprehended being" (p.105). More pointedly, Gauthier states that, in Levinas' view, "the Heideggerian project is ethically problematic because it is oblivious to the needs of strangers" (p.97)—not to mention the needs of other species vis-à-vis their dwelling. Levinas believes, in part, that our refusal to be obliged to the Other is the reason why human beings experience homelessness (p.113)—rather than the forgetfulness of Being. The source and sense of homelessness, for Levinas, "provides the impetus for human fraternity" (p.114)—dwelling together. Gauthier notes that in Levinas' political philosophy, "the home achieves its full dignity when the Other is welcomed" (p.131). In his book *Totality and Infinity*, Levinas (1969) states,

> To dwell is not the simple fact of the anonymous reality of a being cast into existence, as a stone one casts behind oneself; it is a recollection, a coming to oneself, a retreat home with oneself as in a land of refuge, which answers to a hospitality, an expectancy, a human welcome.
>
> (p.156)

Here is the apparent paradox of Levinas' view: the Other evokes a sense of homelessness and this homelessness is mitigated by the infinite obligation to recognize and welcome Others in their singularity. For Levinas, dwelling is the existential foundation of being and becoming human. This said, both Heidegger and Levinas understood human beings to be existentially homeless, which for Heidegger meant the need for roots (e.g., place) and identity, and for Levinas the importance of hospitality toward strangers (Gauthier, 2011).

The lofty language of philosophical or theological reflections on being and becoming can distract us from the very material realities and routine struggles and traumas of dwelling. Historians reveal and sometimes justify innumerable stories of people being unhoused—killed, colonized, etc. (e.g., Barry, 2012; Danner, 2009; Harman, 2017; Lepore, 2018; Zinn, 2003). Orlando Patterson (1982), Cedric Robinson (2016), and Edward Baptist (2014) describe the horrific realities of U.S. slavocracy and the Jim Crow Era vis-à-vis African Americans who were denied social-political dwelling, literally in the sense of being killed or being deprived of resources necessary to thrive. Feminists (e.g., Fraser, 2020; Tronto, 2013) and other liberation philosophers and theologians (e.g., Cone, 1970; Dussel, 1985; Gutiérrez, 1985; Moltmann, 1973) have long pointed out how excluded-included Others are marginalized and oppressed, which means being pushed to live on the fringes of society where they are deprived of goods necessary for their well-being, for dwelling. Sociologists, like Mathew Desmond (2016), depict the deeply painful and disturbing realities of people who are legally (but unjustly) and forcibly evicted from their homes,[7] which often leads to homelessness in a country that has the resources to create homes for everyone. Joe Soss, Richard C. Fording, and Sanford Schram (2011) and Loic Wacquant (2009) provide comprehensive sociological analyses of the precarities of poverty, exposing the systemic realities that leave millions of people food and housing insecure. Housing and food insecurity are linked to systemic apparatuses of racism and classism, which undermine dwelling of persons of color and those who are constructed as lower class. Georg Lukács (1968), Herbert Marcuse (1964), Dany-Robert Dufour (2008), Wendy Brown (2015), Nancy Fraser (2022), Nancy Fraser and Rahel Jaeggi (2018), Jerry Mander (2012), Sayak Valencia (2018), and others address political and economic realities that lead to psychological, political, and economic experiences of alienation and homelessness that result from global capitalism. Political and economic alienation are implicated in the issue of dwelling—materially, psychologically, and socially. Problems in dwelling are not simply associated with those deemed to be citizens. Miriam Valverde (2017), for instance, details the draconian and politically violent immigration policies of the Trump Administration, where people were not only evicted from their homes, but also deported from this country. Add to this the violence committed when states unhouse their own people, as in the cases of evictions, ethnic cleansings, apartheid, social death (Patterson, 1982), and terroristic bombings of civilians (e.g., Danner, 2009). Of course, the psychological traumas of physical and sexual abuse in every culture leave people unhoused in their own bodies, as well as feeling alienated in the world, in their homes, and in their relationships. These examples of unhousement, if you will, are likely to worsen as the effects of climate change deepen and human beings compete for dwindling resources, which I will say more about below.

There are two related points to highlight in this discussion above. First, while human beings can be seen as torn existentially between home and homelessness, it is clear, as Levinas experienced firsthand at the hands of the Nazis, that we are quite capable of furthering all kinds of homelessness for many people, while also privileging the dwelling of particular groups. This also has relevance when considering Western political philosophies and other-than-human species, which I address later. For now, let me remark that the ontological rift between human animals and other species, which is constructed by apparatuses that produce and maintain anthropocentricism, leads to the privileging of human dwelling at the expense of other species, leading to the unhousing or extinction of millions of species. Second, human dwelling is inherently paradoxical. Dwelling is an existential fact (being/actual), as well as something potential (becoming). Put differently, dwelling is both a matter of fact and a matter of intention. While I will say more about this in the section on a psychoanalytic developmental view of dwelling, for now let me simply say that, for Levinas, actualizing one's capacity and potential for dwelling (materially and psychologically) depends on others' intentional actions of welcoming. Hospitality or care actualizes the stranger's potential for dwelling, and it is through dwelling together that human beings actualize, but do not exhaust, their potentialities. The good-enough polis, in other words, is humankind's "most proper dimension" (Agamben, 2011, p.xiii) precisely because it fosters the relational conditions by which potentialities regarding dwelling are actualized.

Potentiality vis-à-vis dwelling also refers to the dwelling of other species. For Agamben (2004), potentiality is what marks all living beings, but human beings have the capacity to not actualize potential (impotentiality) and, even in actualizing potentiality, never exhaust it. All living beings depend on a biodiverse earth to actualize their potentiality for dwelling. Of course, actualizing potentiality for dwelling can be interfered with by destructive natural events and other animals (e.g., killing for food, overpopulation). The destructive realities of climate change threaten the present existent potentiality for and actualization of dwelling for many human beings and other species, but also for the non-existent potentialities of all living beings. Put differently, unfortunately, Western political philosophies promote anthropocentrism, which undermines the needs of more-than-human species regarding the actualization of their dwelling. A degraded earth means there is no place for many species to exist. It also means that extinctions caused by climate change destroy future existent dwelling of those species, which implies that environmental care and ethics are also aimed at the non-existent dwelling of all species.

Embedded in this general discussion are other attributes of dwelling and, with each attribute there are varied challenges, which are examined from a psychoanalytic perspective. Above I claimed that dwelling entails the fundamental question of how are we to live a life in common. A life lived in common presupposes experiences of belonging to a specific people and inhabiting this particular place or land [implacement] (Casey, 2009, p.23).[8] We share a common language, a shared history, a shared ethos, and a collective vision that are yoked to and emerge from speaking and acting together (polis). As Edward Casey points out, "just as every place is encultured, so every culture is implaced" (p.31). Inhabiting this particular space with these particular people means creating spaces of speaking and acting together, which depend on an ethos—narratives and rituals that are held in common—that shapes our subjectivities, our perceptions, and our behaviors. Put differently, the ethos or habitus, to use Pierre Bourdieu's (1990) concept, is internalized and inhabited, providing answers to questions regarding whom to trust, to whom do we owe loyalty, in what are we to believe (civic faith/trust), as well as what and who we are to care for.

Ideally, dwelling as belonging, which depends on mutual personal recognition particularized by a shared ethos and shared identity, necessarily means plurality.[9] Recall from the previous chapter that recognition of Others as persons means there is an excess to the person's experience of suchness or singularity, which exceeds our ability to represent an individual (Dickinson, 2015a, p.34). The consequence is that every human being (and other species) is unique, which implies a diversity within the polis. Good-enough belonging in the polis, to recall Jessica Benjamin's (1995) anthropological perspective, means there is a dialectical tension between likeness in difference and difference in likeness, which ensures plurality. That is, in dwelling together we share a collective identity linked to a particular place (Richardson, 2019), while also affirming differences regarding individual identities.

Of course, one of the challenges of belonging and identity is the conscious or unconscious belief or illusion in sameness. We believe that we must possess the same identity to belong in this polis, which instantiates a loss of the dialectical tension and, concomitantly, the denial or disavowal of plurality vis-à-vis singularity. What remains is a belonging riven by anxiety and insecurity—a form of dwelling that depends on exclusion and division (with the polis), as well as a conscious or unconscious unwillingness to overcome our rootedness and, from a Levinasian perspective, a corresponding loss of the disposition to welcome and care for Others.

Types of dwelling where belonging depends on the illusion of sameness to secure shared identity are tragically common throughout human history. From a psychoanalytic perspective, these instantiations of dwelling and their apparatuses rely on splitting off or disavowal of Others who do not share a group's identity. In addition, there is an unconscious belief that if we do not share the same identity, our belonging and identity will dissolve, which is yoked to varied forms of annihilation anxiety. The recent white supremacist, hateful and fear-laced chant, "Jews will not replace us," is an illustration of annihilation anxiety, profound insecurity, and the illusion of sameness. "Jews," in this context, are perceived and constructed as threats to white supremacists' existence, identity, and dwelling. For white supremacists, Jews do not belong. Those who are Othered (e.g., Jews, native peoples, African Americans) may be killed, assimilated (engulfed), exploited, sequestered, etc., all with the aim of securing dwelling, identity, and privileges for the dominant group. This anxiety is psychosocially comprehensible but existentially false. By this, I mean that belonging is not contingent on sharing identity. Put another way, the belief in sameness is not requisite for dwelling, as Levinas' philosophical perspective of hospitality points out. There are numerous occasions of people dwelling together who do not share the same identity, which is reminiscent of Kant's cosmopolitanism. For instance, the Norwegian town of Longyearbyen has around 2,000 residents, representing 50 nationalities and their respective cultures, living a life in common. To be sure, there must be some degree of sharing a common ethos amidst this lively plurality, but dwelling and belonging do not rest on belief in sameness vis-à-vis identity.

Another related challenge to belonging and identity vis-à-vis dwelling is hierarchical valuations. People who dwell together can share identity, yet some people within the community or society can be marginalized or excluded, while others retain privileges that enhance their experiences of dwelling and belonging. Sexism, classism, ableism, and racism represent systems that produce and maintain valuations of superiority and inferiority within a society and relations of subordination and subjugation. Those constructed, recognized, and treated as inferior are marginalized or, worse, excluded from spaces of speaking and acting together. In other words, while "inferior" others may be considered to possess the civic identity of that society, their political agency is restricted or denied, which means their experience of belonging is undermined not only with regard to social-political recognition, but also in terms of the maldistribution of resources necessary for dwelling. Alain Badiou (2018), referring to the Gulags of the Soviet Union, points out that there was an absence of politics in the camps (we could include U.S. slave labor camps, pp.50–51). Indeed, he argues further that "To put an end to the horror demands the advancement of a politics that integrates whatever has been the cost of its absence" (p.51). Those forced to live a bare life or Fanon's (2008) "zone of nonbeing" (p.xii) are by definition inferior and denied access to society's spaces of speaking and acting together. The absence of interpersonal recognition and dignity. But it is not simply the camps that are problems vis-à-vis inferiority and the absence of mutual recognition and dignity. There are any of a number of instances in so-called democratic nations where misrecognition or non-recognition takes place. Put differently, constructing some citizens or residents as inferior has very real material consequences, in that marginalized people have less access to resources that would enhance their dwelling in society and their physical dwelling, whether we are referring to one's body (e.g., more susceptible to illnesses and lack of healthcare) or one's house, apartment, etc. In brief, misrecognitions tied to beliefs in superiority and inferiority are intertwined with systems of maldistribution of resources that negatively impact experiences of dwelling (see Fraser & Honneth, 2003).

Conscious and unconscious beliefs in sameness, superiority, and inferiority also impact human beings' relations to other species and the earth. Western political philosophies production of the ontological rift between human beings and other species is fostered by these beliefs, negatively impacting the dwelling of millions of other species. In other words, anthropocentric beliefs accompany the convictions that human dwelling takes priority (of higher value) over other species and that other species exist merely for the sake of benefiting human dwelling.

Illusory beliefs in superiority and inferiority vis-à-vis dwelling, from a psychoanalytic perspective, have pernicious impacts on those who are constructed as inferior, whether the inferior Other is in or outside the polis. Of course, to those who rely on apparatuses to "prove" their own superiority and the Others' inferiority, their beliefs are not illusory, but rather a fact. In other words, social, political, and economic apparatuses produce these beliefs, while simultaneously creating the conditions of privilege and oppression. These beliefs and valuations are illusions because they must be continually produced and enforced—by way of violence or threat of violence. I add that these are illusions because there is nothing in nature to confirm either belief, which is especially evident today when we consider that climate change threatens the dwelling of human beings and other species. The possibility of human extinction, in other words, belies any belief in human superiority or the inferiority of other species. Nevertheless, many human beings are dependent on these illusions to secure and privilege their belonging and identity. This reveals unconscious insecurity and accompanying disidentification vis-à-vis "inferior Others" (including other species), as well as a convenient disavowal of their suffering and needs. I add that those who rely on apparatuses to secure their "superiority" also disavow their accountability to and for the dwelling of Othered human beings, which attends a disavowal of our responsibility in undermining the material and psychosocial dwelling of Othered persons and other-than-human species. The realities of racism, classism, sexism, ableism, speciesism, and other forms of marginalization and oppression provide innumerable examples of this problem of human dwelling.

Let me say more about the challenges of belonging as a foundational feature of human dwelling. The ontological rift means that other-than-human species do not share a political identity and, therefore, do not belong, except as they may enhance or serve human dwelling. Therefore, more-than-human species are not considered in political discourse even though they are essential to a biodiverse earth, which is foundational for human dwelling. Non-identity vis-à-vis other-than-human animals means, more often than not, disidentification, and this accompanies instrumental knowing and use of other species to enhance human dwelling and belonging. Disidentification and instrumental knowing accompany disavowal of the singularities of other-than-human species and their particular needs for dwelling (Kovel, 1988, pp.288–293).[10] This disavowal is manifested in our forgetting about them entirely (normative and historical unconscious) or exploiting them because our dwelling is of higher value—so we believe and our apparatuses confirm. This disavowal accompanies the absence of empathy and remorse for the suffering of Othered human beings and other species. To put this in Kantian terms, the categorical imperative, or Løgstrup's (1997) ethical demand to care, which is constitutive for human dwelling, does not include other species. If, however, we acknowledge that a biodiverse earth is necessary for human dwelling, then it would be logical to include other species in the ethics and polity of dwelling. Other species belong precisely because they dwell with us on this one earth, and this means the categorical imperative applies to all species. Thus, the beliefs associated with human superiority and inferiority of other species interfere with the ecological-political realities of dwelling. Ethos and polis include and depend on nature.

Before moving on to other attributes of dwelling, it is important to say a bit about belonging and identity as they pertain to boundaries. Wendy Brown (2010) notes that, since the fall of the Berlin Wall, many nation-states are building walls or other fortifications, which she argues are attempts to further secure the sovereignty of nation-states. The United States builds walls on its southern border, the India-Pakistan border is heavily constructed and armored, and Israel walls off Palestinians. These border walls are also attempts to keep out those who do not share in the nation-state's ethos and identity. We do not want "Them" dwelling with us because "They" are dangerous, dirty, etc. For those Othered persons who make it past the border legally, they are surveilled as they enter the immigration process to become citizens—for people of color in the United States, this means being second-class citizens. For those who find other ways to cross, they are often imprisoned and deported—the denial of their need to dwell—a denial of civic care and civic faith.

Boundaries and borders are also found within nations. For instance, gated communities and apartments with "poor" doors are symptoms of classism and, in many cases, racism. People who can afford to dwell there possess more privileges, keeping poor (read "inferior") people outside the gates, except in cases where they are house cleaners, gardeners, etc. I recall seeing a photograph taken by a drone of a part of a South African city where there was a wall between the very poorest part of the city and a wealthy neighborhood. The contrast was startling. People outside the wall are members of the society and share in the South African national identity, yet they are also excluded and marginalized, which means the resources for their physical well-being and physical dwelling are severely reduced or denied.

Boundaries also pertain to other-than-human species. These boundaries may be physical, in the sense of excluding wild animals. Enclosures or barriers may be constructed to keep some animals out or animals within enclosures (e.g., zoos, cattle and pig farms, etc.). Boundaries may be also informal and inadvertent, which is seen when human beings "develop" a wilderness area, which drives many species out from their dwellings. Boundaries vis-à-vis other-than-human beings more often than not reveal their status in terms of political dwelling, which is another illustration of the ontological divide. More-than-human beings may be included in the polis, but they do not belong except in the sense of serving human dwelling. Species not constructed as useful or constructed as dangerous are excluded from spaces of human dwellings.[11] In each case, disavowal of the needs and sufferings of other-than-human beings pervades our relations with them.

There is an implicit factor in this discussion of political belonging, identity, and boundaries, namely, power and force. I will say more about power and force in Chapter 3, but for now I remind readers of Arendt's distinction between power and force or violence. Power, for Arendt, is defined as people speaking and cooperating together, while force is a synonym for violence, which is characterized by its instrumental epistemology and relations (Arendt, 1970, pp.44–46). In terms of the attributes of dwelling, speaking and acting together undergirds belonging, identity, and boundaries, but force or threat of force can be used to secure types of belonging, identity, and boundaries or exclude Othered human beings and other species. This said, whenever force, as coercion and violence or threat of violence, is exercised by the apparatuses of the polis, we note that the recipients or targets of the violence are excluded from the spaces of speaking and acting together, their identities are marginalized, and their capacity for dwelling is undermined. Of course, marginalized groups often create their own political spaces of belonging and identity, setting up boundaries for their protection. A quick example is and was the use of force and violence against African Americans by social, political, and economic apparatuses that produce and maintain illusions of white supremacy, securing white identity, belonging, and physical and material boundaries over and against African Americans who have been constructed as inferior. Many African Americans have responded by creating spaces for belonging, identity, and agency that rendered and render inoperative white supremacy (churches, political organizations) as a factor in human dwelling. To put this differently, these communities exhibit interpersonal care that makes possible spaces for individuals to exercise their capacity for impotentiality—a capacity linked to ungovernable selves. Moreover, to do so requires the forming of boundaries to actualize their potential for dwelling.

The realities of power and violence are, in Western political philosophies, usually discussed in terms of the political dwelling of human beings. The earth and other species are rarely mentioned, though this is changing as a result of the realities of climate change. Of course, using Arendt's (1958) notion of power as speaking and acting together, other species would not be included because they lack political agency. But so do infants and other human beings who are, for assorted reasons, unable to exercise their agency. They nevertheless belong and dwell with us. Other species belong because they dwell on this one earth, and a biodiverse earth is the ground of all political dwelling. Unfortunately, most human relations with other species are characterized by varied iterations of force, in part, because other-than-human species (and some groups of human beings) are constructed by

Western political philosophies as inferior and, therefore, perceived to exist for the sole purpose of human dwelling. The Anthropocene Age, with its mass extinctions, reveals the systemic violence and brutality of human beings toward other species, which tragically, in the long run, undermines human political dwelling.

There are two other important related attributes of dwelling for all species, namely, vulnerability and dependency. All life exists in relation to and hence vulnerable to non-existence. More specifically, all living species are dependent on the earth for their existence and flourishing, even as they are vulnerable to the destructive elements of the earth. From a different angle, the Anthropocene Age reveals that human beings are a force of nature (Chakrabarty, 2009), which means that, in negatively altering the climate, we[12] imperil the dwelling and existence of millions of species that may eventually include ourselves. We are making ourselves more vulnerable in our desperate attempts to be independent of nature. Of course, vulnerability and dependence exist on a continuum with some species seemingly more vulnerable and dependent than others. In terms of human beings, infants are clearly more vulnerable and dependent for their existence than most adults, but adults, despite resiliencies, defenses, and illusions of self-sufficiency and independence, are nevertheless vulnerable and dependent on this one earth. It may be that our drive in the West to be independent of "nature" through our attempts to "control" nature is, from a psychoanalytic perspective, a way to avoid facing and embracing individual and collective existential vulnerability and dependence.

The issue of vulnerability and dependence also impacts dwelling, as it pertains to human belonging. Racism, classism, sexism,[13] and other forms of marginalization and oppression can be understood to represent attempts to manage the anxieties of vulnerability and dependency through disavowal and projection (Butler, 2004). Apparatuses of white (or male) supremacy split off white insecurities, fears, and anxieties regarding vulnerability and dependency, while attempting to make people of color (and women) vulnerable and dependent, resulting in the diminishment of their psychological and material dwelling. In terms of classism, the wealthy garner vast resources to secure their dwellings and to reduce their vulnerabilities at the cost of making the dwelling of poor people more precarious. Paradoxically and unconsciously, this only reinforces their dependence on subordinating and subjugating people of the lower classes. The point here is that human dwelling is inextricably tied to the existential realities of human vulnerability and dependency, which many human beings attempt to deny through splitting and projection that ends up deepening the precarity of Others, whether Others are a particular group of human beings or other-than-human beings.

The ontological rift between human dwelling and more-than-human species also reflects the issues of vulnerability and dependency. Western philosophies have largely promulgated the belief that human beings are distinct from, if not separate or above, nature. Geoengineering, animal experimentation, factory farming, etc. are examples of this instrumental control and violent means of using nature for human well-being. In these situations, the vulnerability of other species is worsened through human exploitation and neglect, which will likely lead to tragedy for human beings. As Jonathan Schell (2020) remarks, "If we conquer nature, we will find ourselves among the defeated" (p.19).[14] The irony and tragedy here is that human instrumentalizing the earth and other species for the sake of human dwelling exacerbates the present and future vulnerabilities of human existence. As Val Plumwood (2008) argues, an "ecological re-conception of dwelling has to include a justice perspective" when it comes to other-than-human species (p.139). Political justice must also include care.

In summary, human dwelling entails both polis and ethos. The ethos informs those who dwell in common about whom to trust, to whom do we owe loyalty, and for whom and what we are to care about and for. Implicit in both polis and ethos is mutual personal recognition that, at best, affirms singularity and plurality and, at worse, relies on the illusion of sameness for political belonging. As part of dwelling, I indicated that singularity and plurality are linked to what it means to belong as a people—individual and collective identity. Both belonging and identity vis-à-vis dwelling accompany the establishment of boundaries, which are real and imagine. All of this accompanies myriad expressions and exercises of power and force. The other attributes of dwelling highlighted were vulnerability and dependency—a feature of human and more-than-human life. Each of these features of dwelling engenders problems and challenges, whether that refers simply to dwelling with other human beings or human dwelling in relation to other species and the earth.

## Dwelling: A Psychoanalytic-Political Perspective

To further this discussion, I turn to a psychoanalytic developmental-political view of dwelling. Here I contend that psychoanalytic perspectives can contribute to not only an understanding of dwelling, but also political dwelling in the Anthropocene Age. Part of this contribution is to identify what I believe are foundational psychoanalytic premises that, while wildly variable in expression, pertain to all forms of human dwelling.

Nearly a century ago, Otto Rank (1929/2014) argued that "*analysis turns out to be a belated accomplishment of the uncompleted mastery of the birth trauma*" (p.5). Perhaps this trauma was rooted in the fact that the newborn baby is unhoused from a sensorially peaceful, oceanic home of the womb and thrown into a world that is "one great blooming buzzing confusion" (James, 1918, p.488). Both Otto Rank and William James seem to suggest that something necessarily precedes birth trauma or confusion—a nascent ego and some pre-semantic organizations of experience—which Winnicott (1975, p.186) would have agreed with. If these did not exist, how could there be trauma or great blooming confusion? Given this, we might posit pre-representational, embodied experiences of dwelling prior to birth. The womb, in other words, is the first *place* we experience dwelling.

Once thrown into this great blooming and buzzing world, infants are vulnerable and, therefore, reliant on the consistent care of good-enough parents. This care, as elaborated in the previous chapter, consists of personal recognition, which is a foundational feature of attunement and repair of relational disruptions. Care provides the matrix for infants' burgeoning embodied and nascent consciousness[15] and organizations of relational experiences of dwelling. To "inhabit the world in an embodied way" in relation to Others "means that [children] must also inhabit [their] essential sociality, since the contingencies of corporeal life are how and why we are drawn into relations of interdependence with others" (Waggoner, 2018, p.107). Naturally, these early experiences of dwelling are organized semiotically or pre-semantically.

Organizing experience implies a nascent ego. It is not only the construction of presymbolic experiences of dwelling that points to the presence of an ego. It is also that vulnerable and dependent infants surrender to the parents' ministrations, which means there is sufficient presymbolic relational trust to risk asserting needs and desires and to be open to parents' caring responses. The point here is that while infants are dependent and vulnerable, they are not passive. There is a co-participation with regard to the space of "speaking and acting together," which is foundational to presymbolic, embodied-relational experiences of dwelling. I add here that, in this space of speaking and acting together, infants' embodied-relational experiences of dwelling necessarily include nascent presymbolic organizations of self-esteem, self-respect, and self-confidence that subtend infants' agency.

I want to pause here to highlight an important aspect regarding dwelling vis-à-vis psychosocial development. Philosopher John Macmurray (1961) argues that a person is a matter of fact and a matter of intention. The individual *qua* person is an existential fact; however, to experience being a person means that others *intend* to recognize and treat the individual as a person. This applies to dwelling. The infant who is dwelling in the womb is a matter of fact, but it is also a matter of intention with regard to the parents. A pregnant person may decide to have an abortion or the partner may harm the mother, intending to end the pregnancy. After birth, children dwell—a fact—but this is also a matter of intention. For evidence of this, I need only point to the thousands of parental caring acts that are intended to facilitate children's experiences of being with and of dwelling together.

Fact and intention vis-à-vis dwelling can also be framed in terms of potentiality and actuality. Infants' potentiality for dwelling depends on parental care. Biologically, one could argue that a pregnant woman's body is biologically geared to actualize the dwelling of an infant. However, for dwelling to move toward actualization, a woman necessarily cares for her body and is cared for by others, making possible infants' dwelling. People who are oppressed and marginalized face many obstacles with regard to the actualization of their potentialities for good-enough dwelling, as well as the dwelling of their children. Women of color, for instance, have higher infant mortality rates.[16] The claim here is that good-enough care entails a matter of intention and is necessary for actualizing human potential for embodied-relational dwelling, which is the case for children who are vulnerable and dependent, but also for adults who can be oppressed or killed. Put differently, actualizing children's potentiality for dwelling is facilitated by good-enough parental care and societal apparatuses.

To return to a psychoanalytic developmental perspective, I move to Christopher Bollas' (1987) term "unthought knowns." I suggest that early presymbolic, embodied-relational experiences of dwelling are unthought knowns that become intertwined with later symbolic organizations of experiences of dwelling. An adult's oceanic experience, such as surrendering to a symphony, or some other aesthetic experience accompanies the "illusion of deep rapport of subject and object" (p.32), which can be understood as linked to early pre-symbolic experiences of embodied-relational dwelling. Put differently, a deep rapport between subject and object is also a sense of the subject inhabiting and being inhabited by the object—a sense of oneness or union. This is reminiscent of Buber's (1958) notion of I-Thou relations, which includes not only our relations to other human beings but also to animate and inanimate objects.

Bollas' concept of unthought knowns can be understood from another perspective regarding dwelling. Early presymbolic experiences of dwelling, I claim, do not exhibit the deep ontological rift between human beings and other-than-human beings (or other objects). To be sure, infants are partially capable of differentiating between this and that object, but in my view, early capacity for differentiation is devoid of exclusionary beliefs in superiority or inferiority. It may be that infants recognize, to some degree, their profound dependence on parents, who may be seen as powerful dispensers of care, but asymmetry does not, I contend, accompany the belief in parents' superiority or the infant's inferiority—at least in good-enough parent-infant interactions. I think further evidence of the absence of the ontological rift in early organizations of experience is the unthought knowns in adults' aesthetic experiences. The deep relational rapport or dwelling in aesthetic experience is necessarily devoid of beliefs in inferiority or superiority. If one believes one is inferior, there can be no genuine surrender or rapport, only subordination and subjugation. Shame (inferiority) is never an aesthetic experience, but it is an experience of not dwelling or not being at home in one's own body, as well as alienation regarding self and others.[17]

If there is no ontological rift, then the objects at hand and the place (e.g., home) are part of children's experiences of dwelling. This means the materiality of the "place" is woven into and, in part, the ground of children's embodied, psychosocial experiences of dwelling. There is no object without place. The background importance of place with regard to early experiences of dwelling is evident when children experience parental deprivation and impingement. The lack or absence of parental care interferes with children's actualizing their experiences of dwelling. In other words, deprivation evokes distrust, which is not simply aimed at the parent. It encompasses distrust and anxiety about the environment, the place itself, which becomes *unheimlich*, unhomelike. This *unheimlich* that results from trauma includes not simply relational disruption, but a sense of not being at home in this place and in one's body. A patient remarked that he felt at home in a city that was a day's travel from the city he grew up in. Whenever he goes back to where he grew up, he has a sense of deadness. He does not feel at home in the city of his youth. On a more positive note, infants' actualization of their potential for and experiences of dwelling depend on the caring attunements of parents, which means that dwelling is associated not simply with the relation to parents, but is inclusive of the place and its objects.

Since I am mentioning objects and the absence of an ontological rift, let me turn to the first transitional objects and the notion of dwelling. I mentioned in Chapter 1 that the primary transitional object represents parental ministrations (RIGs [Representations of Interactions that have been Generalized]), which includes semiotic organizations of self-esteem, self-confidence, and self-respect that are integral to infants developing agency. Here I want to suggest that the first or primary TO can also be understood as facilitating infants' experiences of dwelling that are under their omnipotent control. Moments of separation anxiety may motivate a turn to the TO to secure infants' experiences of dwelling, which also means the TO, being under the infant's omnipotent control, functions to manage the infant's emotions vis-à-vis vulnerability and dependency. I add here that the TO includes the place, though this is in the background. An example of this is an infant who is with his parents in a strange place, clinging to his blanket. The blanket comforts not only because it represents parental care, but also the familiarity of the place where care was experienced. Children take a piece of home with them when holding onto transitional objects. Adults do this as well. This suggests that the first TO represents infants greater agency with regard to their co-creating dwelling with others.

Secondary transitional objects are taken from the cultural field and also represent (1) parental care, (2) child-parent speaking and acting together, and (3) place. This is when capacities for symbolization become increasingly crucial to organizing experiences of dwelling. As indicated above, earlier embodied, relational semiotic organizations of experience become intertwined, but these are unconscious—unthought knowns. Secondary transitional objects can be further depicted as a bridge to dwelling with others in the larger social-cultural field, which means that children are internalizing and learning how to make use of the culture's symbolic field to dwell publicly with others.

The initial secondary transitional objects, I contend, also are devoid of the ontological rift, especially between human beings and animals. Browse the children's section at the local bookstore and one reads innumerable stories of children interacting with other animals. These animals communicate with children and they dwell together. In the imagination of the authors, other species are different, but they are like us in that they communicate and dwell with us. They are an integral part of public-political spaces children inhabit. The fact that adult authors of children's literature can use their imaginations to entertain and teach children by way of speaking and acting to and with other species suggests there is no ontological rift in their or in children's imagination. Nature and other species are part of human dwelling.

If the secondary transitional object is a bridge to dwelling with others in one's locale, then in making this transition the secondary TO loses its psychosocial function and importance. As Winnicott (1971) writes, "It is not forgotten and it is not mourned. It loses its meaning, and this is because the transitional phenomena have become diffused, have become spread out…over the whole cultural field" (p.5).

Part of the difficulty in making this transition to political dwelling is, in the West, the internalization of beliefs in human superiority and other-species' inferiority that leads to the ontological rift between human beings and other species. What is lost are experiences of place that include animate and inanimate objects as necessary for human dwelling. Naturally, human beings may include other species in their experiences of dwelling, but these are pets or animals constructed for human use.

I want to add a couple of thoughts to further this discussion of psychosocial development and dwelling. In Chapter 1, I offered several examples of the impact of racism on the lives and psyches of African Americans, like Malcolm X, Ruby Sales, Martin Luther King Jr., Ta-Nehisi Coates, and untold others. Racism, and other systems of oppression and marginalization, can literally unhouse people from their homes and even their lives. These systems also make the transition to the public-political spaces of dwelling together more difficult. African American children, for example, have embodied-relational experiences of dwelling with good-enough parents, but in transitioning to the public realm they may have experiences of not feeling at home in public spaces or in their own bodies (Coates, 2015). Fear, anxiety, and distrust make it difficult to have the freedom to exercise their agency. This is due to apparatuses of white supremacy that undermine civic care and personal recognition, disconfirming African Americans' senses of self-esteem, self-respect, and self-confidence that are necessary for the exercise of political agency in speaking and acting together in this place. Many African Americans over the decades have not felt at home in the United States, with many living abroad. I remember a conversation my wife and I had with an African American couple in a café in Venice, Italy. They had lived overseas for years and said they would never return to the United States, except to visit. They felt more at home in the "foreign" country in which they resided than in the United States, and they did not want their daughter to grow up (dwell) in a racist society.

To summarize, a psychoanalytic developmental perspective of dwelling offers a number of contributions to political philosophy. First and foremost, good-enough care is foundational to individuals' actualizing their potentiality for experiences of dwelling with others in a particular place. As indicated above, dwelling is a matter of fact and a matter of intention. Parental caring attunements (including repair) reflect this matter of intention, giving rise to dependent infants' relational trust to assert their needs and desires, as well as to surrender to parents' caring actions. These first experiences of dwelling are presymbolic organizations, which later become enfolded into symbolic organizations. Implicit here is that nascent ego or agency is geared toward actualizing children's potentiality for dwelling. This leads to another contribution, which is that experiences of political dwelling are yoked to unconscious processes and representations (unthought knowns) that are related to earlier embodied-relational organizations of experience of dwelling. A third contribution a psychoanalytic developmental perspective on dwelling offers is that the rift between human animals and other animals does not exist in early childhood. This suggests there is no "ontological" rift, except the one created by Western political philosophies and theologies. This rift, in other words, is a learned illusion, becoming part of the adult persons' experiences of dwelling. If this is the case, then it becomes possible to raise this illusion to consciousness and then to consider constructing a political philosophy of dwelling that is free of this illusion. Let me add here that a psychoanalytic perspective also reveals that when dwelling is dependent on the illusion of the ontological rift, there is a corresponding anxiety and fear of early experiences of dwelling that do not privilege human beings over other animals. Evidence for this are derogatory statements (projections) made toward "native" or "primitive" peoples who are more attuned and adapted to nature (do not have this illusion as the core of their dwelling and do not split off nature from being human) and the history of Western attempts to "civilize" these people who have been constructed as primitive. A fourth and related contribution is that a psychoanalytic developmental perspective portrays the transition from pre-political to political forms of dwelling. This transition can be precarious, not simply because of failures in parental care, but because systemic political apparatuses undermine the experiences of dwelling for some parents and their children.

## The Anthropocene Age as a Crisis of Political Dwelling

Decades ago, long before news of climate change permeated society, philosopher Alfred North Whitehead remarked that "Any physical object which by its influence deteriorates its environment, commits suicide" (in Wood, 2019, p.65). In the case of climate change, suicide with regard to human beings destroying the environment includes the extinction of millions of species. In one sense, our collective actions in degrading the environment is a crisis of political dwelling, precisely because a biodiverse earth is the material condition for political dwelling. An uninhabitable earth (Wallace-Wells, 2020) obviously means there is no place for a polis, no place to dwell. This is the worst possible outcome, but this is not the only reason why the Anthropocene Age is a crisis of political dwelling. We are already in the midst of this crisis and I highlight some of the features of this political crisis.

In the Introduction, I mentioned that U.S. intelligence agencies and the Pentagon take seriously global threats to "national security" (Davenport, 2014). Without a doubt, this means these agencies are planning for future conflicts as states fail, resources dwindle, and mass migrations (already happening) take place within and between states. The acknowledged goal of the United States is to retain its hegemonic position in the world, believing that the United States as a superpower is a stabilizing political influence. In brief, these reports acknowledge that the increasing impacts of climate change will lead to political crises. The reality is the United States and other imperialistic states (Russia and China) are vying for greater economic and political power, which only exacerbates the political crisis. Instead of cooperating to reduce the impacts of climate change, these imperialistic nations, especially the United States, are spending trillions of dollars on military services and weapons. The U.S. budget for defense spending in 2021 was over a trillion dollars, which exceeds the combined military expenditures of China, Russia, Germany, France, Italy, Australia, India, the United Kingdom, South Korea, Saudi

Arabia, and Japan.[18] Martin Luther King Jr. once said that war is the enemy of the poor. I would add that preparation for war is the enemy of the poor, and it is inherently destructive politically with regard to climate change because these expenditures only worsen climate change and undermine the dwelling of millions of species. Consider that military readiness requires vast amounts of energy and includes other environmentally destructive actions (e.g., tanks, heavy equipment, bombs, environmentally destructive chemicals, and displacement of species).[19] There is a tragic vicious cycle linked to imperial nations preoccupied with maintaining political stability. The more they divert resources to preparing for conflict, the more they contribute to climate inaction and environmental destruction, and the more they are leading to greater political instability.

Another feature of imperial states vying for more and more political and economic power has to do with the rise of nation-states and their preoccupation with state sovereignty as *the* form of political dwelling. I will say more about this in the next two chapters, but for now let me say that political arrangements that are wedded to the idea of nation-states make international cooperation toward climate action much more difficult. Each state seeks to pursue its own interests and nations,[20] especially the imperialistic United States, drum up patriotic support that leads to an us versus them approach to international politics. This was clear in the United States when the corrupt 45th president and his cronies opted out of the climate accords. Even if nations sign the climate accords, there is no enforcement because each nation is sovereign. I would also mention that poorer nations are desperate for help, while wealthy global north nations have not offered much in the way resources for poor nations to develop sustainable economies.[21] Poorer nations will experience greater political instability (diminishment of dwelling), leading to migrations and conflicts.

The inherent tragedies of imperialistic states (the United States, China, and Russia) and the competitive milieu of nation-states are linked largely to apparatuses of global capitalism, which undermine dwelling of human beings and other species. The rise and spread of capitalism in the 17th through the 20th centuries has been due to colonialism (Western nations) (Woods, 2017). In the late 20th century, the emergence of the more virulent neoliberal capitalism in the United States and Britain spread throughout the world, primarily as a result of U.S. exercise of political and military power (see, Jones, 2012; Klein, 2007; Mander, 2012; Reich, 2007, 2015; Valencia, 2018; Woods, 2017). The result of the proliferation of neoliberal capitalism includes vast gaps in income and wealth (Piketty, 2014, 2020) and the unrelenting expansion of greenhouse gases. Indeed, Jason Moore (2016) believes that a more apt appellation for our current era is Capitalocene Age. Beginning in the early decades of the 19th century, the climate has changed in pace with the rise of greenhouse gas emissions due to industrialization. Another way to frame this is that, between 1800 and the end of WWII, the total $CO_2$ emissions were at or under 5 billion tons per year. Since 1950, it has exceeded 35 billion tons (and rising).[22] The reason for this massive change is that, after WWII, there was a vast expansion in global capitalism with the United States leading the way.

At a global level, capitalism has for centuries undermined the dwelling (political, physical, and psychosocial) of billions of people, while securing the dwelling for millions. The apparatuses of capitalism, in other words, produce and depend on racism and classism (see Mills, 1983). In terms of the current climate emergency, this means that poorer citizens will lack the resources to protect themselves from negative climate events. For instance, poor persons in the U.S. Northeast currently lack air conditioners during heat waves, making them more susceptible to heat-related illnesses and death—existentially unhoused. Poor persons who are in the paths of devastating hurricanes may be unhoused and, if still alive, be unable to rebuild. Capitalism may not be a problem of political dwelling for the political and economic elite, at least currently. But in time, even the wealthiest will not be able to protect themselves from being unhoused by climate change.

Capitalism, which I will say more about in Chapter 4, can also be seen as politically untenable when we turn to other-than-human species. Capitalism is not only an equal opportunity exploiter of vulnerable human beings, it also, in its preoccupation with profits, exploits other species and the earth. A capitalist mindset neglects the short-term or long-term "costs" of polluting the air, water, and land—unless government regulations and laws rein in the worse offenders. Capitalist mindsets pay little attention to the necessity of biodiversity for human dwelling as it develops factory farms, experiments on other species, etc. In my view, capitalism will be a major factor in the crisis of political dwelling, not simply because of the rapacious, unremorseful pursuit of profits, but because, as a system that structures political belonging, it maintains the ontological rift between human beings and other species and, as the Anthropocene reveals, undermines the very material foundation of political belonging. It is not the internal contradictions that will bring capitalism down, it is a degraded earth and human extinction. To return to Whitehead, capitalism (which intersects with imperialism and nationalism) is and will be the means of the extinction of millions of species and our collective suicide.

I have sketched some of the global, intersecting factors that undermine political dwelling in the Anthropocene. Now I narrow the focus to some of the features of degraded political dwelling in the United States. For decades, researchers and activists have highlighted the deleterious effects of environmental racism (see Taylor, 2014; Zimring, 2017). Homelessness, evictions, inadequate dwellings, and living near polluting factories are just some examples of how environmental racism undermines the physical and psychological well-being of individuals, families, and communities.[23] Environmental racism is produced and maintained by political and economic apparatuses that prevent or obstruct people of color from engaging and being represented in political spaces of speaking and acting together. This, in turn, contributes to undermining their experiences of dwelling—embodied, psychological, social, and political. True, local residents may protest and seek to have local governments clean up toxic environments in their community, but it is altogether another question whether these sites will be cleaned up and people compensated for decades of political inaction. Of course, the reality of environmental racism was present long before anyone was aware of climate change. It is a safe prediction that environmental racism in the United States and elsewhere will only worsen as the climate deteriorates. If history is a guide, political and economic elites will not make changes to address the needs of people of color who are facing climate disasters. Worse, political and economic elites will exploit race divisions to further their opportunistic goals, which we have seen played out in the Republican leadership in the United States over the last four decades. While racism and classism are issues and crises of political dwelling, environmental racism/classism in the Anthropocene Age reveals just how destructive it is for millions of people of color.

Capitalism, nationalism, and imperialism are produced and maintained by innumerable apparatuses that have undermined and undermine the physical, psychosocial, and political dwelling of billions of human beings. There is, in other words, an inherent political crisis of dwelling that exists within these systems—privileging the dwelling of one group while making the dwelling of others more precarious. The frightening realities of climate change have also revealed that these systemic forces are imperiling the dwelling of more-than-human species, which, in turn, imperils human political dwelling. While I will say more in Chapter 4 about these systems as obstacles to climate action, for now I simply note that they represent formidable obstacles to global cooperation toward mitigating the disastrous trajectory we are currently on—a trajectory of being unhoused. It may very well be that the tragedy of human life will be that our creation of global systems of political and economic apparatuses will destroy our ability and the ability of millions of other species to inhabit this earth.

## Conclusion

Psychoanalysis, in my view, is concerned about patients' experiences of dwelling, whether in their own bodies, their families, or communities. If we move out of the consulting room, we can see that dwelling is a political reality. It has been my argument that psychoanalysis can offer insights not only into the unconscious aspects of political dwelling, but also insights into the emergence and development of persons' experiences of dwelling. Put differently, psychoanalysts can develop a psychoanalytic political philosophy that attends to the embodied, relational realities of dwelling with the combined aims of (1) engaging in and contributing to political philosophical discourses around climate change and (2) developing more caring and just ways of dwelling with each other and other species on this one place we call earth. The dire realities of the Anthropocene Age reveal the existential demand to care for each other, other species, and the earth. The likely possibility of extinction means not just an end of the earth as a place for dwelling, but the end of dwelling on this earth.

## Notes

1  Roland Boer (2009) examines the use and abuse of political myths in Judeo-Christian scriptures. These myths continue to shape Western secular notions of the state. Wendy Brown (2010), in part echoing Carl Schmitt, notes that the notion of sovereignty that is "secularized for political purposes *does not lose its religious structure or bearing*, even as it ceases to have the direct authority of God at its heart" (p.70).

2  Todd Mei (2017) argues that "the focus on and recovery of place is crucial for addressing conceptual prejudices which can be tied to forms of environmental and sociopolitical exploitation" (p.110). Edward Casey (2009) adds to this by discussing groups of people who have been displaced and the short- and long-term negative impacts of displacement. This can be understood to refer to particular places, but also the earth as a whole with all of its species.

3  Illustrations of this can be seen in indigenous stories. See Kerven, *Native American Myths: Collected 1636–1919*; Erdoes and Ortiz, *American Indian Myths and Legends*.

4  Martha Nussbaum (2019) identifies some of the key flaws to the notion of cosmopolitanism, which needs to be considered given the issues of plurality and climate change.

5  Philosopher Jeff Malpas (2012) explores Heidegger's work from the perspective of the idea of place. Similarly, Edward Casey (2009) considers the importance of the idea of place as it relates to being. Casey argues it is not possible to conceive of being without place. It is place that is the ground of the possibility of human dwelling. It is not possible to do justice to the notion of place vis-à-vis dwelling, though I acknowledge its importance and will attempt to include it in the discussion of dwelling as it pertains to psychosocial development. See also Malpas (1999, 2006).

6  Todd Mei (2017) argues that "Heidegger see specific problems like the lack of housing as symptomatic of the failure to understand what it means to dwell" (p.130). Of course, Heidegger's affiliation with the Nazis and his antisemitism suggest his failure to understand what it means to dwell.

7  Todd Mei (2017) argues that Heidegger viewed "the lack of housing as symptomatic of the failure to understand what it means to dwell" (p.130). I would add that the failure is not only about human dwelling, but also about how we dwell in this place called earth and with more-than-human species.

8  Todd Mei (2006, 2017) explores the concept of place as it relates to land, which provides a path to reconsider and reimagine our relationship to the earth and to our particular patch of earth/land.

9  Karl Popper (2002) makes clear that a flourishing society depends on diversity or plurality. When belonging becomes connected to sameness (vis-à-vis ethos, identity), then we can be assured this is not an open society but one that will have one segment of the population flourishing at the expense of different Others.

10  Kovel (1988) points out that human beings necessarily make distinctions between themselves and other species, but distinctions do not necessarily lead to separation. People can make distinctions "when they "differentiate from each other" such that "they remain associated, connected, and indeed, mirrored" (p.292). When we make distinctions that lead to separation there is the presence of poor differentiation, disidentification, and disavowal. From a psychoanalytic vantage point, Kovel is addressing the ontological rift.

11  Eva Meijer (2019, 2020) makes a case for the inclusion of other-than-human species in political theorizing because of our dependence on a biodiverse earth. While other animals may not have political agency, they necessarily belong to the polis. Other ecologically minded scholars and activists propose re-wilding areas that have previously excluded other species (see Jepson & Blythe, 2022; Paulsen, Jagodzinski, & Hawke, 2021). It is also important to mention the work of philosopher Peter Singer (1975) whose early work, *Animal Liberation*, sparked a movement that seeks to care for other species and reduce human exploitation of other species.

12  I feel it is necessary to indicate that not all human beings bear the same level of responsibility for climate change, even if they reside in Western societies. Native peoples, poor persons, sustainable communities, etc., have little or no impact on climate change, though they too suffer the effects.

13  Sarah Bracke (2016) and other feminists (e.g., Dodds, 2014; Gentry, 2015; Koivunen, Kyrölä, & Ryberg, 2019) have explored the issue of vulnerability and resistance in

situations of marginalization and oppression. In general, these and other writers identify the problems of vulnerability as well as its power vis-à-vis resisting trauma and oppression. While feminists and other liberative philosophers focus on vulnerability in relation to other human beings, it is necessary to acknowledge the vulnerability of all life and that human beings can deliberately and inadvertently exacerbate and exploit the vulnerabilities of more-than-human species.

14  Alan Watts (1957, pp.174–175) also points to Western preoccupations with conquering nature, as if nature is an object to serve the needs of humanity or that "nature" can actually be conquered.

15  Matt Waggoner (2018), discussing Theodor Adorno's philosophy, notes that "The human experience of dwelling begins with embodiment, with the fact that consciousness is inseparable from the somatic and sensorial" (p.105). "Embodied life," he points out, "contains within its phenomenology a template for what we have been calling dwelling. The necessity of corporeal beings to seek housing in a place and in relation with others is never purely subjective and cannot be individualized" (p.105), which points to both human vulnerability and dependency.

16  Racial and Ethnic Disparities Continue in Pregnancy-Related Deaths|CDC Online Newsroom|CDC,   https://www.cdc.gov/media/releases/2019/p0905-racial-ethnic-disparities-pregnancy-deaths.html, accessed 4 February 2022.

17  Psychoanalysts George Atwood and Robert Stolorow (2016; see also Stolorow, 2014) uses the term "emotional dwelling" to move away from a Cartesian view of the isolated mind, while affirming the fundamental relationality of the mind. I am in agreement, yet I want to extend our understanding of dwelling to include the political and to indicate that in early development there is no ontological rift.

18  U.S. Defense Spending Compared to Other Countries (pgpf.org), https://www.pgpf.org/chart-archive/0053_defense-comparison, accessed 22 February 2022.

19  The military's contribution to climate change – CEOBS, https://ceobs.org/the-militarys-contribution-to-climate-change/, accessed 22 February 2022.

20  It is more accurate to say that the political and economic elites that operate state machinery pursue their interests, which may or may not coincide with the interests of ordinary citizens.

21  How climate change traps poor countries between poverty and disaster – CNET, https://www.cnet.com/news/how-climate-change-traps-poor-countries-between-poverty-and-disaster/, accessed 22 February 2022.

22  See Annual $CO_2$ emissions by world region (https://ourworldindata.org/grapher/annual-co-emissions-by-region)accessed 5 February 2021.

23  Environmental Racism Collection|Environmental Health Perspectives (nih.gov), https://ehp.niehs.nih.gov/curated-collections/environmental-racism, accessed 22 February 2022.

# Chapter 3

# Psychoanalysis, Sovereignty, and Political Violence

What is particular to human dwelling is its ground in ethos and polis. In Western philosophies (and theologies[1]), the ethos and polis of dwelling are inextricably yoked to and dependent on the notion of sovereignty. Throughout the millennia in the West, varied forms of sovereignty have appeared—oligarchies, tyrannies, aristocracies, monarchies, plutocracies, democracies—and, at times, these faded or morphed through revolution into another type of sovereignty. What has remained largely, but not entirely, unquestioned is whether sovereignty is essential to human dwelling in a polis. The very idea of the absence of sovereignty for organizing political life must have nauseated and frightened Hobbes, who railed against the idea of anarchy (political belonging without a ruler) (Ryan, 2012, p.297). Anarchy, Hobbes believed, led only to chaos and violence, because it undermined the necessity for a leviathan or sovereign to provide security and peace through the exercise of political violence or the threat of political violence. Not surprisingly, Hobbes, given his own privileged social position, seemed to ignore the overt and hidden forms of violence perpetrated by sovereign classes and their apparatuses, yet Jean-Jacques Rousseau (2016) seemed to recognize this in the last line of his *Discourse on Inequality*: "that the privileged few should gorge themselves with superfluities, while the starving multitude are in want of the bare necessities of life" (p.126). In the 19th century, Pierre-Joseph Proudhon and others sought to resurrect the idea of anarchy or non-sovereignty, yet today anarchy retains strong negative valences because, in my view, many of us in the West cannot imagine political life or dwelling without some form of sovereignty. To rephrase Frederic Jamison's famous quip, why is it easier to imagine the end of the world than the end of sovereignty?

The notion of sovereignty is not simply a perennial topic for political philosophers and political scientists. It has been and is an issue for psychoanalysts, though not necessarily a conscious one. Consider that in Freud's corpus, there are only six mentions of sovereignty,[2] yet there are numerous references to and explorations of civilization, which covertly introduces or assumes the notion of sovereignty as necessary for the safety and security of human beings. For Freud (1927), human beings are mostly helpless and vulnerable against the relentless, majestic, cruel, indifferent forces of nature,[3] and, therefore, we need to band together (civilization) to control, as much as possible, nature for human benefit. If this is not quite sovereignty or dominion over nature, Freud tacks close to this, recognizing that while the "the

DOI: 10.4324/9781003258827-5

principal task of civilization…is to defend us against nature," which civilization does well (p.15). He and others were under no illusion "that nature has already been vanquished" (p.15). If human beings are not completely sovereign over nature, we have some measure of control exercised by way of civilization. Freud's notion of civilization, however, has, it seems to me, roots in Hobbes' leviathan, which means that while human beings are not sovereign over nature, sovereignty is deemed necessary for human belonging—for civilization. I add that the notion of political sovereignty is evident in Freud's imaginary origin story. In Freud's (1950) *Totem and Taboo*, for example, it is obvious that patriarchal sovereignty is unquestioned and unquestionable. The origins of civilization emerge from the rule of the father and when the father is killed, the sons rule. In addition, this imaginary tale inscribes patriarchal sovereignty into Freud's formulation of psychosocial development, which is another way to universalize and ontologize sovereignty and, in particular, patriarchal sovereignty, which is not divorced from conduct within the context of psychoanalytic therapy. Indeed, Lynn Chancer (2020) points out that Erich Fromm, in reading Freud's case of Dora, understood this to be a "therapist/patient reproduction of patriarchal inequalities of power and powerlessness" (p.98). Freud "perceived Dora's rebellion from a sexist psychoanalytic situation in which she had been cast as an unequal." Fromm believed Dora's leaving analysis was an act of liberation—"a means of exiting the patriarchal and unequal relationship" (p.98). This is not to disparage Freud. Indeed, I noted in the Introduction that Paul Roazen (1999/1968), Eli Zaretsky (2015), and numerous others (e.g., Altman, 2000, 2004; Kovel, 1970; Samuels, 1993) have relied on Freud's work and psychoanalytic theories to examine political life and uncover its unconscious features. My point, however, is that Freud (and other psychoanalysts who followed him) unwittingly and unconsciously accepted the necessity of patriarchal sovereignty for political dwelling, which shaped their work with patients. And this is not at all surprising considering that social imaginaries of Western political philosophies have promulgated the necessity of sovereignty for human dwelling, even as there is debate about what form is suited to human life.

If we shift to the psychoanalytic literature around climate change, the notion of sovereignty, in many cases, is simply not mentioned. Leading analytic writers on climate change, like Donna Orange (2017), Sally Weintrobe (2013, 2021), and Paul Hogget (2019), never mention sovereignty and its relation to climate emergency, suggesting a tacit acceptance of its necessity for human dwelling—though they no doubt prefer liberal democratic types of sovereignty. Of course, these psychoanalysts do identify political-economic apparatuses, in particular neoliberal capitalism and its relation to the state, that shape subjectivity, which undermines our taking action to reduce the effects of climate. That said, the absence of the notion of sovereignty is telling and problematic, which I intend to make clear below.

This is not to say that the concept of sovereignty is completely absent in analytic discourse on climate change. In the relatively few articles where climate change and sovereignty are mentioned, some of the limitations and problems of sovereignty are noted (e.g., Brunning & Khaleelee, 2018; Chalwell, 2017; Covington, 2019). However, sovereignty itself is not considered or explored as a factor in climate change except in three articles (Armstrong, 2017; Clough, 2021; LaMothe, 2021c); two of these articles, however, do not examine it in detail.[4]

Since the notion of sovereignty is a central concept in Western political philosophies, it is incumbent that a psychoanalytic political philosophy concerned about our climate emergency take it up. As in the previous chapter, my method is to offer psychoanalytic considerations as to the unconscious features of sovereignty and how it shapes subjectivity. In addition, I return to a psychoanalytic developmental perspective, arguing that human dwelling rests on anarchic foundations. Given this, it is important to begin by providing some background on the notion of sovereignty as well as identifying its attributes. Included in this section is an explanation and discussion of the relation between sovereignty and political violence,[5] which is a foundational aspect of ecological degradation. Once this foundation is proffered, I move to psychoanalytic considerations.

## Sovereignty and Its Attributes

The notion of sovereignty has roots in ancient Greek philosophers like Plato[6] and Aristotle (Grayling, 2019), though it was a French jurist and political philosopher, Jean Bodin, who, in the 16th century, set out to identify the key attributes of sovereignty instantiated in monarchies. There are, for Bodin (2009), four key features of sovereignty, namely, it entails supreme power (no superior), it is also absoluteness, indivisibleness, and perpetuality. The king has no superior (except God), is absolute in his rule, his power and rule cannot be divided, and his rule is perpetual, handed down to his sons (in rare cases, daughters). This pre-Enlightenment formulation of sovereignty was not completely abandoned by Enlightenment political thinkers, notably in the political philosophies of Thomas Hobbes and John Locke. Indeed, in the 20th century, jurist Carl Schmitt (2005) picks up on Bodin's work, pointing out that it is widely referenced in works on sovereignty, though these works often ignore a core aspect of Bodin's thought. Schmitt writes:

> Bodin asked if the commitments of the prince to the state or people dissolve his sovereignty. He answered by referring to the case in which it becomes necessary to violate such commitments. To change laws or to suspend them entirely according to the requirements of a situation, a time, and a people. If in such cases the prince had to consult a senate or the people before he could act, he would have to be prepared to let his subjects dispense with him. Bodin considered this an absurdity because, according to him, the estates were not masters over the laws…Sovereignty would thus become a play between two parties.
>
> (pp.9–10)

Sticking to his ideas regarding the attributes of sovereignty, Bodin considered the example above to violate at least three of the four attributes.

By the time Carl Schmitt (1888–1985) took up the idea of sovereignty, there had been a number of revolutions (e.g., American, French, and Russian), as well as a struggling democracy in Germany after World War I. Schmitt, in his study of law-making and law-preserving actions of the state, wished to reinterpret Bodin's work. He boldly stated that the central feature of all forms of sovereignty is the state of exception. "The sovereign," he wrote, "is he who decides on the state of exception" (p.5). Besides the fact that Schmitt carried forward the idea of sovereignty embodied in an ostensibly male person, there are two key points here. The sovereign is the one who makes the decision, which might awaken our memory of a democratically elected president who said he was the decider in chief. Schmitt went on to claim that a

> sovereign produces and guarantees the situation in its totality. He has a monopoly over this last decision. Therein resides the essence of the state's sovereignty, which may be juristically defined correctly, not as a monopoly to coerce or to rule, but as a monopoly to decide.
>
> (p.13)

The second and more complicated feature here is the state of exception and its relation to law. The phrase "state of exception" means that the sovereign, as we see in the quote above, can, because of absolute power, decide to set aside laws according to the requirements of a given situation—*extremus necessitatis casus* (p.10). Bodin's absolute power/authority, then, is seen in Schmitt's notion of the state of exception. We might, for instance, think of a state of emergency when the sovereign, for real or imagined reasons of security, has the power/authority to suspend the law—state of exception.

The relation between the law and sovereignty's state of exception needs further elaboration. For both Giorgio Agamben and Carl Schmitt, the "sovereign exception is…the condition for the possibility of the juridical order, for it is through the state of exception that sovereignty creates and guarantees the order the law needs for its own validity" (DeCaroli, 2007, p.53). At the same time, "the state of exception exercises the law as force" (Colebrook & Maxwell, 2016, p.54). Agamben, then, takes on Schmitt's idea that the sovereign stands outside of, but belongs to, the juridical order, which is a paradox. The paradox is yoked to questions of the relations between sovereignty, the law, and violence. "The paradox of sovereignty," Agamben (1998) writes, "consists in the fact that the sovereign is, at the same time, outside and inside the juridical order" (p.15). As he (2005) states elsewhere, "the state of exception appears as the legal form of what cannot have legal form…if the law employs the state of exception—that is the suspension of the law itself" (p.1). Put differently, "As a figure of necessity, the state of exception therefore appears as an 'illegal' but perfectly 'juridical and constitutional' measure" (p.28). Sovereignty, then, "is neither external nor internal to the juridical order" (p.23). While paradoxical,

> The sovereign exception is, for both Schmitt and Agamben, the condition for the possibility of juridical order, for it is through the state of exception that the sovereign creates and guarantees the order the law needs for its own validity.
>
> (DeCaroli, 2007, p.54)

This stated, the paradoxical[7] nature of sovereignty is evident in that the "work of sovereignty precedes the law, creating a regular 'frame of life,' which the law preserves and codifies but does not instantiate" (p.50). One might recall here Freud's early tribal father and his rule over other men and women. As sovereign, his rule precedes the law, but it is later codified in patriarchal apparatuses that preserve the sovereign who, in turn, can suspend the laws.

Before turning to other key attributes of sovereignty, it is important to point out that sovereignty does not simply refer to *a person* exercising the decision about the state of exception. This can be understood in three ways. First, Agamben (2005) points out that "the police are always operating within a similar state of exception" (p.103). The police (and other security forces and institutions) can be understood as the arm of the sovereign's power vis-à-vis the state of exception. Moreover, the police, at least in the United States, often have power to make decisions to use deadly force. That is, an alleged "perpetrator" can be killed without the person's death being considered a homicide (or sacrifice)—Agamben's (1998) term *homo sacer* fits here. This means that the police stand with and belong to the juridical order, while also standing outside it in that they can kill without penalty. This also means that victims of police violence are outside the protection of the law, precisely because the police are protected and fall within the sovereign's state of exception. Second, it is not only the police who can exhibit the state of exception. In the United States, there is a long, sordid, racist history of terroristic lynching and raping African Americans (see Alexander, 2010; Anderson, 2016; McGuire, 2011; Wilkerson, 2020). These acts occurred outside the juridical order, yet done with tacit approval of the white juridical order in that African Americans were denied justice. White supremacists were within the legal order, but not subject to it during slavery and Jim Crow. In one sense, white supremacists decide on the state of exception when they terrorized African American citizens. African Americans were/are included-excluded Others—within the juridical order, but excluded from its protections. They could be killed or raped or economically exploited and these innumerable cases were not considered crimes. African Americans, then, existed outside the protection of human and divine law—bare life (Agamben, 1998, p.83) or Fanon (2008) called a "zone of nonbeing" (p.xii) or what Orlando Patterson (1982) termed social death. Agamben, I believe, would agree with this illustration, as he notes that the sovereign "has the power to decide which life may be killed without the commission of a homicide" (p.142). But it is not just the sovereign, it is also the sovereign classes (white supremacists) who can exercise the state of exception as long as the sovereign permits this.

Similarly, Catherine MacKinnon (1991) notes that violence against women by men has been tolerated by sovereign states (patriarchal rule) for millennia. These acts of violence are permitted by the sovereign and sovereign classes, even though they do not have a basis in law or perpetrated by the state. These acts or threats of violence are political in that they maintain the patriarchal rule, power, and privileges of men.

A third and related point is that there is no such thing as *a* sovereign. The sovereign and sovereign classes exist in relation to apparatuses that carry out the sovereign's decisions (e.g., police, other law enforcement organizations, bureaucracies, etc.). The police are not part of the sovereign classes. They are functionaries of the sovereign. The sovereign classes contain the political and economic elites who identify with and benefit from supporting the sovereign. As Chris Harman (2017) demonstrates, the rise of civilization and concomitantly sovereignty accompanies the rise of sovereign classes and functionaries that are necessary for supporting the ruler and the exercise of state apparatuses or disciplinary regimes. For those who live in so-called democratic nations, it is clear that "democratic sovereignty" also has ruling and economic elites, despite the idea of political equality. This is especially evident when we note vast disparities in income and wealth (Piketty, 2014, 2020), as well as excessive political influence wielded by economic and political elites in constructing laws that benefit the members of the sovereign classes (Gilens & Page, 2014).

Of course, history is also replete with stories of sovereigns who are deposed. Those who are deposed are replaced by a new sovereign and new sovereign classes. Freud's imaginary ur-father apparently lost the support of the sovereign class (his sons) and was deposed, giving rise to a not-so-new male sovereign order. A real-life example is Russia's 1917 revolution (Miéville, 2018). The Tsar was eventually replaced by a putative communist state where everyone was equal, yet in reality the Soviet state and its government created sovereign classes of political elites. The point here is that a sovereign always exists in conjunction with sovereign classes and functionaries, even if these are replaced by way of revolution—ushering in a new sovereign and attending new sovereign classes.

The necessity of sovereign classes for the existence of a sovereign reveals several other features that attend sovereignty. To rule implies a hierarchy (Lechte & Newman, 2015, p.166), which means one's subjects are subordinate: even the sovereign classes are subordinate to the sovereign. In Aristotle's polis, women, barbarians, and children are subordinate to the rule of adult male citizens. In Hobbes' state, the social contract of citizens is that they agree to submit to the power and rule of the leviathan, hopefully obtaining peace and security in return. A representative democracy, like the United States, means that the demos, who elect the representatives, are subordinate to these representatives, who make decisions ostensibly in the demos' interests. This subordination is especially evident when we consider the relation between sovereignty and political violence below.

It is important to mention that relations of subordination are but one small step from relations of subjugation vis-à-vis sovereignty. For millennia, women were (and in many places still are) subordinate in patriarchal societies and in many instances subjugated to male sovereign classes (de Beauvoir, 2011; MacKinnon, 1991; Wollstonecraft, 1996). In the U.S. slavocracy, Black members of society were subjugated by the apparatuses of white supremacy/sovereignty to serve the interests of white people in general and the political and economic elites in particular. Beliefs (more accurately, illusions) in white supremacy were and are at the very heart and origin of U.S. democracy. After Emancipation, white men and women created numerous ways to continue to subordinate and subjugate Black persons. And as Michelle Alexander (2010) writes, the achievements of the Civil Rights Movement were quickly followed by new Jim and Jane Crow laws that were consciously and unconsciously aimed at subordinating and subjugating African Americans—maintaining the sovereignty of white supremacy.

Closely associated with relations of subordination and subjugation are beliefs in superiority and inferiority. The sovereign is by definition superior (and so too the sovereign classes) because the sovereign has the sole "power" to act on the state of exception. Western political philosophies (and theologies) have for millennia largely supported male sovereignty, which attends beliefs in the superiority of men (reason) and inferiority of women (putative lack of reason), which were used to legitimate relations of subordination and subjugation. One might counter and say that in a democracy everyone is equal, which would seem to belie the intertwining of sovereignty and beliefs in superiority and inferiority. I have two replies. First, while I am not knowledgeable of every instance of democracy in human history, I am familiar with some and I find that none of them is free of these beliefs or relations of subordination and subjugation. In Plato's and Aristotle's political philosophies, women were constructed as inferior to men. Charles Mills (1997, 2017) indicates how European political philosophers, who advocated for some types of democracy, tended to view white male Europeans as superior to native peoples who needed "civilizing," which served to legitimate colonization—the subordination and subjugation of peoples deemed to *be* inferior. In the United States, which was and, one could argue, still is a colonizing nation, there are marginalized classes that are constructed as inferior (Isenberg, 2016; Wilkerson, 2020), which legitimates their poor treatment by the state and many of its citizens. A survey of any manifestation of sovereignty will reveal how beliefs in superiority and inferiority accompany relations of subordination and subjugation. There are perhaps no more insidious and destructive beliefs than those of superiority and inferiority.

So far I have been referring to human beings when it comes to relations of subordination and subjugation and attending beliefs in inferiority and superiority. In Western political philosophies, more-than-human species are considered subordinate and inferior to human beings. Human beings, by way of constructed hierarchical taxonomies, are judged to be sovereign over other species because they apparently lack this or that human attribute (e.g., reason)—an attribute that is deemed to give human beings superiority and the apparent lack of which is equated with inferiority. Since human beings "are" superior, so the logic continues, they have the right to exploit other species for human well-being or pleasure or dwelling. This epistemological and "moral" perspective is evident in the extractive and destructive aspects of global capitalism and in its exploitation of other species (factory farms, experimentation). Indeed, the very reality of climate change reveals how so-called human superiority and the subordination of nature are immensely destructive to the earth and other species.

Implicit in this discussion of the attributes of subordination/subjugation and superiority/inferiority is another key attribute of sovereignty and the law, namely, political violence. John Lechte and Paul Newman (2015) contend that the "law always articulates itself through violence which both preserves its boundaries and exceeds them, and violence always establishes a new law.... violence is at the very origins and foundations of the law" (p.128). In brief, the "Law," they point out, "is never free from violence" (p.173). This echoes Foucault's view that the "The law is born of real battles, victories, massacres, and conquests, which can be dated and which have their horrific heroes; the law was born in burning towns and ravaged fields" (in Oksala, 2012, p.40).

There is, however, a deeper connection between law and violence. In DeCaroli's (2007) reading of Agamben, the "law is not the essential function of sovereignty" (p.50). "The work of sovereignty," he writes, "precedes the law, creating a regular 'frame of life,' which the law preserves and codifies but does not instantiate" (p.50). What precedes the law is violence or the threat of political violence. Freud's fictional story about the origins of civilization is an illustration of this. The killing of the tribal father is an act of political violence, overthrowing the sovereign. Yet, this political violence is necessarily preceded by the violence and the threat of violence the father must have employed to subjugate his sons and women. Political violence establishes the sovereign, then the sovereign and sovereign classes create laws (and stories) that legitimate the ruler and ruling bodies, all of which is never far from the threat of political violence.

Political violence not only establishes and maintains the sovereign and sovereign classes (e.g., Hobbes' leviathan), it also can only be exercised legitimately by the sovereign and the state apparatuses, which the sovereign leads (Weber, 2013/1919, p.1; see also Schmitt, 2005). The exercise of political violence outside of the sovereign is illegitimate and a threat to the sovereign classes. In the United States, for instance, the exercise of violence by some Black Lives Matters protestors was labeled by the government and media as a riot. The protestors' violence is considered to be outside the law. However, the state's use of violence to quell a "riot" is judged legitimate. Similarly, revolutionary violence is considered to be outside the law, until the revolution has overthrown the sovereign and sovereign classes. Then the new sovereign claims sole legitimacy in the use or threat of political violence.

It is important to stress that violence is not always physical. Agamben (1998) writes that

> If it is the sovereign who, insofar as he decides on the state of exception, has the power to decide which life may be killed without commission of homicide, in the age of biopolitics this power becomes emancipated from the state of exception and transformed into the power to decide the point at which life ceases to be politically relevant.

(p.142)

Agamben, then, extends violence to include the power to make individuals and groups politically irrelevant, which is a central feature in the inverted totalitarian system present in the United States (Wolin, 2008), as well as in indecent states that employ apparatuses of humiliation to produce and maintain subordinate and subjugated classes (Margalit, 1996). Individuals and groups cannot become politically irrelevant without state (and non-state) apparatuses and disciplinary regimes of humiliation that accompany the threat of physical violence. Non-physical forms of political violence *violate* the political recognition of subordinate and subjugated Others as persons, as citizens (see Soss, Fording, & Schram, 2011; Wacquant, 2009). To violate individuals' recognition and status as persons (denial of self-esteem, self-respect, and self-confidence) is already a form of exclusion and political irrelevancy (marginalized from spaces of speaking and acting together), which is accompanied by material deprivation through failures in the adequate distribution of resources (Fraser & Honneth, 2003). The reality of food deserts, inadequate housing and housing insecurity, dilapidated infrastructure, evictions, and policing of poor persons and people of color are examples of social-political apparatuses of sovereignty that violate, threaten, and create political irrelevancy. The exercise of political violence, in these instances, may entail physical violence, but, more often than not, political violence is exercised through apparatuses that deprive people of rights, protections, and needed resources to survive and thrive.

Sovereignty's apparatuses of political irrelevancy are also yoked to the onto-logical rift between human beings and nature. More-than-human species are, in most nations,[8] politically irrelevant. For many human beings, the very idea of other species being included in the political realm is inconceivable. To be sure, there are political considerations for endangered species and in these cases the protections suggest political relevancy. However, by and large, other species and the earth are politically irrelevant, though some species and tracts of land become politically relevant when they are needed to benefit human dwelling.

The interrelated attributes of sovereignty discussed so far (state of exception, relations of subordination, superiority-inferiority, and violence) are also joined to the attributes of exclusion and identity. Exclusion is a foundational feature of sov-ereignty. As Wendy Brown (2010) notes, sovereignty establishes a political iden-tity and geographical boundary. Those who do not share the political identity are excluded from political life, whether they live outside the geographical boundaries or reside as "aliens" within the boundaries. Aristotle's barbarians may have lived within the boundaries of the polis, but they did not possess the shared identity and were thus excluded from engaging in political life. But this exclusion also entails those who are politically irrelevant, even as they are deemed to be citizens. Women in Aristotle's polis shared in the identity of a particular polis, but, like the barbar-ians, they were excluded from political spaces of speaking and acting together. And, of course, other-than-human beings are barred from political consideration, except in cases when other species can be used for political purposes (e.g., war).

Sovereignty's exclusion functions to reinforce identity vis-à-vis belonging/ dwelling, as well as to legitimate the exercise of hierarchical political power/vio-lence. "Sovereign power," Jenny Edkins (2007) writes, "has to produce a homog-enous and pure 'people' by the exclusion of all that do not count as people in its terms" (p.78). All of this can be recognized in terms of what Carl Schmitt (1996, p.26), echoing Hobbes, considered to be the basis of sovereignty: the friend-enemy distinction. This can be understood in three ways. First, the friend-enemy distinction can refer to the shared identity within a particular sovereign territory over and against Others, who may or may not be enemies. For those external Others who are not enemies, they remain excluded either in terms of the boundary or within the state's boundary as resident aliens, since they do not share a political identity with other members of the polis. These non-citizens are neither friends nor enemies, though they are othered. Second, within the geographical boundaries, sovereigns have power over their subjects, indicating their power to identify who is a friend or enemy, whether that refers to those within the boundaries of the nation or external. Agamben points to this sovereign power when remarking about what the state cannot abide. He (2013) writes, "What the State (or sovereign) cannot tolerate in any way is that the singularities form a community without affirming an identity, that human beings co-belong without any representable condition of belonging" (p.5). As long as the state can determine who is a citizen or resident, there is no threat, but if people take it upon themselves to welcome Others, the state will respond with force. The Sanctuary Movement in the United States during the 1980s is an example. Consider also the rancorous debates over so-called illegal immigration. The anxiety, fear, and hostility result not simply from not having control over the border(s), but also from the perceived threat to American political identity (read white, European). This political identity is inextricably linked to a particular instantiation of (whites dominate, at least for now) democratic sovereignty. Third and relatedly, it is not simply the sovereign that seeks to produce and maintain friend-enemy distinctions; it is also the members of the sovereign classes. In a so-called democracy, ideally all citizens are part of the sovereign class in the sense of believing that they exercise political power vis-à-vis governance of the state. Individual citizens in a democracy (individual sovereigns) believe they have the political agency to identify who is a friend or enemy, whether this refers to other citizens, residents, or people within their own political party. This can be seen in situations where individuals deem other citizens are un-American or RINOs (Republicans In Name Only) or DINOs (Democrats In Name Only). These actions are aimed at homogenizing the group's political identity.

Philosopher Wendy Brown (2010) provides a summary of the main attributes of sovereignty. She writes that

> classical theorists of modern sovereignty, including Thomas Hobbes, Jean Bodin, and Carl Schmitt, suggest that sovereignty's indispensable features include supremacy (no higher power), perpetuity (no term limits), decisionism (no boundedness by or submission to law), absolutism and completeness (sovereign cannot be probable or partial), nontransferability (sovereignty cannot be conferred without cancelling itself), and specialized jurisdiction (territoriality).
>
> (p.22)

In the discussion above, I elaborated on these attributes by highlighting aspects embedded in Brown's summary, namely, state of exception, relations of subordination and subjugation, epistemologies of superiority of the sovereign classes and inferiority of others to legitimate relations of subordination and subjugation, justification for the sole use of political violence or threat of political violence by the sovereign and sovereign classes, and the use of friend-enemy distinction vis-à-vis group and Other identity. While much of the discussion above has understandably centered on human beings, I have also made clear that the attributes of sovereignty extend to other species and the earth, which are constructed as inferior, politically irrelevant, and thus exploitable for the general benefits of human beings' political dwelling and, more particularly, the benefits of political-economic elites.

## A Psychoanalytic Rendering of Sovereignty

Now I want to turn to a brief discussion regarding sovereignty by way of what I call a psychoanalytic-political hermeneutical framework for identifying and describing some of the problems of sovereignty. A political-psychoanalytic framework identifies the conscious and unconscious aspects of agency, motivation, and desire as they emerge from and exist within spaces of speaking and acting together and their attending apparatuses (Arendt, 1958)—in this case apparatuses that produce and maintain sovereignty. I am, in other words, putting sovereignty on the couch. This sets the stage for offering a psychoanalytic-political philosophical perspective that offers an alternative to sovereign relations.

Freud, the scientist, took as his mission to identify the illusions people hold, believing that these illusions, in particular religious illusions, were ultimately detrimental to human progress (e.g., science). Winnicott would have agreed that some illusions are detrimental to human beings, though he also made room for benign, if not necessary, illusions (e.g., the infant's illusion of omnipotence) in human life. Both Freud and Winnicott recognized that human illusions have real material effects, which may be benign, positive, or negative. In my view, the belief that sovereignty is necessary for human political belonging is an illusion that has both negative and positive results. Sovereignty certainly has functioned to keep a people together with some degree of political peace and stability, though the cost to non-sovereign classes, foreigners, and other-than-human species has often been quite steep. The Anthropocene Age, in particular, reveals just how destructive the belief in human sovereignty over nature is. Nevertheless, we are left with the question of why sovereignty is an illusion and what are its unconscious collective features.

Sovereignty, both as an idea and political reality, is a human artifice or social-political imaginary that emerged with the Neolithic revolution and one that is not necessarily universal or timeless. In other words, many political philosophers believe that sovereignty has always been necessary for human belonging or civilization, and this is universal. Apparently, they overlook the fact that there are and have been human beings who form a community or polis and who do not believe in human sovereignty over nature or that sovereignty is existentially necessary for human belonging and survival. The belief in the necessity of sovereignty for human dwelling is an illusion precisely because it is not existentially necessary.

The belief in human sovereignty over nature is also a deadly illusion, especially when it is joined to the artifices or social imaginaries of capitalism, imperialism, and nationalism, which are taken up in the next chapter. It is precisely the impending climate disaster and likely extinction of human beings that reveal and confirm that we are not sovereign over other species or the earth. Of course, human beings can exercise a great deal of control over other species and, in some cases, over the earth, but limited control is not a confirmation of sovereignty. In short, a reason the belief in the existential necessity of sovereignty is an illusion is that reality disconfirms this despite the fact that human beings continue to construct apparatuses that produce and maintain beliefs in human sovereignty.

Closely allied with the belief in human sovereignty are the illusions of human superiority and the inferiority of other species. Again, we note these are illusory because of the realities of the Anthropocene Age. The possible extinction of human beings at our own hands (with some being more accountable) is a clear repudiation of the belief in human superiority. Just as the reverse is true: the extinction of the dinosaurs is not confirmation of their inferiority, only their bad luck. I seriously doubt we would consider the likely survival of cockroaches or bacteria as evidence of their superiority or our extinction as evidence of human inferiority, though it would indicate the tragic nature of human beings. That said, I do think a species that is responsible for the extinction of millions of other species can hardly consider itself to be superior. In short, any valuations of superiority or inferiority are strictly human creations rather than existential features of other species and the earth.

We can return to Freud to posit an unconscious source of the belief in the necessity of sovereignty. Freud (1927) had a particular view of nature and its relation to civilization.[9] While ambivalent about civilization, Freud believed it was necessary for human survival. Sure, there may be people who wish to abolish civilization so that "nature would not demand any restrictions of instinct from us, she would let us do as we liked" (p.15). However, nature has "her own particularly effective method of restricting us. She destroys us—coldly, cruelly, relentlessly" (p.15). "With these forces," Freud continued, "nature rises up against us, majestic, cruel and inexorable; she brings to our mind once more our weakness and helplessness" (p.16). Like Hobbes, the state of nature, for Freud, is not something to be desired, because human beings would even be more helpless and weaker against the implacable forces of nature. Setting aside the anthropomorphizing and feminization of nature, which begs for analysis, it is clear that human beings are helpless before the powers of nature. Indeed, it is human helplessness before the dangers of nature that, Freud believed, motivated human beings to come together to create civilization—the leviathan that demands partial renunciation of instinct for protection. Besides the idea that human beings are somehow distinct from and in opposition to nature (Agamben's ontological rift), there is the argument that we construct civilization to protect ourselves from danger and existential feelings of vulnerability and helplessness. Civilization and sovereignty are artifices that give human beings a sense of control, power, significance, and self-esteem (yoked to beliefs in superiority), which screen our profound helplessness, vulnerability, insignificance, and imper- manence before a seemingly cruel and indifferent "mother" nature upon which we are utterly dependent.

We can also take note of human helplessness, vulnerability, and self-worth in the way many human beings perceive and treat other species (and Othered human beings). Factory farms, animal experimentation, and hunting as a sport are instances that reveal our desire to exploit other species for our benefit or mere pleasure, pro- viding many of us with a sense of entitlement and control/agency, while reinforc- ing the helplessness of these species in the face of human cruel indifference. Put differently, many human beings who exploit other species are projecting onto them their own sense of helplessness and vulnerability, while securing belief in their own agency and power. The affirmation of human dominion and the correspond- ing projection of helplessness and vulnerability means that we disidentify with the suffering of other species—traumatic sufferings many human beings have caused. We do not, in other words, actualize our potentiality for empathy, because to do so would entail some recognition and accountability for our own helplessness, vulner- ability, insignificance, and impermanence, not to mention letting go of our illusory beliefs in privilege and superiority.

The absence of empathy (speciesopathy, if you will) and disavowal of account- ability can be further understood in light of Donnel Stern's (1997) use of weak dissociation, which is discussed in the Introduction. To recall, this type of dissocia- tion, Stern follows closely with Herbert Fingarette's (1969) philosophical analysis of routine self-deception in human life. Fingarette wrote,

> it is when we judge that there is a purposeful discrepancy between the way the individual really is engaged in the world and the story he tells himself that we have the complex but common form of self-deception in which we are interested.
> (p.62)

This self-deception, from Fingarette's perspective, results from not spelling out (nar- rating) one's engagement in the world or, better, spelling out one's engagement such that one misinterprets the action, while also disavowing the consequences of these actions. Stern (1997), building on Fingarette's analysis of self-deception, argued that some non-pathological forms of spelling out are illustrations of weak dissociation. Weak dissociation, for Stern, involves narrative rigidity, which means that persons organize their experiences such that their actions and consequences are narrowly spelled out, omitting actions, consequences, meanings, and affects that do not "fit" the dominant story. Inflexible narration, in other words, means that those ideas, mean- ings, values, and affects that are unconsciously perceived to contradict the dominant- conscious narrative are excluded or unformulated and, therefore, outside awareness. In weak dissociation, Stern argued, we spell out only what

> we believe we can tolerate, or that furthers our purpose, or that promises a feel- ing of safety, satisfaction, and the good things in life; we dissociate the meanings

that we believe we will not be able to tolerate, that frighten us and seem to threaten the fulfillment of our deepest intentions.

(p.128)

As a result, "of so insistently turning our attention elsewhere...we never even notice alternative understandings. Focal attention under these conditions is controlled by the intention to enforce narrative rigidity" (p.132). The presence of weak dissociation's narrative rigidity is seen in the mountains of books (philosophical, religious, human science novels, etc.) that produce and maintain the idea of sovereignty. This narrative rigidity becomes clear when we note the collective anxiety, fear, and hostility directed toward people who espouse anarchy. Anarchy is a threat to sovereignty and its illusions. In my view, Hobbes' leviathan and Freud's civilization exemplify rigid narratives that screen fear and anxiety linked to helplessness and vulnerability, as well as existential insignificance and impermanence. They screen out, in other words, fear and anxiety associated with the loss of a powerful leviathan intended to keep us safe and secure. Their stories are self-deceptions in that they promulgate the illusion that sovereignty or civilization is existentially necessary for human dwelling. Weak dissociation, then, is evident in the tendency for human beings to overlook the suffering and needs of other species, as well as our culpability in their suffering. In brief, both Freud and Hobbes believed that, without civilization or sovereignty, life would be untenable, which explains, in part, why there is so much animus and rigidity when faced with narratives of anarchy—a rigidity that reveals the presence of weak dissociation.

The irony of Freud's view of nature and civilization is that human beings, in the West, because of "civilization" and belief in human sovereignty, exhibit cruelty and indifference toward other species and the earth. By relying on projection and weak dissociation, we refuse to acknowledge and accept our dependence and helplessness, our insignificance and impermanence, while many of us are indifferently participating in the extinction of other species and the degradation of the earth. Human beings will not become extinct because of "nature's" cruel indifference, but because human beings have acted cruelly against "nature." In other words, the ontological rift constructed by Western political theologies and philosophies of sovereignty is based on the illusion of human distinctiveness and separation from "nature," representing a refusal to acknowledge and accept our (and other living beings) helplessness, vulnerability, and dependency. Freud's beliefs, in my view, are clearly linked to Western political epistemologies that promote the illusion of the necessity of sovereignty, while also mystifying this fabrication and projecting our helplessness, dependency, insignificance, and impermanence onto other-than-human species.

Of course, it is not simply other species that are targets of projection. So-called Western civilization has spawned numerous colonizing sovereign states that have used violence and the threat of violence to extract resources from colonized lands and peoples. Many of these Western civilized peoples obtain a sense of esteem and control by subordinating and subjugating Othered human beings. A psychoanalytic interpretation is that Western civilizations construct apparatuses that promote projection and weak dissociation, which accompanies the exploitation of Othered peoples, exacerbating their vulnerability and helplessness, as well as projecting onto them insignificance. This distracts so-called civilized peoples from their existential helplessness, vulnerability, and insignificance. Of course, within these sovereign nations, there are Othered citizens (Native peoples, African Americans) and residents (e.g., persons who are undocumented) who are subjugated to benefit members of the sovereign classes. Sexism, classism, and racism are occasions that illustrate the sovereignty of one group over other groups with the subordinate and subjugated groups forced by virtue of the apparatuses of the sovereign classes to experience helplessness and vulnerability.

This general view of the psychological sources of sovereignty overlooks other unconscious features of sovereignty among the sovereign classes. William Connolly notes, "The aura of sovereignty is sustained through the mystique of the sacred" (in McLoughlin, 2016, p.26). Evidence of the aura of sovereignty is observed in Abrahamic religious traditions that celebrate the absolute sovereignty of God, which means that God's sovereignty is unquestioned and unquestionable. It is but a small jump to transfer the aura of God's sovereignty to a human being and attending members of the sovereign classes. Connolly, like Schmitt, argues that this religious aura is manifested today in secular constitutions (p.99). This "aura" can be further understood as the ability of the sovereign and sovereign classes (and attending apparatuses) "to produce (and reproduce) forms of subjectivity that consent to, and even defend, the conditions that make sovereignty, and the subordination it entails, possible" (DeCaroli, 2007, p.45). This production of subjectivity takes place "beneath political mythologies sanctifying the 'right to rule'" (p.45), providing an appearance of autonomy from the powers that created sovereignty and its institutions. Dickinson and Kotsko (2015), commenting on Agamben's views of glory, argue that "politics today functions as a thinly veiled religious spectacle, complete with its own calls for glory" (p.250). Glory (democracies, spectacles of acclamation) is produced by rituals and narratives that function to legitimate, constitute, and perpetually reproduce religious and secular forms of sovereignty, while mystifying not only its fictional origins, but also the beneficiaries of sovereignty. Sovereign classes, like the "all-powerful" Oz, do not want the curtain to be pulled aside, revealing the artificial nature of the benefits and necessity of sovereignty. To be exposed would be to face the loss of privileges and their feelings of specialness—experiences of singularity that are dependent on relations of subordination/subjugation of Othered persons and beliefs in sovereign classes' superiority.[10]

There is one other feature of the dynamics of sovereignty to address. As noted above, sovereignty's political violence is used to establish and preserve relations of subordination/subjugation and attending beliefs in superiority and inferiority. This is where we can glimpse the inherent mimetic and tragic instability at the heart of sovereignty. Relations of subordination and subjugation and beliefs in Others' inferiority are based on the denial and diminishment of the subordinated/subjugated

Other's potentiality/impotentiality, singularity, and agency. The sovereign classes' sense of singularity and agency is dependent on constructing subordinated Others as inferior and restricting their political agency. The mimetic instability of the sovereign's political violence is that it is based on treating existential illusions as facts, which, in turn, requires that subordinate and subjugated people accepting "reality" as fact. Of course, to do this depends on sovereign classes' apparatuses and political violence or threat of political violence. The mimetic feature here is that subjugated classes, eventually, though not always, want to return the favor. This can be restated in terms of the psychoanalytic concept of projective identification. The sovereign classes split off and project (by way of apparatuses) onto subjugated persons inferiority/insignificance, vulnerability, and dependency so as to shore up their self-esteem (belief in superiority) and deflect anxiety and fear associated with vulnerability and helplessness. Yet, non-sovereign classes often wish to return the favor. Throughout history, subjugated classes have often overthrown the sovereign classes, only to initiate their own form of sovereignty. Two illustrations will help here. The first is Malcolm X's autobiography (Haley, 1964). Malcolm X refused the sovereignty of white supremacy and believed in the Nation of Islam's mythic story on the origins of black superiority and white inferiority, though the Nation of Islam lacked the social, political, and economic apparatuses to enforce humiliation onto white people—a view he later rejected. The second illustration of projective identification and sovereignty is taken from the cover of the *American Spectator* (June 2014)—a conservative magazine—that reveals the anxiety and fear of the political-economic sovereign elites vis-à-vis the loss not simply of their lives, but their power, prestige, and privilege. The illustration depicts a bespectacled and paunchy white rich man being led to the guillotine surrounded by a mob. An official of the mob is raising a bloody copy of Thomas Piketty's book *Capital in the 21st Century*. Near him is a guillotine with a bloody blade, suggesting that many other wealthy people had already been guillotined. This image hearkens back to the terroristic political violence of the French Revolution in the 18th century. With regard to the present, the anxiety revealed in this cover art is associated not simply with death, but the catastrophic loss of power, prestige, and privilege of the sovereign classes. To put it another way, the rage and desire for justice of members of poor, subjugated classes are evident in violently overthrowing the sovereign wealthy. The so-called lower classes, weary of bearing the anxiety of economic vulnerability and dependency associated with scarcity, loss, and desolation (Marris, 1996), revolt, instilling fear and helplessness in those who are in the sovereign classes. Both the Nation of Islam's myth and the cover art of the *American Spectator* reveal not only the communicative operations of weak dissociation and projective identification, but also the sometimes mimetic, tragic nature at the heart of sovereignty.

The other aspect of the tragedy of sovereignty is that the communicative dynamics of projective identification and weak dissociation cannot be applied to "nature" as an object in general or other species in particular. These psychoanalytic concepts refer to human beings alone, though this does not mean nature and other species are not objects of human projection, as noted above. "Nature" and other species (as far as I know), however, do not return our projections, which means that projective identification does not quite fit, even though it is a heuristic conceptual tool. Gaia, for instance, will not seek out revenge for what human beings have wrought, even as most human beings continue to grip their illusions of sovereignty. Nevertheless, what can be noted is that weak dissociation and projective identification, which accompany beliefs associated with sovereignty, are foundational to our tragic trajectory. Consider Jonathan Schell's (2020) comment: "If we conquer nature, we will find ourselves among the defeated" (p.19).

## A Psychoanalytic Political Philosophical Perspective: Non-sovereignty and Belonging

Given this discussion above, I now offer a psychoanalytic, political philosophical perspective that proposes non-sovereign relations as foundational for human belonging—a belonging that takes into consideration our dependence on a biodiverse earth and the necessity of care for actualizing potentialities—not exhausting them. This said, the previous chapters proffer a psychoanalytic political philosophical perspective, which I refrain from repeating here, but intend to build on. My focus will be on considering psychoanalytic developmental insights and applying them to a political philosophy—a philosophy that eschews human sovereignty as a way of organizing social relations and our relations to other species and the earth. In other words, social relations organized in anarchic ways exemplifies a politics of nondomination. As Alain Badiou (2018) write, "There is a political capacity in the order of nondomination" (p.67) and that capacity, in my view, is the capacity for anarchic relations with other human beings and more-than-human species. And to quote Jacques Rancière: "Politics is, in the strict sense, anarchic" (in Bensaïd, 2012, p.26).

Let me begin by returning to the comments about Freud. Freud, like Hobbes and Rousseau, imagined human beings in the state of nature, which he then posited as a central feature of human psychosocial development. It is apparent that Freud was seeking to present his idea of development, but he unconsciously and unwittingly ontologized patriarchal sovereignty and this reveals, to my mind, his political philosophy. Of course, this was not unique to Freud. Alice Miller (1998) has demonstrated how European "experts" of child development in the 19th century used theology and "secular sciences" to promote breaking children's will so that they would obey and accept their subordinated status vis-à-vis parents who were sovereign or represented the sovereign (God and/or political authority). If we can inflect psychosocial development with political notions of sovereignty, then it is also possible to imagine human development that is free of sovereignty and to conceptualize power and authority in other ways. This does not necessarily mean that I am universalizing or essentializing the following perspective. Instead, I am offering a way to imagine relations that are anarchic[11]—without rule—and where authority and power are linked to and founded by care.[12]

In a non-scientific and informal "poll," I have not met one parent who believes they are sovereign over their infants, though a few parents feel as if there are days and nights when their infants are sovereign and parents are subjugated to their needs. Interestingly, some psychoanalysts, beginning with Freud (1926), use the notion of sovereignty when referring to infants (e.g., Bromberg, 1983; Corte, 1997; Ghent, 1992; Kessler & Kessler, 2019; Schiller, 2018), but this is a metaphor masquerading as a fact. The notion of sovereignty is deeply complex and cannot be attributed to infants, though certainly parents can shape their relations with children based on conscious and unconscious aspects of culturally specific ideas of sovereignty. I suggest, however, that good-enough parental attunements to infants have nothing to do with sovereignty and its attributes. The care of good-enough parents, in other words, does not involve subordinating or subjugating their children through the use of violence or the threat of violence, though clearly good-enough parents possess and wield a great deal of power in caring for their children. Neither do parents hold the belief that their infants are inferior and they, as parents, are superior. Good-enough parents do recognize the vulnerability and dependence of their children. While parents possess considerable psychosocial capacities, infants have only potentiality. Vulnerability and dependency, then, are not framed in terms of beliefs in inferiority and superiority, except perhaps in cases where parents are wildly insecure. In short, the parents' care is radical in the sense of being the root of early anarchic relations/experiences.

There is much more to be fleshed out here. To begin, parents' caring attunements, which include repairs of relational disruptions, represent a type of belonging or togetherness that is marked by recognition of infants' singularities. In terms of infants, early experiences of belonging, rapport, and singularity, which are initially potential and made actual by parental care in spaces of speaking and acting together, are organized semiotically—pre-representational organizations of rapport and senses of self-esteem, self-confidence, and self-respect. These unthought knowns become part of later, more complex organizations of belonging and singularity—a belonging and singularity that have nothing to do with sovereignty and its attributes. Let's return to an illustration from Chapter 1. I referred to activist Ruby Sales' depiction of her parents' care for her and other children in the midst of a society that was organized by the sovereignty of white supremacy. It is worth requoting her. She writes:

> I grew up in the heart of Southern apartheid. And I'm not saying that I didn't realize that it existed, but our parents were spiritual geniuses who created a world and a language where the notion that I was inadequate or inferior or less-than never touched my consciousness. I grew up believing that I was a first-class human being and a first-class person, and our parents were spiritual geniuses who were able to shape a counterculture of black folk religion that raised us from disposability to being essential players in society.[13]

Ruby's parents were well aware of the pervasiveness of white sovereignty in a so-called democracy and their anarchic care for their children rendered the apparatuses of power and authority vis-à-vis racism inoperative.[14] Put differently, they sought to use their authority and power—power to care—to protect their children from the attributes of white supremacy, not by offering a new version of sovereignty, which one would find in Malcolm X's (Haley, 1964; see also Payne & Payne, 2020, pp.260–261) early adoption of the myths of the Nation of Islam, but by creating spaces for them to develop a sense of singularity and belonging, wherein they exercised their agency in speaking and acting together. In other words, these early experiences of singularity and belonging were without her parents' ideas of ruling over her—an anarchic caring relation, which gave rise to unthought knowns of belonging and rapport. These unthought knowns of early childhood become intertwined with later complex organizations of singularity and belonging, as well as moments of exercising capacities for actualizing potentiality and impotentiality.

Relatedly, the parents' anarchic caring also gives rise to an ungovernable self (LaMothe, 2021b)—a self capable of exercising impotentiality and, therefore, not determined by the apparatuses of oppression. In terms of Ruby's activism, she certainly sought and seeks justice by removing (rendering inoperative) the apparatuses that promote the sovereignty of white supremacy and replacing them with a more democratic and just versions of sovereignty. So, we can see that the notion of sovereignty continues to appear, but for her and Martin Luther King Jr., democratic sovereignty represents relations of mutual-personal recognition and equality, as well as civic care and civic justice. Nevertheless, I suggest there is an early anarchic strand to her version of democracy—a strand rooted in early childhood and its anarchic relations of care and belonging. I add and stress that the anarchic relations of consistent parental care led to her sense of singularity, belonging, as well as the emergence of an ungovernable self—a self capable of impotentiality and, therefore, not captive to or determined by the political-economic apparatuses of racism.

A question may arise regarding parents and their use of aggression in caring for their infants and their infants' aggression. That is, since sovereignty is founded on political violence and the threat of violence, we might enquire as to the relation between violence and aggression as it pertains to the care of infants, as well as infants' aggression toward their parents. Good-enough parental care does entail the use of aggression, as Winnicott (1990) notes when he addresses setting boundaries with difficult children. But this aggression is ideally aimed at the well-being of children, even if they are unable to understand this. It is not an aggression meant to establish the rule of the parents or to subjugate their children. The aggression in good-enough parental care, then, is not violent—it does not violate children's embodied-psychic integrity. Violence and the threat of violence do fall under the heading of aggression, but they are inimical to caring relations. Aggression, framed in terms of care, is for the sake of children and, at some level, children recognize this and trust their parents. I suspect that Ruby's parents were, at times, aggressive in their care, but this did not interfere with Ruby's sense of being a first-class person.

These initial experiences of belonging/rapport and singularity, I argue, are anarchic in nature—at least in situations of good-enough parental care. But this raises two questions: What happens to these experiences, since most adults obtain some notion of sovereignty from social-political apparatuses and participate in spaces of speaking and acting together that are framed in terms of sovereignty. How are we to understand these anarchic experiences of belonging and singularity in light of the Western ontological rift between human beings and other species? To address these questions, I return to Winnicott's (1971) notion of transitional objects.

We need not repeat what was discussed regarding transitional objects in the previous two chapters. Stated simply, the primary transitional object represents the anarchic care evident in parent-child interactions, which enables children to experience belonging and singularity with another object—not a cultural object—as well as actualize impotentiality [Winnicott's (1965) "right not to communicate" (p.179)]. For Winnicott, children have an experience and belief in omnipotence as they make use of the transitional object. This omnipotence includes, at times, aggression. This seems to suggest that the seeds of adult sovereignty are rooted in omnipotence, but this would be incorrect for three reasons. First, Winnicott viewed the experience and belief in omnipotence as both necessary for creating external reality, which would suggest the first steps toward acknowledging the singularity of objects. Second, children's omnipotence vis-à-vis the TO is a way of creating and possessing belonging and singularity in the absence of the parents. Third and relatedly, omnipotence here is not about ruling over the object. The intersection of omnipotence and sovereignty comes later, once children grow up having internalized the notions of sovereignty from their culture's apparatuses. In brief, this first transitional object represents an anarchic relation of care and experiences of belonging and singularity that are under the infant's omnipotent control.

The second transitional object appears as children begin to internalize and make use of complex cultural symbol systems. One of my favorite illustrations of this is the comic strip Calvin and Hobbes. Hobbes is a stuffed tiger who is very much alive in the mind of Calvin—but appears only as a stuffed animal from the perspective of adults. They play and laugh together, argue and make up, and comfort each other. In brief, there is a deep sense of rapport and belonging between the two that emerges in Calvin's imagination. This sense of belonging, while under the omnipotent control of Calvin, depends on the mutual care-aggression between Calvin and Hobbes. The relation is an anarchic space of speaking and acting together. Calvin and Hobbes are best friends, and it is inconceivable that one rules over the other or that one is superior to the inferior other. Instead, as friends, there is mutual recognition and care, which provides the matrix for actualizing potentiality and impotentiality—ungovernable selves.

Calvin and Hobbes are not an anomaly. There are mountains of children's literature that animate other species, giving them agency and feelings. These other-than-human animals possess their own singularity and with human beings experience a sense of belonging. In general, this literature displays no ontological rift, no claims of superiority-inferiority, no beliefs in sovereignty. As in the Calvin and Hobbes comic strip, there are anarchic relations, where the notion of sovereignty simply does not apply. It is important to mention that children's literature, for children who are reading, often has issues and challenges associated with sovereignty.

C. S. Lewis' *Narnia Chronicles*, for instance, imports Christian notions of divine sovereignty. Interestingly, Aslan, a sovereign god, is represented as a lion, but he nevertheless is sovereign. My point here, though, is that early secondary transitional objects are not yet touched by political and religious beliefs about sovereignty. This means that these early objects and experiences of belonging represent anarchic relations of belonging and are not yet part of the ontological rift.

Winnicott argued that transitional objects are not mourned, because children simply become more involved in the socio-cultural field of objects and relations. In so doing, the subjectivities of children begin to be largely shaped by the cultural-political narratives of their polis, which suggests not only buying into the necessity of sovereignty for human belonging, but also accepting, unwittingly, the ontological rift and human dominion and superiority over other species. This raises a question: What happens to these early anarchic relations and experiences where there is no ontological rift? I think we see glimpses of this in adult life. First, adults write children's literature, so at least in their imaginations, there is an anarchic bridge to the world of other species and a recognition that we are all part of this one world. Second, philosophers like Buber (1958) argue that individuals can have I-Thou experiences with other species and geographical spaces. I-Thou experiences by definition are anarchic, because the "Thou" is not subordinate, subjugated, or inferior. Moreover, I-Thou relations necessarily entail distinctions vis-à-vis other species, but distinction as differentiation is not separation, not rift (see Kovel, 1988, pp.288–292). I add that I-Thou relations entail the presence of impotentiality or ungovernable selves who are not captive to I-It epistemologies and relations. There are also religious persons and theologians who would agree with Buber. Francis of Assisi and theologian-scientist Teilhard De Chardin were able to conceptualize and experience a life where I-Thou relations with other species and the earth are possible, even necessary.

We might consider these I-Thou experiences as signifying the presence of unthought knowns linked to early childhood where anarchic care gives rise to a deep sense of rapport and belonging, whether that is to an individual object (or person) or to the cosmos. But it is not only I-Thou experiences in adult life that serve as evidence of anarchic relations. There are innumerable routine occasions in adult life when a person cares for another and this care is not related to apparatuses of sovereignty. This could be a friendship. It could be a nurse caring for an ill patient. An adult child cares for a dying parent, a person helps an older man cross the street, an individual tends to a lost dog, and a neighbor clears the driveway and sidewalks for an elderly person are just some common examples of care that are not tied to or have anything to do with sovereignty or even I-Thou experiences. While I will say more about this in a later chapter, a foundational aspect of psychoanalytic psychotherapy is anarchic care for the well-being of the patient.

If we consider the above developmental perspective, what are its implications for a psychoanalytic political philosophy? The above is not my attempt to offer a state of nature that undergirds a specific political philosophy of or a justification for an anarchic polis. Even if I were to do so, I am not sure how practical it would be, given the seemingly impervious hegemony of political philosophies that serve as apparatuses producing and maintaining the belief in the necessity of sovereignty for human belonging. What I am suggesting is that, in the midst of our political belonging structured by ideas of sovereignty, there are innumerable routine occurrences of anarchic relations and care. Indeed, I would take a leap and contend that anarchic care is a necessary feature for the very existence of political belonging, even those dominated by sovereignty. An illustration of this is seen in the TV series *Deadwood*. Deadwood was a town in South Dakota, while South Dakota was a territory—outside the sovereignty of the U.S. state. There was a great deal of violence and ruthlessness as various factions sought to gain control or be *de facto* sovereign over the town. Yet, in the midst of the brutality, machinations, and absence of I-Thou relations were numerous acts of care—care that was neither instrumental nor linked to subjugation, superiority-inferiority, or violence. Even in this dystopian town, there were acts of anarchic care, which kept the town from imploding into violent chaos. A psychoanalytic political philosophy, then, can affirm and encourage this existential reality of anarchic relations that found human belonging and give rise to ungovernable selves.

To suggest that anarchic care is a necessary foundation of the polis is connected to both the developmental view described above and the idea that sovereignty is a tragic artifice and illusion. In other words, a psychoanalytic political philosophy can expose the illusion of human sovereignty and posit an existential reality of anarchic relations. First, how do we know with some confidence that sovereignty and its ontological rift are illusions? I mentioned this above, but let me return so that this becomes contrasted with anarchy. I stated that these illusions of sovereignty are not universal.[15] There are other types of belonging and attending narratives that do not depend on sovereignty or beliefs in an ontological rift. Second, sovereignty depends on artificial apparatuses that continually produce and maintain the beliefs in its necessity for human belonging. The ongoing creation of human artifices indicates it is an illusion and not something "discovered" in the state of nature. Of course, illusions have real effects. Indeed, the Anthropocene Age reveals how destructive these illusions are. Third, the illusions of sovereignty and ontological rift contain a tragic contradiction. The more and more we hold onto these illusions, the more we can be sure that the effects of climate change will continue, likely leading to the extinction of human beings. This extinction will demonstrate that there is no ontological rift and that human beings were never sovereign. *Anarchic relations, by contrast, do not carry an internal contradiction, in part, because these relations are rooted in existential facts.* Anarchic relations of care, in other words, are existential facts because anarchic care founds the movement from potentiality to actuality, as noted in the developmental perspective above. Anarchic care, at least with regard to early life, creates belonging that is not reliant on artifices to produce it.

I am also suggesting in this psychoanalytic political philosophy that human beings can refuse the ontological rift, can refuse beliefs in the necessity of sovereignty for human belonging, can refute human superiority and privilege, and can exercise impotentiality of ungovernable selves. In rendering these apparatuses inoperative, we, as ungovernable selves, are free to engage in relations of anarchic care with other human beings, other species, and the earth. Will this be enough to alter the dire trajectory we are currently on? This is an understandable question, even though it seems to depend on unlikely positive results to accept this perspective. Put differently, this question suggests positive results are necessary to confirm an ethical-political stance, as if we accept only those means that will achieve desired outcomes. Instead, the above points to a categorical ethical demand and relation to other human beings, other species, and the earth, the means of which is radical, anarchic care—a means not contingent on positive results. Put differently, sovereignty and its attending ontological rift are tragic illusions that have and are causing untold damage to Othered human beings, other species, and the earth. A psychoanalytic philosophical perspective acknowledges the necessity of a biodiverse earth for any political philosophy regarding human dwelling and belonging. This acknowledgement can give rise to ethical relations of belonging and dwelling, even if ethical, anarchic relations will not stem the tide of global warming.

## Conclusion

The aura of sovereignty and attending ontological rift appear to be unquestionable, existential or even ontological facts of human life, which are produced and reproduced through various apparatuses that facilitate the internalization of these beliefs. We may protest, vote, and discuss the political state of affairs, but most of us never seem to question sovereignty itself. I am reminded of the movie The Wizard of Oz. Dorothy, who desperately wishes to return home, is told to seek out the powerful wizard of Oz—the unquestionable sovereign of the city. When she and her friends encounter the "wizard," there is a great and frightening spectacle (use of machines and deception—apparatuses of aura) demonstrating his superior power, the threat of violence, and their inferiority and subordination. They are initially captivated and terrified by the aura of power and possible violence of the sovereign of Oz, yet we espy a frail older gentleman, because Toto, Dorothy's dog, unmasks him. A "non-human" animal from the ontological rift exposes the illusion of the sovereignty of the great Oz. He is simply an old, insecure white man. Unlike this movie, sovereignty and its aura vis-à-vis human beings have been and are revealed in the ecological devastation of the Anthropocene Age. The growing number of extinctions are unmasking the tragic illusions we hold. Once unmasked, once we are aware, we will not, like Dorothy, find a magical way to return home. But we, like her, might discover we are home and we can choose an ethical-political stance of anarchic caring relations that bridge the ontological gap, even given the tragic trajectory of climate change.

## Notes

1 Judeo-Christian theologies ontologize sovereignty, making it an attribute of God. Lest one think that political theologies, which serve as apparatuses for the production and maintenance of sovereignty, have little to do with modern political philosophy, we need

to recall German jurist Carl Schmitt's view that "All significant concepts of the modern theory of the state are secularized theological concepts" (in Agamben, 2005, p.36). The ontologizing of sovereignty serves to make this attribute of the state unquestionable, except perhaps to heretics and anarchists. Recently, the idea of the non-sovereignty of God vis-à-vis political dwelling has been taken up by philosopher John Caputo (2006) and political theologian Ryan LaMothe (2021a).

2  Freud (1900, 1914, 1918, 1926, 1933) uses the term in different contexts, ranging from intrapsychic to religious-political to international. In any case, my point here is that, for Freud, sovereignty in human life is taken for granted.

3  Freud views human beings as animals, though he also differentiates human beings and nature, suggesting that human beings are somehow separate from nature even as they are part of nature. This is not simply an awkward formulation. It reveals, in part, what Agamben called the ontological rift between human beings and other species that is created by Western philosophies. This rift, as discussed below, is intertwined with the notions of sovereignty. I add two other points. First, Freud's appellations regarding nature reveal an antagonist relation marred by "nature's" cruelty and indifference. He obviously overlooked the long history of the cruelty and indifference many human beings exhibited and exhibit toward othered human beings, other species, and the earth itself. Second and relatedly, nature is anthropomorphized. Nature is not and cannot be indifferent or cruel, only human beings, as far as I know, can manifest these attributes.

4  In a recent article, I (2021) have discussed the problem of sovereignty vis-à-vis climate change and while I use some of what I have written in this chapter, the focus is different.

5  Since political violence is a central factor in political change (or stopping political change), I will return to it in Chapter 5.

6  Karl Popper (2002) argued that Plato's fundamental philosophical question vis-à-vis the polis was "who should rule." This he contended has led to a number of problems in Western political philosophies, hiding key paradoxes and problems, not the least of which is the tendency toward Platonic tyranny (pp.114–129). Popper then goes to address the importance of democratic institutions in a democracy. This chapter focuses more directly on the issue of sovereignty itself—an issue that attends democracies as well.

7  While I will focus on a couple of paradoxes of sovereignty, it is worth mentioning that Wendy Brown (2010) identifies six paradoxes of sovereignty: (1) Sovereignty is both a name for absolute power and a name for political freedom; (2) Sovereignty generates order through subordination and freedom through autonomy; (3) Sovereignty has no internal essence, but rather is completely dependent and relational, even as it stands for autonomy, self-presence, and self-sufficiency; (4) Sovereignty produces both internal hierarchy and external anarchy; (5) Sovereignty is both a sign of the rule and the jurisdiction of law and supervenes the law; 6) Sovereignty is both generated and generative (pp.53–54).

8  There are rare exceptions. Bryant Rousseau (2016) discusses New Zealand's parliament that has two political representatives who represent the land and species of two geographical areas.

9  Freud, in my view, when referring to civilization is primarily referring to European civilization and adopting Western political views of sovereignty, even if Freud never mentions this.

10  It is important to mention that, during Freud's life, European states, along with the U.S., controlled most of the world. Civilization was a trope and mystification used to legitimate colonization—sovereignty over subjugated "primitive" peoples. Curiously, in the indexes of Freud's 22 volumes, there is no reference to Western imperialism or colonization. Freud was exercised about religion, but not about the destructive illusions of science and political beliefs around imperialism and Western sovereignty. The absence of this, during a time when there were anti-imperialist and anti-colonial organizations, suggests that Freud admired and benefited from civilization and in particular being in

the sovereign classes (educated, bourgeois). So, perhaps Freud's defense of civilization, and by implication sovereignty, reveals an unconscious motivation to retain his social-political and economic privileges and status.

11  Anarchy comes from the Greek and means without sovereign or ruler. The concept emerged during the time of Thomas Hobbes, who was horrified at the prospect, linking anarchy to social-political chaos and violence. While French philosopher Pierre-Joseph Proudhon in the 19th century embraced the idea of anarchy as foundational to his political philosophy, Hobbes' appellations regarding anarchy remain today. Readers may have negative views of anarchy, which I believe reveals how effective apparatuses of sovereignty have captured our psyches. Why is it that we can imagine the end of the world, but not the end of sovereignty?

12  Adam Phillips (2021b) makes a similar case when discussing psychoanalytic therapy and linking this to parent-child relations.

13  Ruby Sales—Where Does It Hurt?|The On Being Project – The On Being Project, https://onbeing.org/programs/ruby-sales-where-does-it-hurt/#transcript, accessed 16 November 2021.

14  For Agamben, "inoperativity" means to deactivate the functioning of apparatuses, which does not mean that these apparatuses cease operating or do not continue to have effects (Prozorov, 2014, pp.31–34).

15  A reader might point to the "fact" of sovereignty among other species. Ants and bees have queens. Some social animals have pack leaders, like wolves, gorillas, etc. To suggest from this that sovereignty exists in nature and is therefore not an artifice would be to elide the fact that we use a human concept to explain the behavior of other species.

# Chapter 4

# Psychoanalysis and Systemic Obstacles to Climate Action

## Capitalism, Nationalism, and the New Imperialism

In an interesting chapter on obstacles, Adam Phillips (1993) writes, "Consciousness is of obstacles" (p.91). In psychosocial development, we become aware of desire and need when we encounter obstacles—hopefully obstacles that we learn to manage, instead of the obstacles managing us. For Phillips, an "aim of psychoanalytic treatment may be to enable the patient to find, or be able to tolerate, more satisfying obstacles to contend with" (p.86). This is a plausible view, but there are notable omissions in Phillips' discussion that reveal a tragic dimension of human existence. There are obstacles that human beings create (artifices) that are not recognized as obstacles by the creators, but as necessary for human belonging and fulfillment—at least for some. We might think of the apparatuses that produce and maintain racism, sexism, classism, and other forms of exploitation that are dangerous obstacles to those who are marginalized, while viewed by the privileged as necessary and desired. Aristotle certainly did not conceive his politics to be obstacles to women's flourishing, even though the polis he imagined and lived in was thoroughly patriarchal and sexist (and classist or elitist). Racists similarly never see themselves and their artifices as obstacles, though most people of color are conscious that racism is a destructive obstacle and not something to be tolerated. Those who create the obstacle may hardly be aware that it is an artifice *qua* human construction, arguing that the artifice is existentially "natural" or God-given. Similarly, there are artifices, not seen as obstacles, that are tragic, precisely because they are not perceived to be or experienced as obstacles, leading to destruction or death. The soldiers and leaders of Troy viewed the wooden horse as a gift and a sign of their success in overcoming their enemies. In fact, the wooden horse was an obstacle that led to their downfall. Iago is not seen as an obstacle by Othello, which leads to a tragic ending. Sometimes it is only in recognizing that something is killing us that we become aware that it is an obstacle, which may, as in the case of Troy and Othello, be too late. To paraphrase Camus (1947, p.69), when an artificial obstacle starts to kill you, you have to get to work on it, if it is not already too late.

In this chapter, I identify three interrelated systemic, global obstacles—obstacles to stemming the tragic trajectory of climate disaster. These obstacles, which are human artifices, are capitalism, nationalism, and new imperialism. While some people recognize these as barriers to working toward reducing or stopping greenhouse

DOI: 10.4324/9781003258827-6

gas emissions, most people view them as necessary or inevitable for human dwelling. Other individuals may even believe they are not only not obstacles, but provide answers to climate change (e.g., Wagner & Weitzman, 2015). A possible, perhaps, likely tragedy is that the majority of human beings will not become conscious of this dangerous trinity until these obstacles kill us and numerous other species. I begin by briefly defining each obstacle, while also arguing that these obstacles are interconnected. In this section, I explain how these macro systems have contributed to climate change and how they impede gaining any traction toward effective climate action. This is followed by a critique of these obstacles using psychoanalytic concepts, which is the typical psychoanalytic approach to addressing social, political, and economic issues. Here I want to explain, relying on psychoanalytic concepts, how it is that many people are tragically not conscious that these obstacles threaten human existence, as well as the existence of millions of other species. In the last section, I shift to a different psychoanalytic approach. I identify some of the key premises and principles of a psychoanalytic political philosophy, which become part of a hermeneutical framework for further critiques of capitalism, nationalism, and imperialism vis-à-vis the climate emergency. Also included in this section is a discussion on how a psychoanalytic political philosophy provides ideas regarding how to respond to these (and other) obstacles.

As is my habit, I offer some caveats and clarifications before beginning. First, capitalism, nationalism, and imperialism are deeply complex social imaginaries that cannot be adequately defined or examined in one chapter, let alone a book. Given this, my aim is not to be exhaustive but rather heuristic, highlighting major features of these stumbling blocks so I can critique them using psychoanalytic concepts, while further developing a psychoanalytic political philosophy. Second, this chapter follows the previous chapter on sovereignty and political violence for good reasons. Sovereignty is itself an obstacle, because it is founded on and perpetuates the ontological rift. Add to this that capitalism, nationalism, and imperialism are inextricably yoked to sovereignty and sovereign classes, which exacerbates and extends the ontological rift that is tragically undermining the dwelling of human beings and other species. While my main focus is not to explicate the relation between sovereignty and these barriers, I will briefly indicate the intersection. Third, it is necessary to make clear that I do not see this trinity of obstacles as the only barriers to climate action, but in my view they are systemic realities that undermine global cooperation in helping those already suffering the effects of climate change, as well as undermining real and effective climate action. Finally, there is a growing body of literature on petrocultures and their contribution to climate change and their obstructing climate action (Kerber, 2017; Orpana, 2021; Szeman, 2017, 2019; Wilson, Carlson, & Szeman, 2017). My focus on capitalism tacitly includes the notion of petrocultures in that it is impossible to imagine the rise of capitalism in the West and globally without also seeing the rise of petrocultures. I add that even if it is possible to move toward a culture that is not reliant on oil, capitalism would remain a significant problem for billions of human beings, other species, and the earth.

## A Trinity of Obstacles in the Anthropocene Age: Capitalism, Nationalism, and Imperialism

We will face many barriers and challenges in the years ahead as global warming continues. When it comes to individuals and small communities, some of these obstacles are easier to overcome than others. Persons can decide to eschew or reduce their consumption of meat, since the mass production of animals for consumption is a significant contributor to greenhouse gasses. If people and groups can afford it, they can purchase solar panels and electric vehicles to reduce or eliminate their carbon footprint. Individuals may seek out clothing and other products (bicycles) that use sustainable resources, like bamboo. Others may re-wild their property, planting trees as a carbon offset. These are laudable efforts, yet when we take a few steps back and survey the landscape, there are massive hurdles that may not be scalable. In this section, I focus on three obstacles, beginning with capitalism.

Markets, Ellen Woods (2017) explains, have long been a part of civilization, though, historically, markets have been subordinate to other representational systems that organize society.[1] Millennia ago, Plato and Aristotle, for instance, reluctantly accepted the reality of markets and money, believing that "involvement with the exchange for profit can easily incite the desire for wealth for its own sake" (Brown, 2015, p.90), which, in turn, undermines political belonging because it creates alienation among the haves and have-nots. While markets have been part of civilization for millennia, in England during the 16th century, according to Woods (2017), we see the origins of capitalism in the promulgation of agrarian laws (p.105), which reduced the commons and led to mass movements of people to the cities, where they tried to eke out a living. Eventually, the beliefs and practices associated with capitalism were instantiated in the liberal philosophies of John Locke, Adam Smith, David Ricardo (and others); codified into English law; and spread to other countries often through imperialistic practices (pp.125–166).[2] Katerina Pistor (2019) details how the emergence of capitalism can only be understood in light of sovereign classes using or promulgating laws, court actions, policies, and programs that furthered capitalism's dominance in organizing society. By the 20th century, Western societies were market societies, rather than societies that had markets or subordinated markets to the society (Cox, 2016; Dardot & Laval, 2013). As Chris Harman (2017) writes, "Capital had stamped its impact everywhere in the world by 1900" (p.379), resulting in vast increases in wealth for the upper classes and imperial states, while negatively impacting the lives of numerous citizens in Europe, the United States, and especially colonized peoples.

As capitalism spread throughout the world, it became monolithic, while at the same time taking on different appearances at different times and places. This suggests that when we are talking about capitalism, we necessarily recognize its variability. Consider these iterations: classical capitalism (Mann, 2013; Wolff & Resnick, 2012), laissez-faire capitalism, supercapitalism (Reich, 2007), neoliberal capitalism (Harvey, 2005; Jones, 2012), state-corporate capitalism (Beckert & Desan, 2018; Duménil & Lévy, 2011), state-run capitalism (e.g., China), democratic capitalism (Wolff, 2012), and gore capitalism (Valencia, 2018). Even within these varied discourses, there are nuances, complexities, and contestations. Given this, we can make a general claim that, in whatever guise, capitalism represents a complex semiotic system or social imaginary comprising ideas, narratives, treatises, laws, rituals, and other practices that order social relationships and institutions vis-à-vis financial exchange, property, and profit.

Let's delve a bit more into this general definition to obtain greater clarity. Capitalism as a complex semiotic system is "organized... around the institution of property and the production of commodities" (Bell, 1996, p.14). These commodities are determined by a "rational" calculus of cost and price—the commodification of goods and services—and the market law of supply and demand.[3] Peter Hudis (2015a) notes that "Marx insisted that the aim of capitalist society is not to enrich human needs and capabilities, but rather to augment value. Capitalism...has one over-riding goal of capitalists: to accumulate value for its own sake" (p.176). Value here is inextricably tied to the primary aim, which is profit. Whatever the iteration of capitalism, its aims and values are productivity and profit or the accumulation of capital for the purposes of reinvestment, market expansion, and greater profits. Profit, then, is the central value, motive, and *telos* that largely determines "rational" decisions about expanding production, seeking larger market share, wages, hiring, benefits, expenditures, etc. Labor and wages, for instance, are inextricably linked to and ostensibly determined by material production, services, supply and demand, and, naturally, the overarching aim of securing profit (Wolff & Resnick, 2012, p.39). Surplus labor and value are integral to overall profit, which is kept by the owners or shareholders of the business. In addition, the means of production, in classical capitalism, are privately owned, whether by an individual, family, or stockholders (more precisely, socially constructed legal entities called corporations that have stockholders). In terms of the relation between consumers and producers, Adam Smith touted the "invisible hand" of the market, whereby each individual "rationally" maximizes his/her self-interest in a milieu whereby supply equals demand, thus increasing the wealth of producers and shareholders, while providing goods and services to consumers (Hendricks, 2011, p.152). Each subject, then, is self-referential, maximizing his/her self-interest, which, it is believed, will lead to an overall "good" for the society. This "good" is understood primarily in terms of wealth, which is measured by what we call the GDP (gross domestic product).

Before moving to discussing how capitalism is an obstacle, it is important to bring in the other two social imaginaries, namely, nationalism and imperialism, because they intersect with each other and capitalism. As Woods notes, the roots of capitalism lay in late-16th-century England, which is curiously around the time of the emergence of nation-states in Europe. The rise of modern nation-states has been attributed to the Peace of Westphalia (1648). The Peace of Westphalia entailed two treaties, one ending the 30-year war and the other the 80-year war. From these European treaties emerged beliefs that nations had their own inviolable sovereignty and territory, though this did not end further transgressions between nation-states. Put differently, nationalism asserts that each nation should pursue its self-interests, which, of course, may result in working with other nations toward mutually shared interests. Within these nation-states, citizens believe they share a collective national identity, which is linked to the particular nation-state.[4] Put differently, citizens, in general, believe they share a common identity, origin, history, and language(s), even amidst diversity. In addition, nationalism refers to persons' loyalty and devotion to a larger group—country and state.

In a seminal work, Benedict Anderson (1983) offers further thoughts and insights about nationhood. He argues that the very possibility of imagining a nation resulted from the loss of several cultural conceptions (e.g., feudalism) that had previously gripped the minds of men and women during the Middle Ages (p.36). The rise of nationalism accompanied what Anderson called imagined communities—a felt (imaginary) sense of comradeship "regardless of inequality and exploitation that may prevail" (p.7). Nations are imagined communities in two senses. First, they are socially constructed realities. That is, the nation is created by a people and does not exist prior to its emergence within a particular geographic region—a region that comes to be called or constructed as the boundaries of the nation. The nation, in other words, does not naturally exist in nature. Second, a nation is an imaginary in that it provides a felt sense of belonging that depends on the fiction of sameness (we all share the same identity) and the construction of Others—those who are not citizens. Even though people do not know each other directly, the idea of being one people provides citizens with a sense of belonging, which is felt to be real, though it is imaginary. Of course, imaginary belonging does not mean there are no real effects. In the United States, for example, numerous wars have been fought by appealing to national identity-belonging.

Yet, it is overly reductionistic to say that a nation is simply a collectively held *idea* that evokes a sense of belonging or comradeship and shared identity. The *idea* of a nation accompanies what Charles Taylor (2007) called social imaginaries. Social imaginaries are a complex array of social practices, rituals, ceremonies, and narratives that, when considering the notion of nation, are formalized and legitimized by way of social-political institutions. Social imaginaries that support the notion of the nation also comprise objects (e.g., flags, statues, and buildings), which, in the minds of the people, evoke consciously or unconsciously the cognitive schema of my/our nation. For instance, the nation's political institutions enact legislation that identifies a day to commemorate those who sacrificed for the mother/fatherland. Local towns have parades, the media retell stories of bravery, and groups place flags on the graves of the fallen. These are very concrete, socially constructed practices that are linked to a complex array of signifiers representing the idea of the "nation," which further establishes an imaginary sense of shared identity and belonging. A nation, in short, does not have an existence that is independent of its construction by a group of people or the socially constructed practices that maintain its existence. Citizens and their social imaginaries/apparatuses, then, produce and reproduce the nation.

Let me return to capitalism and its relation to nationalism. As capitalism begins to take hold in Europe, each nation is sovereign over its capitalistic markets. So, within a nation-state, capitalists pursue markets and profits, all of which are tied to and dependent on the sovereign and sovereign classes for legitimation. Within the nation, there is, for most citizens, a shared sense of identity and belonging vis-à-vis the nation, but this occurs in relation to classism and inequalities that are exacerbated by capitalism. Classism fosters stratified groups of belonging—each having their own culture (Fussell, 1983; Sayer, 2005)—and group identity. Put differently, in a nation-state, capitalism, as Rousseau noted,

> bound new fetters in the poor, and gave new powers to the rich…fixed forever the laws of property and inequality; converted clever usurpation into an inalienable right and for the sake of the few ambitious men, subjected all mankind to perpetual labour, servitude and misery.
>
> (Rousseau in Eagleton, 2011, p.199)

Between nation-states, things become a bit trickier, with nations trying to protect their own markets, placing tariffs on goods from other nations or forming pacts with other nations to compete against other nations (e.g., imperialistic nations cooperating to establish economic zones in China in the 19th and early 20th centuries). Of course, more recently, powerful nation-states have decided that it is in their interests to cooperate with other nations to establish collective rules of the capitalistic game (e.g., G8, Indo-Pacific Trade Agreement). Nevertheless, nation-states are primarily concerned with protecting their markets at home, while seeking to facilitate the expansion of markets outside their borders, which places them in competition with other nation-states.

It is important to stress here that market societies are nations and that markets become part of what it means to be a nation. This is especially true in nations with a history of imperialism, like the United States. It is common in the United States for citizens to identify capitalism as integral to what it means to be a sovereign nation, as well as one's identity as an American. Capitalism has been integral to this nation's birth and "development." Any suggestion of altering the capitalist system heightens anxiety and hostility. People who advocate anything that is contrary to capitalism are labeled as socialists, communists, and un-American by the media and politicians. Capitalism, in the American context, also becomes linked to the notion of political freedom, while socialism is seen as undemocratic, robbing people of their so-called freedoms. Congressman Tom Cole is merely one of those who decry socialism as un-American.[5] Cole's view is common and one that is supported by numerous government and non-government apparatuses, including the media. Indeed, by and large, the media depends on the capitalist system for financing, making media outlets disinclined to offer alternatives or to critique the idea that capitalism is not essential to the nation.

Another phenomenon developed during this time of the rise of capitalism and nation-states was Western imperialism. Of course, it is true that imperialism existed long before the rise of imperial powers in Europe and the United States (e.g., Roman Empire, Persian Empire). But what took place in Europe was the intersection of capitalism, with its insatiable drive for markets and profits, with nationalism, giving rise to numerous imperialistic nations. For instance, Ellen Woods (2017) notes that "in England, its economic logic became not just the driving force of the domestic economy but also an instrument of imperial domination beyond the boundaries of England" (p.162).[6] England was not alone. Many European nations (e.g., Belgium, Britain, Netherlands, France, Germany, Spain, and Portugal) became imperialistic, seeking to secure markets and profits by colonizing and exploiting other peoples. Imperial nations competed with each other and often fought wars to safeguard their colonial acquisitions. Indeed, WWI and WWII can be seen as wars conducted by and for imperial powers.

In the early 20th century, European and U.S. empires covered wide swaths of the world. The French Empire covered over 5 million square miles with a population of over 65 million. France had colonies in Africa, Southeast Asia, and the South Pacific. In 1920, the British Empire was the largest official realm in the world. It controlled one-quarter of the earth's surface. It had territories on every continent and ruled some 500 million people. The U.S. empire had political and economic control over Central America, Cuba, the Philippines, Hawaii, and other territories. It is estimated that European imperial powers, combined with the United States, controlled over 80% of the earth by the early 20th century. After WWII, an era of postcolonialism emerged in Africa and Asia with peoples seeking to shed the yoke of colonization and become nations, having their own sovereignty, territorial integrity, and identity. Did this mean that imperialism faded into the background? To answer this question, we must first understand what the definition of imperialism was prior to the end of WWII and how imperialism changed.

Traditionally, an imperial nation or empire was understood to possess "formal political control of one state over another's external and internal policy" (Lundestad, 1990, p.37). For instance, the United States, as an imperial power, actively pursued in the late 19th and early 20th centuries acquisition of Cuba, Puerto Rico, the Philippines, Hawaii, etc. Policies, such as the Monroe Doctrine and the notion of Manifest Destiny, "legitimized" U.S. territorial, economic, and political interventions in Central and South America, all of which included capitalistic expansion, including formal and informal acquisition of land and tacit control of governments. Historian Paul Kennedy remarks, "From the time the first settlers arrived in Virginia from England and started moving westward, this was an imperial nation" (in Stone & Kuznick, 2012, p.xv; see also Herring, 2008).

Once WWII ended and there were emancipatory surges in colonized countries, the old definitions of imperialism no longer applied. A new imperialism emerged. Geir Lundestad (1990) argues that an empire like the United States no longer had colonies, but instead established "a hierarchical system of political relationships with one power clearly being much stronger than any other" (p.37). Similarly, Julian Go (2012) defines new imperialism "as a sociopolitical formation wherein a central political authority (a king, a metropole, or imperial state) exercises unequal influence and power over the political processes of a subordinate society, peoples, or space" (p.7). The power used to gain client states or to gain influence over other nations is not merely political, but rather an amalgam of economic and military power. Both Go and Lundestad contend that imperialistic nations, like the United States, China, and Russia,[7] need not have direct, formal political, and territorial control. More particularly, Go (2012) and Fergusson (2004) argue that after WWII the United States became more of an informal empire, preferring indirect rule—exercising influence and political and economic control over societies and client states that were not colonies. As Go (2012) notes, the "imperial state keeps these nominally independent territories in line or compels them to meet its interests, but does not declare sovereignty over them" (p.11).[8] Worse, as Naomi Klein (2007) painstakingly details, imperial nations can destabilize other nations without having to resort to war or the threat of war. For instance, Klein notes the collusion of U.S. government leaders and economic experts (Friedman and other economists from the Chicago School) to destabilize governments and economies (Chile, Argentina, Brazil, etc.) during the 1970s, 1980s, and 1990s in an effort to install capitalistic systems that favored U.S. and European interests (see also Reich, 2007, pp.44–45).

The intersection of capitalism, nationalism, and (new and old) imperialism is revealed by someone who had firsthand knowledge of each. General Smedley Butler, winner of two Congressional Medals of Honor, called himself a "gangster for capitalism" (Bacevich, 2005, p.142). General Butler, reflecting on his years in the U.S. military, remarked:

> I spent thirty-three years and four months in active military service.... And during that period, I spent most of my time as a high-class muscle-man for big business, for Wall Street, and the bankers.... Thus, I helped make Mexico and especially Tampico safe for American oil interests in 1914. I helped make Haiti and Cuba a decent place for National City Bank boys to collect revenues in. I helped in the raping of a half a dozen Central American republics for the benefit of Wall Street.... In China I helped to see Standard Oil went its way unmolested.

> (quoted in Johnson, 2004, p.169)

This highly decorated general clearly understood the essential link among U.S. capitalism, nationalism, and imperialism. Today, the United States, China, and Russia represent the world's new imperialistic nations. China is actively seeking markets and client states in Africa, Central and South America, and Asia. Russia has a client state in the Mideast and is attempting to extend its influence in previous Soviet republics. The United States is competing with both nations to maintain political and economic hegemony. My point here is that these imperial powers are not merely seeking power; they are also seeking influence to expand and secure their markets.

Here I want to begin to elaborate how these intersecting social imaginaries represent significant contributors to global warming, as well as systemic obstacles to climate action. Since the early 19th century, $CO_2$ levels have risen, corresponding to the rise and expansion of capitalism in Europe and the United

States, as well as intensifying colonization efforts by imperial Western nations (and China). This expansionism continued, but carbon dioxide levels began to skyrocket in the decades after WWII, which reflected global expansion of capitalism initiated by the United States and its attempts to control markets through the Bretton Woods agreement (1944) and the establishment of the World Bank and International Monetary Fund.

Let's take a closer look at the numbers associated with the rise of $CO_2$. Citing the National Oceanographic and Atmospheric Administration (NOAA), Michael Northcott (2014) points out that "CO2 levels rose at 1.5 ppm from 1750 to 1950 [and] from 1950 to 2010 they rose at an average of *14 ppm per decade*" (p.5). In 2018, NOAA reported the highest rise of $CO_2$ emissions ever recorded.[9] Gernot Wagner and Martin Weitzman (2015) note that current carbon dioxide levels are at 400 ppm[10] and the last time they were that high was over 3 million years ago during the Pliocene Era, when "sea levels were up to 20 meters higher and camels lived in Canada" (p.10). They point to the International Energy Agency's (IEA) estimates that "the world is currently on track to increase total greenhouse gas concentrations to around 700 ppm by 2100" (p.31).[11] Nearly 100% of climate scientists acknowledge that these increases are almost entirely due to human activities, and these activities center primarily around capitalism and two imperial states, the United States and China. They are the biggest current offenders, but European nation-states, especially former imperial nations, are culpable as well. Given the pervasiveness of capitalism and its massive contributions to climate change, Jason Moore (2016) believes we should call the current era the Capitalocene Age, but in so doing we must also take into account the relation between capitalism and imperialistic nation-states.

Some economists, like Wagner and Weitzman (2015), acknowledge that capitalism is a major systemic factor in global warming, but they argue that the market can be harnessed to reduce greenhouse gas emissions and slow, if not curtail, the rise of global warming. Matthew Paterson and Peter Newell (2010) have a similar argument. For them,

> the issue is less whether we have climate capitalism or not, but what sort of climate capitalism we end up with. Capitalism of one sort or another will provide the context in which near-term solutions will have to be found.

(p.161)

While I can appreciate efforts to try to rein in the deleterious effects of capitalism, these approaches are, at best, naïve when one reads the sordid history of capitalism (and imperialism) and the vast income and wealth inequalities that exist within and between nations (see Piketty, 2014, 2020). We also need to remember that there were attempts to reform capitalism in the early to mid-20th century, introducing numerous regulations or protections (Keynesian capitalism). Even during the earliest days of these reforms, economists and philosophers (e.g., von Hayek, von

Mises, Friedman) were gathering and planning to undermine these protections (Jones, 2012). They were exceptionally successful in advancing neoliberal capitalism around the world, beginning in the late 1970s. Sayak Valencia (2018) calls this type of capitalism "gore capitalism" because of its devastating effects on the lives of millions upon millions of people, not to mention the destructive extractive impacts on the environment (e.g., fracking, Mountain Top Removal [MTR]). As Aldo Leopold notes, "We abuse the land because we regard it as a commodity that belongs to us" (in Harvey, 2016, p.161).[12] David Harvey adds to this stating, "It is hard in the light of these problems (environmental) not to conclude that there is something about money valuations that makes them inherently ant-ecological, confirming the field of thinking and of action to instrumental environmental management" (p.167). The point here is that economists who advocate for a kinder, more environmentally friendly capitalism are profoundly and tragically naïve, to say the least, because capitalism as a system promotes an ethic of exploitation and profligacy and its imbrication with political power apparatuses and sovereign classes of nation-states insure its continuation. In short, capitalism is both a main source of climate change and an obstacle to addressing it.

In addition to capitalism, nationalism and the new imperialism of the United States, China, and Russia also present barriers to climate action. Nationalism is mainly exclusive, focusing on each individual nation's self-interest. This accompanies intense competition for resources, especially given global capitalism. Nations are not likely to accede to the demands of collective cooperation vis-à-vis climate action if they perceive it will be costly to its markets or citizens. Of course, we know there have been international agreements, like the Rio Conference (UNFCCC), the Kyoto Protocol, and the Paris Agreement, which suggest that there is global cooperation among nations on reducing greenhouse gas emissions. At the United Nations Summit in 2009, wealthy countries committed to provide $100 billion a year to poorer nations to help with the effects of climate change. Jocelyn Timperly (2021) breaks down the finances and finds that wealthy nations have fallen far short of their pledges. Add to this the fact that global emissions by the United States, China, and Russia continue to grow, indicating that cooperation among nations is lacking, and I would argue this is precisely because these powerful nations continue to function as market societies bent on market expansion and profit, as well as focusing primarily on their own national interests.

Nationalism and capitalism possess a kind of logic that is compelling in the short term, but will have tragic, destructive consequences in the long term when it comes to climate change. Indeed, the logic of market nations (especially imperial nations) is an obstacle to climate action. The United States is the largest arms dealer in the world with Russia and China following a distant second and fifth.[13] The logic here is that nations need armies and navies to secure their territorial borders and insure national sovereignty. For imperial nations, like the United States, weapon manufacturing and sales are not only good for business; they are also necessary for maintaining global hegemony. Martin Luther King Jr. once remarked that war is the enemy of the poor, but we could add that preparing for war is not only an enemy of the poor, it is enemy against climate action.

Consider another recent example of the logic of nationalism and capitalism. In February 2022, Ukraine was once again invaded by Russia. Previously, Russia had invaded and taken over Crimea and the Donbas region in eastern Ukraine. Many nations have affirmed the idea of the national sovereignty and geographical integrity of Ukraine after Russia's invasion. Sweden and Finland, affirming their own national sovereignty, have shifted their neutral status and formally asked to join NATO, which has only inflamed the nationalistic tendencies of many Russians. Also, billions upon billions of dollars have been directed to Ukraine for their military, as well as billions for humanitarian efforts. We do not know for sure the costs to Russia, but it is clear Russia is spending billions to achieve its political and military goals. NATO nations responded to the desperate cries of Ukraine's government for help, which was also an attempt to stem Putin's imperial expansionist agenda—so the logic goes. The logic of identarian and geographical integrity vis-à-vis nation-states is compelling, as is the capitalism that funds the war. But if we step back and consider the logical trajectory of this type of thinking, we can see that it is also a massive systemic barrier to climate action. Not only are nations pitted against each other in this conflict, exacerbating climate change and environmental destruction, but they are also distracted from longer-term threats to humanity (and other-than-human species).

## A Psychoanalytic Perspective on Obstacles

Philosopher Axel Honneth (2012) situates the "I" and "we" within the context of their horizons, which includes the social-cultural milieu, other species, and material objects. To understand oneself and others requires recognizing that the "I" and "we" cannot be separated from this horizon, for the horizon or circumstance (geography and history) is inextricably a part of "I" and "we." In terms of the relation between societal structures and the self, Erich Fromm argued that the family is "the chief medium through which the child's formation is oriented toward the surrounding society" (in Durkin & Braune, 2020, p.3).[14] Psychoanalyst Roy Schafer (1959/1990) held a similar view, though identifying the psychosocial mechanism for the societal shaping of subjectivity. Schafer realized that the concept of internalization is useful for understanding not only psychosocial development but also the process of accepting an ideology (p.xi),[15] such as the ideologies associated with racism, sexism, classism, etc. Schafer believed this concept, which is used in social theory, can account for how the "oppressed and exploited [come] to accept and even idealize the socioeconomic and ideological system in which they and their oppressors are serving as participant-victims" (pp. xi–xii). Internalization, for Schafer, refers to "all those processes by which the subject transforms real or imagined regulatory interactions with his environment, and real or imagined characteristics of his environment, into inner regulations and characteristics" (p.15). Around the same time and in a different context of exploited peoples, Frantz Fanon used psychology to understand the link between the psychological struggles and sufferings of colonized peoples and the political, economic, and cultural apparatuses of imperial nations. Fanon believed, rightly, "that the body, suffering and anxiety are always politically and racially situated" (Gibson & Beneduce, 2017, p.124). Nelson Maldonado-Torres (2022), commenting on the work of Frantz Fanon, notes that subjectivity is "formed at the nexus of social structures and collective attitudes" (p.91), which in Fanon's context was the oppressive colonization of Algeria. Using Schafer's and Fanon's perspectives, we can claim that the systemic obstacles identified above have myriad apparatuses that facilitate the internalization of various beliefs, values, meanings, and purposes. That is, these systemic apparatuses form, but do not determine, the subjectivities of those who reside in societies. This perspective can deepen our understanding of how our collective subjectivities, which are integrally connected to these obstacles, are or can be obstacles to climate action. In this section, I rely on psychoanalytic concepts to further understand just how significant these obstacles are by delving into subjectivity.

Before beginning, it is important to note that psychoanalysts concerned about climate change have considered larger systemic realities, their impact on subjectivities, and how all this impedes our ability to cooperate toward effective climate action. Sally Weintrobe (2010) demonstrated how consumer greed is linked to narcissistic entitlement, which she argues is associated with the belief in one's superiority. Using the concepts of splitting and identification, Weintrobe depicts how all of this obstructs action toward climate action. In a later work, Weintrobe (2021) depicts how the apparatuses of neoliberal economics and neoliberal culture have undermined mindfulness by infantilizing and regressing residents of market societies to being mere unthinking consumers (p.114). Michael Rustin (2013) makes use of Melanie Klein's notions of paranoid-schizoid and depressive positions and argues that these are related to systemic apparatuses and our destructive stance toward other-than-human species and the earth. Rustin also points to the need to move into a depressive position so that we might adopt a caring attitude and behavior toward other species and the earth. From a different tack, Donna Orange (2017) argues that in the United States most of us have internalized racist, sexist, and classist beliefs and values, all the while developing a historical and narrative unconscious that makes it impossible to be accountable, to mourn, and to change. Put another way, Orange is positing that the historical unconscious is an obstacle to taking collective climate action and, by becoming conscious, there may be hope. Paul Hoggett (2019) examines, in part, the social-cultural beliefs and practices that obstruct climate action. Put another way, he asks why and explores how psychoanalysts (and others in the human sciences) are asleep at the wheel in relation to the present and looming realities of climate change.

In this section, my approach is similar, though I use the concepts of internalization, identification, and weak dissociation to understand how the apparatuses associated with capitalism, nationalism, and new imperialism have shaped our subjectivities to overlook, disavow, rationalize, and moralize the destructive actions of human beings (not all human beings) toward other species and the earth. In so doing, I am arguing that the degree to which we participate in and identify with these systemic obstacles, we ourselves are obstacles to climate action.[16]

Roy Schafer (1990) contends that:

> the idea of internalization can be a valuable resource to all those who are concerned with the psychology of the individual. But the utility of the idea of internalization is not limited to the studies of individuals. Those theorists and researchers who are concerned with social processes and history have used this idea extensively.... (I)nfluential contemporary contributors to general social theory have emphasized in their writings on historical and cultural topics the internalization of ideologies and their modes of comprehending the world and being in it.
>
> (p.xi)

Shafer continues arguing that the process of internalization aids us in understanding how some oppressed and exploited people come "to accept and even to idealize the socioeconomic" and political systems that are implicated in their suffering (pp.xi–xii). Similarly, this concept can help us understand how the systemic social imaginaries of capitalism, nationalism, and imperialism shape our collective subjectivities in the West such that we wittingly or unwittingly become sources of climate inaction.

Shafer devotes an entire book to this concept, but for my purposes a definition will get us started. Simply stated, internalization *"refers to those processes by which the subject transforms real or imagined regulatory interactions with his environment, and real or imagined characteristics of his environment, into inner regulations and characteristics"* (p.9). These processes begin in early childhood, as children initially internalize the beliefs, values, and meanings associated with their parents' use of the extant cultural symbol system. Children, in other words, make use of the symbol system at hand to organize experience, which means they have internalized and are shaped by the symbol system at hand. Parents reading to their children is an illustration of these processes.

This becomes more complicated when children begin to watch TV and other media devices. Children and adults are bombarded with thousands upon thousands of images, advertisements, and stories, which shape their subjectivities and behaviors. I remember a mother recounting how her four-year-old son came down to the breakfast table and fashioned a piece of bread into a gun, that he then used to "shoot" his older sister. The mother was shocked, because they did not have a TV and both parents worked hard to read stories to their children that did not have images or words related to gun violence. Where did this come from, she wondered. Somehow this child had internalized what he had seen and heard in the public realm.

From an early age, we also internalize the narratives and attending beliefs and values associated with capitalism, nationalism, and imperialism. Children observe parents using credit cards or cash to purchase goods. Birthdays and holidays become occasions for more consumption. Some parents introduce their children into the economic system by paying them for weekly household chores, teaching them that work is to be remunerated. They may even encourage or require their children to save a portion, which is further education into the capitalist system. Children attend various public events (sports, school functions, etc.), where people stand for the national anthem. Along with this, they are told stories in their classes and watch TV shows and movies that provide an idealized view of, for instance, the United States. They internalize the belief in U.S. exceptionalism, which accompanies their close identification with and reliance on nationalism for a sense of identity and belonging (Machin, 2020).

Let me be more explicit about internalization in adult life vis-à-vis capitalism, nationalism, and imperialism. Many social critics and scholars[17] (e.g., Brown, 2001, 2015; Dufour, 2008; Durkin & Braune, 2020; Lukács, 1968; Marcuse, 1964), since Marx, have pointed to how the apparatuses of capitalism produce subjects as *homo economicus*, who are alienated from others and sometimes from their own experiences, sense of self, and body (Hochschild, 2012a, 2012b; Illouz, 2007, 2008; Sandel, 2012). Anita Chari (2015) points out that a market society produces subjects that are "hypermobile, entrepreneurial neoliberal subject(s) who must assume the burden of risk that the state no longer shoulders" (p.9). Terry Eagleton (2003) concurs, adding, "Capitalism wants men and women to be infinitely pliable and adaptable" (p.118), which means, according to Wendy Brown (2015), that subjects, having internalized the beliefs and values of the market, are "subordinated to the market" (p.108). Similarly, sociologist Jennifer Silva (2013) studies persons on the lower end of the class divide who have internalized market dogma, which asserts that they are solely responsible for their failures or successes, overlooking how the larger system is implicated in their struggles. Finding it difficult to obtain a college education, incurring large debts, and being limited to low-wage jobs, working-class men and women blame themselves, believing they alone are responsible for their economic woes in a market society (pp.72–73). In the same vein as Silva, Brown (2015) uses the term "responsibilization" to refer to "forcing the subject to become a responsible self-investor and self-provider" (p.34). At the same time, "subjects are constructed as labor or labor power, as commodities or creatures of exchange, as consumers, clients, entrepreneurs, or self-investing human capital" (p.83). The subject, then, as "human capital…is at once in charge of itself, responsible for itself, and yet a potentially dispensable element of the whole" (p.110). These scholars demonstrate that our internalization of market beliefs shapes our behavior and perceptions. Moreover, they reveal that these beliefs have varying detrimental psychological and physical impacts, especially on marginalized and oppressed people (see, Piketty, 2014, 2020; Soss, Fording, & Schram, 2011; Wacquant, 2009).

The internalization of capitalistic narratives and rituals can be further understood in terms of weak dissociation. Recall that weak dissociation, for Stern (1997), involves narrative rigidity, which means that persons organize their experiences such that their actions and consequences are narrowly spelled out, omitting actions, consequences, meanings, and affects that do not "fit" the dominant story. The story becomes part of our assumptive world—unquestioned and unquestionable. Margaret Thatcher's credo that there is no alternative to capitalism is an illustration of how capitalism has become sacrosanct and necessary for "freedom" and societal well-being. It is not only residents of the market society who cannot imagine an alternative; it is also that the apparatuses of the government, media, and other economic entities keep alternatives from being presented. When their weak dissociation is threatened, anxiety is evoked and then transformed into hostility toward those who offer alternatives. It is not that Thatcher and other political leaders were/ are ignorant of alternatives to neoliberal capitalism. They simply keep saying there is no alternative and disparaging any slight move to challenge their position, which reinforces weak dissociation.

Weak dissociation also applies to the rigid narrative associated with nationalism and imperialism. As mentioned earlier, we come to believe that our only way of political belonging is by way of nationalism. To play off of Thatcher's credo, there is no alternative to nationalism. And even this thought cannot be thought, because any alternative is unthinkable. We become unwitting propagators of nationalistic beliefs and, therefore, we often become obstacles to climate action because many of us in the West want to hold onto the privileges and wealth that result from belonging to our nation and its market society. This is exacerbated in imperialistic nations, because state and non-state apparatuses continually produce and maintain beliefs in exceptionalism, which are seemingly unquestionable existential truths. The United States has a long history of promoting beliefs in U.S. exceptionalism, beginning in part with Thomas Jefferson who dubbed the United States an empire of liberty, arguing, with exuberant grandiosity, that "no constitution was ever before as well calculated as ours for extending extensive empire and self-government" (Fergusson, 2004, p.34). This was not simply a politician's exaggeration. In the first half of the 19th century, Alexis de Tocqueville (2004, pp.700–703) observed the widely held belief that the United States is an exceptional nation and, therefore, superior. Numerous writers since have highlighted U.S. exceptionalism and superiority, which are evident in the enshrined and shared official narratives that we tell about ourselves and in our public rituals (cf. Bacevich, 2002; Fullbright, 1966; Hedges, 2002; Hillman, 2004; Johnson, 2006, 2010; Niebuhr, 1957; Ryn, 2003). Indeed, any public figure who challenges these popular beliefs or, better, illusions, as Barak Obama did while running for president in 2008, can expect to be excoriated. The internalization of this belief is further cemented by weak dissociation. Thus, when this belief in exceptionalism structures our subjectivities, we function as obstacles to climate action, precisely because we collectively work to maintain exceptionalism. Exceptionalism, whether linked to one's nation or imperial nations, produces, more often than not, exclusion, fierce competition, and conflict instead of cooperation and inclusion.

Identification is another concept, closely associated with internalization and weak dissociation, that helps explain how individuals can be obstacles to climate action. A few years ago, I was behind a pickup truck, idling until we had a green light. Several bumper stickers caught my attention. The first was "I [heart] capitalism." On the other side of the bumper was "America, Love It or Leave It." I thought this driver wonderfully portrayed his identification with both capitalism and nationalism/imperialism. No doubt if one questioned either, one would be disidentifying with the United States and, in so doing, not be considered a true American. Intense identifications or what Donald Meltzer (1975) called adhesive identifications, in relation to a nation (and, for many people, capitalism/market society), undermine reflective functioning and complex thinking, which make it difficult to find areas of cooperation with people of different views or those who are Othered, especially noted in relation to climate refugees and financial and technical support to poorer nations already suffering from the impacts of climate change. Worse, intense or adhesive nationalistic identifications, such as patriotism (LaMothe, 2009), can lead citizens to support unquestioningly the nation's political-economic leadership—leadership that spends billions on weapon research and production, which results in war and other forms of political violence or threats of violence. In situations of intense, affective identifications with one's nation, global cooperation toward climate action can be diminished or non-existent. Thus, we, as residents of market nations, become part of the obstacles of capitalism, nationalism, and imperialism. Put another way, the above discussion helps explain why so many of us are asleep at the wheel or, if not asleep, indifferent to the dangers of our trajectory, because we have adopted the habitus and its privileges of capitalism, nationalism, and imperialism.

Being asleep at the wheel also pertains to more-than-human species and their suffering. The trinity of obstacles above is social imaginaries that unconsciously reproduce the anthropocentrism of the ontological rift between human animals and other animals. From the angle of weak dissociation and identification, we (I am thinking mainly Western Europeans) preserve our privileged place vis-à-vis other species, believing we are superior and can legitimately exploit other species. I suggest that, from this perspective, weak dissociation and identification accompany projection onto other species of human beings' anxieties associated with existential impermanence and insignificance, as well as existential vulnerability and dependence on nature. In other words, weak dissociation, identification (and disidentification), and projection shield human beings' existential vulnerability and dependency by locating vulnerability, dependency, impermanence, and insignificance in other-than-human species. This accompanies a disavowal of not only the singularities of other species, but also their needs for survival and flourishing. This disavowal can be understood diachronically and synchronically as the construction of historical and normative unconscious. The trinity of obstacles we internalize, in other words, is obstacles to recognizing our own cosmic impermanence, insignificance, vulnerability, and dependency. Also, as subjects of this trinity, we fail to recognize the existential necessity of attending to the needs and sufferings of other species, since the viability of any polis depends on a biodiverse earth.

Before shifting to the next section, I want to briefly mention another psychological feature that does not fall under the categories of internalization, weak dissociation, and identification, but that is a function of this trinity of obstacles. Many people realize that we face significant challenges to climate action, precisely because of systemic systems and their apparatuses discussed above. I have heard (and have felt myself) people say, with some resignation tinged with despair, that there is nothing that can change the trajectory we are on because of these hegemonic systems. There is a felt sense of helplessness and powerlessness when facing these systems that organize societies and international relations. This is completely understandable, but when we succumb to these thoughts and feelings, we become obstacles to climate action. We may be awake at the wheel, but we are not trying to steer.

## A Psychoanalytic Political Philosophy and Climate Obstacles

The typical stance of psychoanalysts (and other critics) critically engaging cultural, political, and economic realities is to use psychoanalytic concepts to depict psychosocial dynamics and unconscious features. This method has borne a great deal of fruit over the last century. Yet, I suggest a psychoanalytically informed political philosophy can provide a hermeneutical lens for highlighting, in this case, other features associated with capitalism, nationalism, and imperialism as sources of climate change and obstacles to climate action. Stated differently, a psychoanalytic political philosophy focuses on the caring relations necessary for the psychosocial and material survival and flourishing of the residents (including other species) of the polis. Social imaginaries or apparatuses of the polis are critically assessed in terms of the degree they interfere with these aims. As discussed in previous chapters, we cannot therefore have a deeper and more complex understanding of the polis and its aims without recognizing its dependence on a biodiverse earth and its interconnection with all other poleis. To establish, briefly, a hermeneutical lens, I identify other foundational premises of a psychoanalytic political philosophy. From there, I will proceed to examining the obstacles identified above.

Foundational Premises of a Psychoanalytic Political Philosophy:

1  Human beings are vulnerable and dependent vis-à-vis a biodiverse earth.
2  Human survival, flourishing, and belonging/dwelling (polis and its spaces of speaking and acting together) depend on caring relations, which depend on interpersonal recognition. Caring interhuman relations make possible the actualization of individuals' potentialities, as well as the exercise of the capacity for impotentiality—political agency and freedom. In terms of other species, care entails respect for their singularities and potentialities, since the polis or human dwelling rests on a biodiverse earth. Caring relations, whether interhuman or directed toward other species, depend on the construction of social imaginaries/apparatuses that promote and maintain care.
3  Caring relations foster civic trust and both found spaces of speaking and acting together—space existentially dependent on a biodiverse earth. Communicative

spaces of speaking and acting together include relational repairs, which restore civic trust.

4  Caring relations include respect and care for the land/earth. "When see the land as community to which we belong," Aldo Leopold writes, "we may begin to use it with love and respect" (in Harvey, 2016, p.161).

5  Negatively stated, human belonging/dwelling is not contingent on the belief in and apparatuses of sovereignty—apparatuses that generate hierarchical relations and illusions of superiority and inferiority.

6  There is, in reality, no ontological rift between human beings and other species (or the earth), except when created by human artifices. This means that a psychoanalytic political philosophy affirms the necessary interconnection and interdependence of all species vis-à-vis dwelling, as well as our existential insignificance and impermanence.

Given these premises, let me turn to considering the obstacles above. In examining the effects of global capitalism in the 21st century, Saskia Sassen (2014) remarks that "we face shrinking economies in much of the world, escalating destructions of the biosphere all over the globe, and the reemergence of extreme forms of poverty and brutalization" (p.12). She argues that "predatory 'formations,' a mix of elites and systemic capacities with finance as a key enabler" are increasingly involved in brutal expulsions from what she calls life spaces, which can be homes, habitable areas of cities, etc. (p.13). Christian Parenti (2011) likewise argues that there is a "collision of political, economic, and environmental disasters," which he calls the catastrophic convergence (p.7). Parenti writes:

> Between the Tropic of Capricorn and the Tropic of Cancer lies what I call the *Tropic of Chaos*, a belt of economically and politically battered postcolonial states girding the planet's mid-latitudes. In this band, around the tropics, climate change is beginning to hit hard. The societies in this belt are also heavily dependent on agriculture and fishing, thus very vulnerable to shifts in weather patterns. This region was also on the front lines of the Cold War and of neoliberal economic restructuring. As a result, in this belt we find clustered most of the failed or semi-failed states of the developing world.
>
> (p.9)

Parenti and Sassen are highlighting the reality that catastrophes of global warming are exacerbated by political-economic systems (e.g., neoliberal capitalism) that rely on violence, oppression, and marginalization to secure privileges for the few. Put another way, as nation-states compete for dwindling resources and as imperial nations pursue extending their political and economic influence, we will, as a Pentagon Report predicts (Davenport, 2014), greater political violence within and between nations, likely leaving imperial nations better situated to secure dwelling for most of their people (though not necessarily for marginalized residents as a result of classism and other forms of oppression).

But we do not necessarily need to point out capitalism's predatory role in relation to climate change. Capitalism, in whatever form, is inimical to political belonging/dwelling because it is founded on exploitative relations that secure wealth for the few, while overlooking or denying the existential and political needs of lower classes. In terms of the political premises above, care is not constitutive of capitalism. And when care, whether regarding human beings or other species, is present, it is instrumental with regard to the objects of capital. For instance, some business owners care for their workers (human and other-than-human) only to the extent that workers' performances reach the business' aims of profit and market expansion. Workers are not cared for in and of themselves. Workers may be trained to "care" for the consumers/clients, but again this is not care for the flourishing of their clients (see Hochschild, 2012a; Illouz, 2007, 2008), unless it is tied to marketing a product.

Someone may counter, saying that capitalism organizes many societies around the world, so it certainly does appear to be effective with regard to belonging. In one sense this is true, but organizing political societies on the basis of capitalistic rubrics leads to reduction of the space of appearances, as well as undermines non-instrumental caring relations in society. Aristotle, for instance, recognized the central problem of economic exchange millennia ago. He argued "that any polis which is truly so-called…must devote itself to the end of encouraging goodness… such as will make the members of a polis good and just" (Barker, 1971, p.119). Encouraging goodness, in my view, requires caring relations. When citizens become focused on "nothing further than matters of exchange and alliance, they would have failed to reach the stage of a polis" (p.119). Aristotle recognized that privileging economic exchanges as a way of organizing social relations in the polis undermines human beings as political animals. Indeed, the very notion of *homo oeconomicus* was inimical to Aristotle's view of the polis, considering such a creature as unnatural (Brown, 2015, p.91). The underlying problem, he noted, was that "involvement with the exchange for profit can easily incite the desire for wealth for its own sake" (p.90), which would conflict with and likely undermine notions of the common good, the good life or weal (well-being) for all the polis' residents, civic trust, and justice. Aristotle's (and Plato's) concerns about economic exchanges vis-à-vis organizing the polis are also echoed, in different ways, in Judeo-Christian scriptures. Scholar Richard Horsley (2009) notes the consistent condemnation in scripture of centralized economic power, because it undermines the "covenantal communitarian protection of people's rights to an adequate livelihood" (p.67). In a similar vein, Martin Hengel argues that "Jesus attacks mammon with utmost severity where it has captured men's hearts, because this gives it demonic character by which it blinds men's eyes to God's will—in concrete terms, to their neighbor's needs" (in Capper, 2009, p.71). Bruce Longenecker and Kelly Liebengood (2009) likewise contend that a key theme in Christian scriptures is the warning that economic exchanges may end up promoting greed and neglecting the needs of the poor. Yes, a polis can be organized primarily through economic relations, but this will be a diminished polis wherein caring relations are instrumentalized and spaces of appearances and civic trust are attenuated, leaving large swaths of the population struggling to survive.

Of course, this is only referencing human beings in the polis. The realities of climate change reveal how the ontological rift harms other species and the earth. Capitalism is founded on this ontological rift, splitting off other species from human political belonging. Greed and neglecting the poor are also connected to how the singularities and needs of other species are disavowed. It is not simply, then, that economic relations diminish the polis' space of appearances and non-instrumental care; they undermine, as Nancy Fraser (2022) notes, the very foundation of the polis, which is a biodiverse earth. David Harvey (2016) adds to this, commenting that "money valuations" are "inherently anti-ecological, confining the field of thinking and of action to instrumental environmental management" (p.167). Harvey also mentions Freud and Ferenczi in recognizing

that there is something morally or ethically questionable or downright objectionable to valuing human life in terms of discounted lifetime earnings and 'nature' (for example, the fate of grizzly bears and spotted owls as allowed to continue to dwell on this earth) in monetary terms.

(p.167)[18]

By contrast, a psychoanalytic political philosophy, in critiquing market societies, confirms that non-instrumental care is essential to caring for the habitat and other species. To return to Aldo Leopold's comment, when we see land as a foundational to community and material well-being, we, in my view, experience an ethical demand to respect and care for the land and its inhabitants—something that capitalism undermines and ignores. Leopold writes that

It is inconceivable to me that an ethical relation to land can exist without love, respect and admiration for the land, and a high regard for its value. By value, I of course mean something different than mere economic value. I mean value in the philosophical sense, so that a ting is right when it tends to preserve the integrity, stability, and beauty of the biotic community. It is wrong when it tends otherwise.

(in Harvey, 2016, p.170)

In short, to respect and care for nature is to acknowledge that we are part of and dependent on nature.[19]

Implicit in this discussion of capitalism is the reality of nation-states. A nation-state organizes political belonging in terms of sovereignty, circumscribed identity, and geography. While nation-states are relatively new phenomena, Plato's and Aristotle's politics, while not rooted in the idea of a nation-state, did have elements of these features of political belonging. A barbarian might have resided in the polis, but he did not possess an identity of that polis because he came from beyond the boundaries of the polis. Nevertheless, he was under the rule of the polis governing authority and had few rights. So, clearly, political belonging has long depended on sovereignty, identity, and geography. We can also suggest that within the nation-state, the premises above can be said, ideally, to operate. Mutual personal recognition, civic trust and care, and vibrant spaces of appearances can exist within a nation-state. This said, the nation-state is, in its essence, politically exclusive and exclusionary. Agamben (2013) points out that

> what the State cannot tolerate in any way…is that the singularities form a community without affirming an identity, that human beings co-belong (co-dwell) without any representable condition of belonging…. For the State, therefore, what is important is never singularity as such, but only its inclusion in some identity.
>
> (p.85)

While this may not be a problem for political philosophers who point out that democratic nation-states organize political life effectively, it is a problem in terms of a psychoanalytic political philosophy that addresses the realities of the Anthropocene Age.

Preoccupation with geography and identity with regard to political belonging will only continue to exacerbate international tensions and conflicts, while undermining global cooperation. In my view, a psychoanalytic political philosophy, while not eschewing the importance of identity, promotes the capacity for recognizing likeness in difference and difference in likeness (Benjamin, 1995). This means that political belonging can include all human beings (and other species), since we are all residents of this one earth, which nation-state thinking cannot get its head around. I am not suggesting that a psychoanalytic political philosophy promotes a world government, but instead promotes the idea of human belonging or dwelling that is not contingent on a particular identity and geography. This political view is seen in Agamben's (2013) coming community wherein members "co-belong without any representable condition of belonging," that is, "without affirming identity" (p.5). I hasten to add here, given the discussion regarding psychosocial development and its relation to other species in the previous chapters, the coming community should extend to other species. A psychoanalytic political philosophy eschews the ontological gap and contends that there is likeness and difference and difference in likeness with regard to other living beings, since we all come from and depend on the earth. In terms of the polis' space of appearances, human beings who lack political agency and speech (infants, infirm, etc.) are represented, as are other species that lack political agency and speech. The survival and flourishing of human beings who belong in a polis depend on the recognition of the necessity for the inclusion of other species—near and far.

Imperialism is nationalism on steroids and is anti-political in relation to those who are not citizens of the metropole. It is not simply that the colonized are exploited and exist on the margins of the imperial polis' spaces of appearances, the land and other species are instrumentally exploited. A psychoanalytic political philosophy would reject an iteration of imperial states precisely because the existence and well-being of the imperium's citizens depend on the exclusion and exploitation of colonized others (including other species). If care is directed toward the colonized, it is, like capitalism, instrumental, and paternalistic—a diminished, impoverished type of care. At its core, a psychoanalytic political philosophy cannot support a polis that depends on relations of exploitation and the exclusion of other poleis for its survival. More positively, a psychoanalytic political philosophy highlights political caring that maintains the dialectical tension between likeness in difference and difference in likeness, which fosters spaces of speaking and acting together that are inclusive even in the midst of contestation.

The apparatuses that produce and maintain capitalism, nationalism, and imperialism intersect and are, in various ways, sources of climate change and obstacles to climate action. In this section, I also argue, albeit briefly, that this trinity may organize a society, but, from the premises of a psychoanalytic political philosophy, this political organization is deeply flawed in terms of mutual personal recognition, civic care and trust, political agency, and spaces of appearances, and respect for the earth and other species. This is true when considering relations within the polis, but also relations among those who are not citizens of the polis, whether that refers to those who reside in the polis or those external to it. I also want to point out that this trinity depends on the ontological rift, which a psychoanalytic political philosophy rejects as illusory, recognizing that, in the long term, this ontological rift threatens the very existence of the polis vis-à-vis a depleted earth that is unable to support human life and the lives of millions of other species. More positively, rejecting the illusion of an ontological rift affirms the categorical, ethical demand to care and the concomitant caring inclusion of other species and the earth in political thinking and practice.

## Conclusion

"Human beings," John Gray (2013) writes,

> are animals that have equipped themselves with symbols. Helping deal with a world they do not understand, symbols are useful tools; but human beings have the inveterate tendency to think and act as if the world they have made from these symbols actually exists.
>
> (p.132)

Gray is not suggesting that the symbolic artifices we construct do not exist, but that we believe or act as if they exist independently of human beings. Capitalism, nationalism, and imperialism comprise complex symbol systems that some human beings have created and believe to be essential for organizing the polis and for human survival and flourishing. Most of us overlook or deny that these particular artifices are sources of climate change and obstacles to climate change. Psychoanalytic concepts can provide the interpretive framework for understanding the psychology of resistance to recognizing how this trinity is undermining life, whether in reference to human beings or millions of other species. In addition, a psychoanalytic political philosophy provides an artifice that critiques and counters this trinity by showing how the apparatuses of capitalism, nationalism, and imperialism diminish the polis and, in the long term, threaten the very existence of political belonging. More positively, a psychoanalytic political philosophy accepts those political artifices that bridge the ontological gap by first acknowledging it as a destructive illusion and reality and, second, by offering the possibility that political care includes human beings, other species, and the earth.

## Notes

1  Woods (2017) addresses and critiques various theories regarding the origins of capitalism. Apologists for capitalism tend to think that every kind of exchange of goods represents the seeds of capitalism, which Woods undermines by demonstrating the differences between markets and why some pre-capitalist cities did not develop into capitalist economies, while other cities in Europe did. One of the values of her cogent work is recognizing that there are alternatives to capitalism.

2  Two points are worth mentioning here. First, some philosophers were critical of capitalism. Rousseau, as noted at the start of the chapter, noticed how destructive capitalism and fetishizing property were. Karl Marx was famously critical (Eagleton, 2011). Marx (1964), who was influenced by Hegel's critique, wrote, "[T]he lords of land and the lords of capital will always use their political privileges for the defense and perpetration of their economic monopolies." Second, even philosophers like Adam Smith (2003), the patron saint of capitalism, were concerned about its excesses.

3  I have placed the term "rational" in quotes to suggest the underlying illusion that the so-called market or those involved in the market make rational, objective decisions. Any casual observer of the rises and falls of the stock market notes the presence of greed, fear, hubris, anxiety, and anger, which all play a large role in making "rational" decisions. I add here that the notion of "rational" vis-à-vis capitalism is a kind of rationalism that is associated with the advancement of each individual's self-interest. It is instrumental and individualistic. This is decidedly different from a rationalism associated with making decisions with regard to the interests and needs of others vis-à-vis the common good.

4  Karl Popper (2002), in critically examining Hegel's philosophy, argued that nationalism intersects with historicism and has a tendency toward totalitarianism (pp.274–275). While the latter is debatable, there is a clear tendency for nationalism to be exclusionary, denying rights and justice for those outside its borders and sometime within its borders, as in the case of the U.S. and its treatment of African Americans.

5  Socialism is Un-American|Congressman Tom Cole (house.gov), https://cole.house.gov/media-center/weekly-columns/socialism-un-american, accessed 8 June 2022.

6  See also Walter Mignolo (2011) for a discussion of the relation between Western capitalism and imperialism.

7  In the 21st century, Russia's taking over Crimea and invasion of Ukraine and Russia's client state Belarus reveals a mix of the old and new imperialism. The response of NATO nations has been to punish Russia economically, indicating that Russia's main goal was not the pursuit of markets in attacking Ukraine, but rather to make Ukraine into a client state like Belarus.

8  Go (2012) argued that "Empires are involved in *imperialism*, which is the process by which they are established, extended, and maintained. They often have *imperial policies*,

which are official and stated plans and practices by which power is exercised" (p.7). From Go's perspective, the United States is an informal empire that is imperialistic, devising strategies and deploying tactics to maintain and extend economic and political influence over client states. Evidence of this is the approximately 725 known American military bases in over 38 foreign countries and over 254,000 military personnel in 153 countries (Johnson, 2004, p.154; 2010). While the United States is not an occupying force in these countries, save one, the presence of these military bases and the use of regional "proconsuls" (Bacevich, 2002, 2005; Chomsky, 2003, 2005; Johnson, 1999, 2004, 2006, 2010) and economic power (see Young, 2005, p.40) to alter the policies and actions of foreign countries are all signifiers of the presence of an American Empire. A recent example of attempts to maintain U.S. hegemony is President Barack Obama's policies (e.g., Pivot to East Asia) that involve building up military strength in the Pacific region, as well as maintaining and extending political and economic influence in this area of the world (Drysdale, 2012).

9  Global carbon dioxide growth in 2018 reached 4th highest on record | National Oceanic and Atmospheric Administration (noaa.gov), https://www.noaa.gov/news/global-carbon-dioxide-growth-in-2018-reached-4th-highest-on-record, accessed 20 May 2022.

10  As of May 2022, it is 420 ppm. Global Monitoring Laboratory - Carbon Cycle Greenhouse Gases (noaa.gov), https://www.esrl.noaa.gov/gmd/ccgg/trends/monthly.html, accessed 18 January 2022.

11  Two interesting facts that Wagner and Weitzman (2015) highlight is that the effects of greenhouse gases were originally discovered in the 19th century (p.35). The second interesting fact is that King Edward I "established the first air pollution commission in 1285. In 1306, he made it illegal to burn coal," though the law was soon vacated (p. 21).

12  The concluding part of this quote is instructive: "When we see land as a community to which we belong, we may begin to use it with love and respect" (p.161). Later he writes, "It is inconceivable to me that an ethical relation to land can exist without love, respect and admiration for the land, and a high regard for its value. By value, I of course mean something far broader than mere economic value; I mean value in the philosophical sense…a thing is right when it tends to preserve the integrity, stability, and beauty of the biotic community" (p.170).

13  Global arms trade: USA increases dominance; arms flows to the Middle East surge, says SIPRI|SIPRI, https://www.sipri.org/media/press-release/2019/global-arms-trade-usa-increases-dominance-arms-flows-middle-east-surge-says-sipri, accessed 8 June 2022.

14  There is, for Fromm, a kind of feedback loop. A person's sense of self is formed in relation to social structures, which means the person adapts to and supports these social structures.

15  Joel Kovel (1988) held a similar view when he addresses neuroses that emerge from living in a market society. "The neurotic individual," he writes, "fits the bill exactly by virtue of the split between deeper layers of his subjectivity and his internalization of the rationalized reality principle of abstract commodity logic" (p.124).

16  I recognize that many of us participate in market societies and are citizens of imperialistic nations. It is very difficult to avoid these three obstacles, unless we live completely off the grid. So, it would be better to say that there are degrees of participation and accountability with regard to being sources of climate change and obstacles to climate action.

17  Even economists like Stiglitz (2012, 2015) and Reich (2007, 2015), who wish to save capitalism, note the excesses and psychosocial sufferings associated with what some call neoliberal capitalism or late capitalism.

18  Harvey (2016) uses the term "biopiracy" to refer to capitalism's pillaging of the earth's resources, leading to habitat degradation (p.260). It is an apt term, in that capitalism, while within and dependent on the "law," is, in one sense, outside the law of nature.

19 Harvey (2016), in discussing Marx, points out that "estrangement from immediate sensuous engagement with nature is an essential moment in consciousness formation. It therefore is a step on a path of towards emancipation and self-realization. But herein lies a paradox. The never-ending estrangement of consciousness permits reflexivity and the construction of emancipatory forms of knowledge; but it also poses the problem of how to return to that which consciousness alienates us from" (p.205). He is addressing this in relation to capitalism, but we could easily apply this to Western political philosophies that produce and maintain the ontological rift. What Harvey and others seem to ignore is that self-reflexivity is not necessarily contingent on estrangement. The capacity for self-reflexivity, from a psychoanalytic perspective, is dependent on the capacity for differentiation. If we consider the narratives of native peoples, like Plenty Coups (Lear, 2006), Chief Seattle, or Black Elk (Neihardt, 2014) we would see that the ontological rift and estrangement from nature are not evident. It would be demeaning and incorrect to suggest that their capacities for freedom and reflexivity are somehow less than Westerners.

# Chapter 5

# Psychoanalysis, Political Change, and the Issue of Hope

Professor James Jackson Putnam met Freud while he was lecturing in the United States and they began a friendly correspondence for several years. In one missive, Putnam observed that he knew individuals who had been analyzed but were seemingly no better as human beings (Hale, 1971, p.186). Putnam believed that psychoanalysis should have, for some patients, an ethical consideration that entails acknowledging "the calls of 'loyalty'" (p.168). Freud responded,

> I quite agree with you that psychoanalytic treatment should find a place among the methods whose aim is to bring about the highest ethical and intellectual development of the individual. Our difference is of a purely practical nature...I do not wish to entrust this development to the psychoanalyst.
>
> (p.171)

Freud, later in the letter, regards the great ethical element in psychoanalysis is truth (p.171), which I understand to mean raising what is unconscious to consciousness, as well as ridding oneself of illusions. In a subsequent correspondence, Freud writes, "The unworthiness of human beings, including analysts, always has impressed me deeply, but why should analyzed men and women in fact be better. Analysis makes for integration but does not of itself make for goodness" (p.188). This exchange represents an agreement that psychoanalysis, as a talking cure, is a hermeneutical exploratory method that raises unconscious material to consciousness. The differences between Freud and Putnam centered principally around the ends or aims of this method. For Putnam, analysis should lead to more ethical persons who understand their commitments, while Freud focused on psychic integration and truth—facing and discarding one's infantile illusions. Another difference between these men was that Putnam located psychoanalysis within the context of community and society. That is, Putnam, in my interpretation, viewed psychoanalysis, at least one feature of it, as contributing to the well-being of the community and society. Freud, as a medical doctor, shied away from this, focusing instead on psychoanalysis as facilitating psychological changes for individual patients, eschewing any role of the analyst as teacher of virtues (p.171).[1]

DOI: 10.4324/9781003258827-7

While discussions about change, method, and ends vis-à-vis psychoanalysis continued long after Freud and Putnam corresponded, a key shift quietly took place after WWII in the United States and Algeria. Nigel Gibson and Roberto Beneduce (2017) write, "In 1946…a group of black psychologists and psychiatrists decided to offer clinical assistance to the poor and marginalized people in Harlem, who, because of racist attitudes of health professionals had no easy access to health facilities" (p.32). This group recognized that apparatuses of racism were having (and have) deleterious effects on the psyches of African Americans. This interracial group decided to name the clinic after Paul Lafargue, "an Afro-Cuban French physician and Karl Marx's son-in-law" (p.32). Richard Wright, who was tangentially involved in the clinic's development, wrote that the clinic "violate[s]… the contemporary metaphysical canons of organized medicine in America" (p.33). Another famous writer, Ralph Ellison (1995/1953), wrote,

> As such, and in spite of the very fine work it is doing, a thousand Lafargue (psychiatric) clinics could not dispel the sense of unreality that haunts Harlem. Knowing this, Dr. Wertham and his interracial staff seek a modest achievement: to give each bewildered patient an insight into the relation between his problems and his environment, and out of this understanding to reforge the will.
>
> (p.302)

Having read Richard Wright's article, psychiatrist Frantz Fanon (2008/1952), practicing in the context of the brutal French colonization of Algeria, came to a similar, though psychoanalytically inflected, view of therapeutic change and ends. Fanon argued that therapy aims (a) "to *'consciousnessize'* [the patient's] unconscious, to no longer be tempted by a hallucinatory lactification," and (b) "to enable [the patient] to choose an action with respect to the *real source of the conflict*, i.e., the social structure" (p.80; emphasis mine).

Putnam may have been concerned with some patients' obligations or loyalty to community and society, but the interracial staff at the Lafargue clinic in New York and Fanon[2] in Algeria were concerned with the political and social betrayals and lack of social obligation in racist societies, and their psychological effects on marginalized and oppressed persons. Neither the Lafargue clinic nor Fanon viewed the aim of therapy as adaptation or adjustment or mere integration, but rather as (1) assisting patients to become aware of the social, political, and economic sources of their suffering (Turner & Neville, 2020) and (2) to choose an action in relation to those sources. Put another way, in a racist society traditional therapy that focuses simply on the individual's unconscious and family of origin mystifies the sources of patients' sufferings and, therefore, colludes with oppressive political apparatuses (LaMothe, 2018).

Implicit in liberative therapies, such as these, is the issue of the relation between change vis-à-vis the consulting room or clinic and political change and its methods. Fanon accepted that change in Algeria required political revolution, which included political violence, though "he acknowledged that armed struggle can also lead to brutality that is psychologically costly even if it is politically organized and justified" (Gibson & Beneduce, 2017, p.6). As a psychiatrist, he was not suggesting that political violence is *the* choice for patients who suffered from colonial oppression, but as a public-political figure, Fanon accepted that liberation from France required political violence. This said, he was ambivalent about political violence, because he saw its impact on the psyches of victims, as well as those who used violence, whether they were colonizers or rebels. Moreover, Fanon's view of change with regard to working with patients depended on empathy and unconditional understanding, which he, in part, gleaned from the works of Sandor Ferenczi (Gibson & Beneduce, 2017, pp.210–215). However, empathy and understanding are not the means of political revolutions, which depend on methods of violence and the threat of violence. This points to a conflict between psychoanalytically informed methods of change and traditional methods of political change. There is, in other words, an apparent divide. The very process of psychoanalysis is inimical to violence as a method of change, yet when we move to the political arena, violence, historically and philosophically, has been justified and promoted, whether we are referring to the issue of sovereignty, just war theory, or revolution. The methods of change in the consulting room and those of the polis appear to be irreconcilable, which may be a reason for compartmentalization by politically engaged therapists when it comes to parsing out the relation between psychoanalytic processes and those of political change.

In this chapter, I address the issue of political violence as a method of change from a psychoanalytic-phenomenological perspective. I argue that political violence, while understandable in some situations, is not justified, whether we are simply addressing interhuman political violence or the political violence toward more-than-human species. If political violence is not justifiable as a method for political change, then what methods are available? Here I turn to features of the psychoanalytic political philosophy developed in the previous chapters to argue that care, as a political concept, is a justifiable method of political change because it respects the singularities of all human beings, other species, and the earth. Political forms of care include aggression (e.g., civic transgressions, civil disobedience, and nonviolent protests), but not aggression associated with political violence. Since the issue of political change raises questions of hope vis-à-vis the systemic obstacles to climate action and mass extinctions discussed in the previous chapter, the last section discusses the relation between caring political methods and hope. I claim that, given the psychological complexity of human beings, caring actions are not contingent on hope and, therefore, not necessarily obstructed by eco-despair. Stated differently, I consider climate hope to be a problem, which is resolved by focusing in the present on political care—care for Othered human beings, other species, and the earth.

A few caveats and clarifications are necessary before beginning. First, some political philosophers believe that human beings are naturally violent and, therefore, we must find ways to limit political violence. For instance, in the West, there is a great deal of literature on political violence, and much of the discourse centers on the moral rationalization for nations going to war (*jus ad bellum*), rules governing the conduct of war (*jus in bello*), and expectations regarding actions toward the defeated (*jus post bellum*). Much ink has also been spilled on questions of using political violence to overthrow a government and, as noted in Chapter 3, the legitimate use of violence vis-à-vis sovereignty. These discourses, in my view, essentialize political violence and collapse the categories of aggression and violence. I think it is safe to say that human beings have the capacity for aggression, but not all human beings and communities are inherently violent or necessarily depend on political violence to maintain social order. Yes, there is a great deal of political violence, but I would suggest that many societies and communities display innumerably more acts of care than acts of violence. Indeed, only failed and failing states exhibit the imbalance between care and violence. A second related comment is that while I will argue that political violence as a means of change is not ethically justifiable, this does not mean I am proposing a kind of strict pacifism. I do believe there are times when political violence is completely understandable, especially when considering populations that are horribly oppressed and exploited. In Fanon's Algeria, given the brutal colonization of the French, a turn to political violence in hopes of becoming an independent nation was understandable. However, as I intend to make clear, political violence is neither morally nor politically justifiable. I am trying to remove any justification and, in so doing, invite remorse, even when the political aims are good, but the means are not. I also want to raise awareness that historically political violence has included the exploitation, sufferings, and deaths of more-than-human species—species largely exempted from political discourses regarding the ethics of political violence. So, one feature of this argument is that any discussion of the ethics of political violence needs to include the harms done to other-than-human species and the earth. Third, I need to make clear that I am not addressing all forms of violence, such as the violence an individual uses to protect themselves. The focus is on political violence used as a means of attaining political ends. Fourth, the aim of this chapter is to argue that if we consider the consulting room or clinic to be inextricably yoked to social, political, and economic apparatuses, then there should be a correlation between the ethical methods used in the clinic and those of the political realm. Yes, they are distinct, but not radically so. If we advocate or accept political violence as a means toward political change, while eschewing any type of violence vis-à-vis psychoanalytic change, then we will rely on the defenses of compartmentalization, denial, and rationalization. Instead, a psychoanalytic political philosophy for the Anthropocene Age avoids compartmentalization and argues against irreconcilable differences in methods between the political arena and the consulting room. Finally, the Anthropocene Age reveals just how much violence human beings have done and are doing to each other, other species, and the earth. The fierce urgency of now calls us to remove justifications for political violence not simply as a matter of our survival, but because it is the morally correct approach if we are to respect all human beings, other species, and the earth that supports all life.

## What Is Political Violence?

Elizabeth Frazer and Kimberly Hutchings (2020) note that "The concept of violence and the concept of politics are vague and contested" (p.2). This section, then, offers a general definition of political violence and focuses on the types of political violence.[3] This will enable more clarity about political violence, before arguing that it is not justifiable.

Broadly speaking, political violence involves the threat or use of force[4] by individuals and groups to secure or safeguard political, economic, social, and/or cultural goods (e.g., identity, resources, and privileges) within a polis (or between states), while depriving Othered human beings and other species of resources needed to survive and thrive. All perpetrators and supporters of political violence, whether they are in the dominant group or the oppressed group, justify their use of force by way of narratives, philosophies, theologies, etc. Those in the dominant group also legitimize force through laws, policies, etc. (e.g., Jim Crow), while oppressed and marginalized groups justify political violence by way of grievance narratives and philosophies of revolution/liberation. Those who advocate for political violence rarely consider, because of the ontological rift, the impacts of political violence on other species. Indeed, other species are often used in the exercise of political violence within and between states. We need only to watch the films or look at the pictures of police using dogs to intimidate and harm peaceful protestors in Selma or the use of horses to disrupt protests or remove native peoples. There is also a long history of using animals in the prosecution of wars.

Political violence can be direct or indirect. Direct political violence involves what one would typically expect to observe in a society. Examples include use of police (and parapolice) or military (and paramilitary) forces to quell protests or insurrections. Direct political violence can also include non-governmental terroristic practices such as lynching, public beatings, executions, bombings, and torture. From another direction, political violence is also evident in situations where citizens riot or rebel, using force to effect political and economic changes. Indirect forms of political violence are more difficult to detect and are not usually acknowledged as violence. Environmental racism and classism are examples of systemic indirect political violence that leads to illnesses and shortened lifespans of marginalized citizens (e.g., Blackburn & Epel, 2017). Decades of Jim Crow laws and new Jim and Jane Crow laws and policies also represent indirect (and direct) political violence that suppresses African American voting, restricts and undermines education, denies access to resources (medical, food deserts, etc.), and impedes gaining financial wealth (Alexander, 2010). Judith Butler's (2020) discussion of political violence furthers this view. She writes that political "violence operates as an intensification of social inequality" (p.142), which is evident in the intersecting apparatuses of racism, sexism, and classism. There is, for instance, the indirect political violence of neoliberal capitalism, with its extractive and exploitive tendencies and maldistribution of resources such that the rich garner vast amounts of wealth at the expense of the so-called lower classes, undermining their well-being (e.g., Desmond, 2016; Klein, 2007; Piketty, 2014, 2020; Valencia,

2018),[5] not to mention the wake of environmental destruction resulting from the political violence of capitalism. Worse, Johanna Oksala (2012) notes that political violence "is inherent to the rationality of neoliberal governing" and "it effectively depoliticizes violence by turning it into an essentially economic rather than a political or moral issue" (p.136). In other words, indirect political violence is often mystified by state and non-state political-economic elites, which means it is excluded from philosophical-ethical discourses regarding political violence.

Indirect political violence also attends ostensible nationalistic and patriotic reasons for defense of the nation. For instance, during the Cold War (and today), the United States and U.S.S.R. spent hundreds of billions of dollars on nuclear arsenals and military equipment and training. The rationale was the doctrine of Mutually Assured Destruction (MAD) as a way to deter outright war—but not proxy wars. Indirect political violence was (and is) evident in the vast amounts of money and resources that were rendered unavailable to address the needs of poor persons (or the environment), whether within the United States, the Soviet Union (Russia), or so-called third world countries—countries that were often used for proxy wars between the United States and the Soviet Union. The conscious or public intent of political leaders was to avoid nuclear war[6] and maintain imperial hegemony, but their construction of foreign and national policies and laws resulted in deprivation vis-à-vis poorer citizens (and other marginalized persons), not to mention environmental damages. Some readers may wonder whether this is political violence, but when a state, like the United States, spends trillions of dollars on "defense," it is also denying people resources needed to flourish. Deprivation occurs not only as a result of force and exclusion from political spaces of influence and power. To recall Martin Luther King Jr.'s assertion: "War is the enemy of the poor." I add to this, contending that the preparation for war also reveals indirect types of political violence that deprive disenfranchised members of society from resources necessary for survival and flourishing.

Another insidious form of indirect political violence involves the deliberate exclusion of marginalized persons from representation in the history of the nation or, if represented, marginalized persons are represented in humiliating ways (Saïd, 1979, 1994). All of this cannot be accomplished without the aid of political, economic, and cultural apparatuses. As Miguel De La Torre (2017) writes,

> To be written out of the story becomes a terrorist act, in which the memory of the marginalized is replaced by the fictitious story of their oppressors, robbing them of identity, of centeredness, of authentic being. Such a terrorist act is more insidious than physical harm, for it devastates the soul, the spirit, the mind, the very essence of a people.
>
> (p.32)

De La Torre describes a form of indirect violence that excludes people from the space of speaking and acting together and from the collective memories that support this space. These Others are not seen as having or meriting political agency, past or present, and as such they are deemed insignificant with regard to collective memory. Put differently, Othered individuals are denied civic trust and fidelity, which means that they are not recognized in terms of their singularities. Worse, othered groups, like enslaved people or indigenous people, are deprived of their culture (Lear, 2006), leaving them on the margins of the dominant society and deprived of resources. All of this is accomplished by political, economic, and social policies, programs, narratives, and practices that exclude or marginalize people from political-economic power. This indirect violence is often accompanied by direct forms of violence, especially whenever exploited people speak out and resist.

It is necessary to reiterate that both direct and indirect forms of political violence impact more-than-human species and the earth. Since other species are not considered to be integral to the polis' spaces of speaking and acting together, they are largely ignored in discussions regarding political violence and are written out of history. The exploitation or instrumental use of other species (e.g., factory farms, experimentation) is, from my perspective, political violence primarily because it is aimed at privileging human dwelling. The discussion of the three sources of climate change and obstacles to climate action in the previous chapter reveals an intersection of direct and indirect forms of violence toward other species. When E. O. Wilson (2005) predicts that half of the known species will be extinct by the end of this century, he is inadvertently pointing to the consequences of both direct and indirect forms of political-economic violence. Most of us may not be directly involved in the extinction of a species, but our collective actions are moving us quickly toward this event. Extinctions, in short, are necessarily the result of violence, and the Anthropocene Age is unique from other extinction events because it is, from my perspective, the result of direct and indirect political violence.

In this general overview of direct and indirect political violence, we can discern basic types of violence, as well as its aims. For instance, Johan Galtung (1975) identified and described structural violence in relation to the political. Structural or systemic violence is evident in the social, political, and economic institutions (apparatuses or disciplinary regimes) that, along with socially held narratives and policies, legitimate and justify the practices or threats of force toward particular groups (Ruggiero, 2020). For instance, the rise of the Black Lives Matter movement is a response to the structural violence directed toward African Americans by police (Goldberg, 2009; Soss, Fording, & Schram, 2011; Wacquant, 2009), which is supported by local, state, and national laws and policies that shield police officers from responsibility for the consequences of their violent actions, which includes acts of intimidation, which are forms of indirect violence. Add to this environmental racism, which depends on structural violence, forcing impoverished communities of color to live in conditions that violate their health. There is structural violence in neoliberal capitalism's classism, which is supported and promulgated by state and non-state apparatuses that legitimate theft of workers' pay and benefits, increasing their precarity. Structural violence is also evident in social and political institutions that deny or restrict people from participating in the polis' space of appearances (e.g., voter suppression laws).

Structural violence is attended and supported by symbolic or epistemic violence and De La Torre's point, previously noted about marginalized people (and other species) being excluded from history, is an example. Epistemic forms of political violence "damage people through a process of denigration and exclusion" (Frazer & Hutchings, 2020, p.3). According to Hannah Arendt (1970), epistemic violence entails the systemic misrecognition or nonrecognition of some residents such that they are marginalized from participating in the space of appearances—speaking and acting together. By excluding people from these spaces, by denying their singularities and potentialities, they are left out of or sidelined from historical memory—both normative and historical unconscious vis-à-vis the dominant groups are applicable here. This has long been true with regard to women in the West, whose equality has been denied, through coercion, threats of violence, and violence. Politically constructed as having less capability (e.g., potentiality in reason, deliberation) and, therefore, less trustworthy, women were (and in some places continue to be) restricted from access to and engagement in public, political, and economic spaces. This is political violence for two reasons. First, to subordinate or subjugate persons (e.g., women, people of color), while also denying them access to resources to actualize their potential, is accomplished only by epistemic and structural political violence and threat of violence. Second, a cursory glance at the 70-plus years of women agitating for the right to vote in the United States (1848–1920) reveals that political violence and the threat of violence were directed toward women activists. Epistemic and structural violence are also evident in the long sordid history of racism in the United States, wherein indigenous people, African Americans, and other people of color (Latinx, Chinese, Japanese, etc.) have been and are discriminated against, kept from exercising political agency, and denied access to resources to empower their flourishing. And to shift to more-than-human species, non-recognition of the singularities of other species is accomplished by epistemic and structural types of political violence. The constructed political insignificance of more-than-human species, in other words, is evident in their exclusion from Western historical narratives, which is a form of epistemic violence. Ironically and tragically, this omission will return to haunt us when our habitats are unlivable.

The aims of political violence are varied. States pursue political violence to maintain sovereignty, identity, and territory. Imperial states also engage in direct and indirect forms of political violence to expand their economic and political power, as well as their territory. Groups in positions of power within a state seek to maintain their power, wealth, status, and privileges through the use of direct and indirect structural and epistemic forms of political violence. Those who suffer under the heel of political oppression may use political violence to overturn the government via insurrections and revolutions (Arendt, 1970). Others may use political violence to change unjust institutions and practices. Persons on any point of the political spectrum may resort to political violence for fear of losing cherished moral, theological, or philosophical traditions. Instances of political violence also emerge out of despair or the refusal to mourn, with the aim of causing malignant destruction. The January 6 insurrection in the United States represented, in my view, a demonstration of white fear of losing their dominance in a society that is increasingly diverse. The insurrectionists' violence, in other words, signified a refusal to mourn and let go. Of course, many of these aims outlined here may overlap. To shift to the realities of climate change, we can safely predict that varied types of political violence will be used by those seeking change and those seeking to remain ensconced in the soporific embrace of neoliberal capitalism, nationalism, and imperialism.

## Dynamics of Political Violence and Why It Is Unjustifiable

Now I want to change direction and argue that political violence is not justifiable. Johanna Oksala (2012) comments that

> Thinkers from Plato to Hobbes, Machiavelli, Sorel, Clausewitz, and Schmitt have built their understanding of the political on the recognition of the irreducibility of violence in human affairs. More recently scholars such as Chantal Mouffe and Slavoj Žižek have emphasized the ineliminability of violence from the political domain.
>
> (p.3)

At best, in these views, we can only hope to limit violence or find constructive, justifiable ways to use it, because it is an inevitable part of human nature and political belonging. It may be that political violence is ineliminable, but it does not logically follow that we must find ways to justify it. The typical method of justification involves attending to the ends (e.g., justice) of the varied means of political violence. Yet, I am interested in *the moment and relation* of political violence from phenomenological and psychoanalytic perspectives, not to provide justification, but rather to indicate why political violence, in and of itself, is not justified, whether we are speaking of human beings or other species.

While political violence can appear to be efficient (Oksala, 2012, p.109), "the price," Hannah Arendt (1970) remarks, "is very high; for it is not only paid by the vanquished, it is also paid by the victor" (p.53). We have a fairly good idea about the ways the vanquished pay the price, but the ways the victors pay a price may be less obvious. It is clear that decades of political violence during the Jim Crow Era, directed toward terrorizing African Americans and restricting or denying their participation in the polis' space of appearances, had deleterious impacts on African American individuals and communities. Yet, Eduardo Porter (2020) provides evidence that the racist beliefs that undergirded political-economic policies aimed at harming African Americans also negatively impacted and impacts the education and health of poor white people.

The cost of political violence is also high because it begets more violence (Arendt, 1970, p.80), as well as social, political, and economic alienation. As Judith Butler (2020) notes, political violence "does not exhaust itself in the realization of a just end; rather, it renews itself in directions that exceed both deliberate intention and instrumental schemes" (p.20).

The mimetic nature of political violence is costly because victimizers must be continually vigilant and constantly maintain disciplinary regimes that produce mis-recognition or non-recognition, while also fueling and projecting a steady stream of fear and hatred toward the objects of political violence. The targets are con-structed as inferior and, therefore, are objectified or depersonalized, while the per-petrators of political violence depend on the illusion of their "superiority" for their senses of self-esteem, self-confidence, self-respect, and political agency. Civic care, trust, and fidelity, in other words, are associated with privileged political spaces of speaking and acting together, while marginalized and oppressed Oth-ers are misrecognized and distrusted, receiving fewer of the resources (civic care) that are needed to survive and flourish. Add to this, political violence entails the collapse or diminishment of the space of speaking and acting together toward Oth-ered "inferior" individuals and groups. These "inferior" Others are denied politi-cal agency, which means they are deprived of self-esteem, self-confidence, and self-respect as they appear in dominant political spaces. Othered individuals are not regarded as *belonging* in these spaces and, therefore, are not trusted to act in these spaces—creating an eclipse of political belonging and dwelling. This eclipse can be understood in terms of Orlando Patterson's notion of social death (political death), Agamben's (1998, p.83) depiction of bare life, and Fanon's (2008) "zone of nonbeing" (p.xii). Each of these terms comes from reflecting on the dynamics and results of political violence vis-à-vis marginalized groups.

A question may remain as to exactly why political violence and the threat of violence must be continually produced, especially when we consider terms like "zone of nonbeing" or "social death." Recall Agamben's claim that actual-izing one's potentiality, which depends on good-enough caring relations, does not exhaust potentiality. There is always an excess. Political violence can, of course, result in an absolute denial of persons' potentialities through murder, but as long as individuals are alive, there is excess, which means that oppressed indi-viduals possess ungovernable selves. The reality of ungovernable selves leads to the ongoing production of political violence and threat of violence. Put another way, to acknowledge that social-political apparatuses support forms of political violence, which function to deny political agency and force people to the fringes of society, is not to suggest that marginalized people are devoid of self-esteem, self-respect, and self-worth—political self/agency and suchness. As noted in many situations, families living under oppressive conditions work to provide children with a sense of self-worth and agency by way of their care, thus mak-ing inoperative the apparatuses of violence and misrecognition, which creates a space for practicing the ethical demand to care. Put differently, families and com-munities, through acts of inoperative care, create spaces of appearance wherein members experience singularity, actualizing but not exhausting their potential for political agency. Recall that activist Ruby Sales

> grew up believing that I was a first-class human being and a first-class person, and our parents were spiritual geniuses who were able to shape a counterculture of black folk religion that raised us from disposability to being essential players in society.[7]

Martin Luther King's (1998) sense of somebodiness parallels this statement. They each experienced sufficient interpersonal recognition, care, and trust in the spaces of speaking and acting together in their homes and churches such that they could experience singularity and exercise their agency to appear, which provided them with the political resilience to face direct and indirect forms of structural and epistemic violence. No matter how oppressed and marginalized people are, there are seeds of ungovernable selves ready to resist. This is why political violence must be continually produced and why it often leads to mimetic violence in the form of revolutions from "below."

There is another avenue to explore here that will help move us toward why political violence is not justified and why it is anti-political. The previous discussion already points to psychological aspects of political violence, such as constructing and perceiving the targets of violence as inferior. Inferiority is projected onto Others, which splits off or dissociates Others from being integrated into one's self-understanding. This accompanies a loss or diminishment of the capacity for mentalization or self-reflection, which is evident in a lack of empathy, compassion, and accountability for the harm done to others.[8] Indeed, before, during, and after an act of political violence, the devaluation of the Other results in the absence of accountability, which attends rationalization and moralization of the harm done. Justification of political violence, in my view, is, from a psychological perspective, a way to disavow guilt and remorse. Consider, for instance, Hobbes' leviathan. The leviathan (which actually comprises particular human beings and apparatuses) is permitted and justified in using political violence or the threat of violence to ensure civic order. In my view, this is simply a sophisticated philosophical argument that rationalizes and moralizes political violence so that those committing harm do not have to be accountable or feel remorse. Similarly, any cursory reading of the history of political violence toward enslaved persons reveals incredible feats of rationalization and moral justification for horrendous, despicable acts toward African Americans. Putting on my psychoanalytic hat, I would argue further that projection, splitting, moralization, and rationalization keep people from taking accountability for harm done, thus avoiding guilt/shame, as well as their own existential fragility, impermanence, and insignificance. The Other is perceived to be fragile and insignificant. It is the Other who does not belong. Add to this, the reality that the presence of psychologically shared defenses and the absence of accountability and remorse mean the targets of political violence are not politically or socially grievable. To reflect, to take accountability, and to grieve are political acts that acknowledge that the Other possesses singularity and belongs in the polis. Without accountability, remorse, and grief, there is no possibility of repairing the political fabric.

This same psychological perspective pertains to other species. The ontological rift is itself a symptom of political violence, and the Anthropocene Age reveals just how violent many human beings are when it comes to other species (Singer, 1975). Most of us give little thought to the sufferings and traumas of other species (Linzey, 2009), because we project inferiority and impermanence onto other species, and split off with regard to the polis; unless, of course, they are constructed as needed to meet human needs and desires. We moralize and rationalize all forms of violence toward other species and, as a result, we do not take accountability for harms done and we experience no remorse. Other species, then, are not grievable, because they are constructed as inferior and lacking significance, from the perspective of Western political narratives. If other species were grievable, we might have to change our relations to them and to deal with the chronic eco-sorrow for the species that are becoming extinct because of human violence.

Above I mentioned the mimetic nature of political violence vis-à-vis human beings, which can be understood as a type of enactment, to use a psychoanalytic concept. Judith Chused (1991) contends that "Enactments occur when an attempt to actualize a transference fantasy elicits a countertransference reaction" (p.616). While this term commonly refers to an interaction between therapist and patient, it can also be applied to the interactions involving political violence. Those who perpetrate political violence project onto their targets fantasies (e.g., inferiority, superiority) associated with objectification (or denial of singularity) and relations of subjugation and disrespect. The targets of political violence often reject and resist these projections, while also engaging similar fantasies. Consider Malcolm X's (Haley, 1964) early adoption of the Nation of Islam's mythology, which constructed white people as inferior. This was connected to Malcolm X's legitimation of political violence against white people who threatened African Americans. Martin Luther King also struggled with rage and with fantasies of violence. Both are examples of enactment or mimesis that accompany political violence. Let me add that enactments do not pertain to other species who suffer violence and who do not return the favor.

Now I turn to explain more explicitly why political violence is not justifiable. Forms of political violence entail a moment and relation that are fundamentally antipolitical. The moment of political violence is, by definition, inimical to the very nature of what the polis is. If we agree that politics is humankind's "most proper dimension" (Agamben, 2011, p.xiii), then we can observe that political violence undermines or destroys this most proper dimension for those who are the targets of violence or the threat of violence. Put another way, this most proper dimension of humanity depends on caring relations of interpersonal recognition that foster spaces of speaking and acting together wherein individuals (1) experience a sense of interpersonal trust, (2) actualize their potentialities without exhausting their potential (singularity), and (3) obtain senses of self-esteem, self-confidence, and self-respect that are necessary foundations for political agency. In brief, from a phenomenological perspective, the *moment and relation* of political violence signifies a contradiction—in the moment of political violence, there is no polis, no proper dimension, even as those who act violently are speaking and acting together. Political violence, at its core, is anti-political because it rests on the denial of political belonging in relation to the targets of violence; therefore, it is not justifiable.

This can be further understood in terms of Arendt's distinction between power and violence. "Power and violence," she (1970, pp.44–46) writes,

> are opposites; where one rules absolutely, the other is absent...This implies that it is not correct to think of the opposite of violence as nonviolence; to speak of nonviolent power is actually redundant. Violence can destroy power; it is utterly incapable of creating it.

> (p.56)

Political power entails acting together, which includes contentious discourses. There must be a minimal level of interpersonal recognition, respect, trust, and care for acting together in the polis. When political power morphs into forms of political violence, political power ceases to exist. In a politically polarized society like the United States, we see a decline in political power, as varied political groups (and representatives) subtly or overtly advocate violence toward their opponents. When this occurs, the larger polis is fractured into political enclaves that seek to justify and secure belonging by securing a particular identity through different modes of violence. Political violence clearly has aims, but these aims are not political in the sense that the moment of violence is not and cannot be an exercise of political power because Others are excluded from participating in the polis. To be sure, individuals act together to perpetrate political violence, but in relation to the targets of political violence there is no civic care, no civic trust, just brute force that is the absence of speaking and acting together.

I add here that political violence is not justifiable because it denies the Other's potentialities, both in disavowing the Other's potentiality vis-à-vis being a person and obstructing the actualizing potentiality of political agency. Recall that actualizing one's potentiality means undergoing a change, and undergoing a change depends on good-enough caring relations. Political violence represents the absence of care.

Would this view hold true for the understandable revolutionary violence directed toward oppressors and political-economic apparatuses that support, for example, racism? Would political violence be justifiable as a means to overturn unjust apparatuses like racism? While I certainly agree that the ends of political, economic, and cultural freedom sought by those who are oppressed are just, the *means* of political violence are not justifiable, because in the moment of political violence, the target is objectified or depersonalized and denied political belonging—force is present, while power, care, and personal recognition are absent in this relation. From a phenomenological perspective, political violence is fundamentally anti-political and, therefore, not justifiable even when we consider the ends to be just.[9]

Let me add that capitalism, nationalism, and imperialism depend on political violence and the threat of political violence to attain varied aims, whether we are talking about human beings, other species, and/or the earth. So, I argue that factory farms, mountaintop removal (MTR), animal experimentation, etc. fall under the category of political violence, because other species are included-excluded Others who are used without consideration for their singularities and without remorse for their suffering and death. What we are seeing in the Anthropocene Age is systemic structural and epistemic violence toward other species and the earth, which is result-ing in the degradation of the biosphere. This reveals how human political violence is undermining the very material foundation of the polis. To destroy one's habitat is an act of political violence, because it undermines the very existence of the polis. Can we not see that this is a kind of collective madness? Can we acknowledge that it is therefore unjustifiable?

In summary, I contend that political violence toward other human beings is not justifiable because it excludes them from spaces of speaking and acting together and denies their existential potentiality (singularity) and political agency. Political violence toward other species is not justifiable, because it excludes other species from the political realm, denies their relevance for political dwelling, and disavows their singularities. Indeed, I assert further that the construction of the ontologi-cal rift has its origins in the violent (epistemic and structural) exclusion of other species. For species that reside in the polis, political violence is evident in the justification or legitimation of their violent instrumental use or exploitation for the benefit of human belonging and dwelling. Since the polis depends on a biodiverse earth, other-than-human species, while lacking political agency, are nevertheless part of political belonging. In my view, political violence rejects this, which means political violence toward other species is anti-political and not justifiable.

## The Ethical Means of Political Change

If political violence is not justifiable as a means of political change, then what means of change are ethical? I believe Martin Luther King's (and others') choice of nonviolent resistance as a means of political change was a recognition that politi-cal violence is not justifiable, despite having just ends (Mantena, 2018). To pre-serve the possibility of a space of appearances between African Americans and white people, King believed that recognizing and treating whites, regardless of whether they were racist, as persons and, therefore, as political agents was and is necessary for the possibility of creating spaces for speaking and acting together among African Americans and white Americans. Forms of nonviolent resistance (e.g., civil disobedience, protests, and boycotts) represent an exercise of political power by ungovernable selves (ungovernable vis-à-vis apparatuses of oppression) who acknowledge that those who espouse hatred and violence are nevertheless persons who belong in the polis and who have political agency (self-esteem, self-confidence, and self-respect). In other words, nonviolence as a method of political change renders inoperative the rubrics of apparatuses that promote political violence, creating a space and possibility of political power and belonging even between groups who are at odds. In addition, nonviolent resistance can be understood as rendering inoperative the mimetic nature or enactment of political violence. In brief, to retain a complex political self and agency, to exercise the capacities for mentalization and deliberation in the presence of intense emotional moments, and to take accountability for one's actions toward others require individual and collective discipline in using nonviolent resistance as a method for seeking political change.

Given the realities of the Anthropocene Age, nonviolent methods for seeking political-economic changes include rendering inoperative apparatuses that promote and justify the objectification of and violence toward more-than-human species.[10] If we are to overcome the ontological rift, we must necessarily find ways to include and care about the needs and habitats of other species in our political deliberations. We need to attend to and care for the singularities of other species for their sake and, secondarily, our sakes. The real work of today and tomorrow is to foster sustainable cultures and societies, which entails embracing the ethical demand to respect and care for each other, other species, and the earth. This cannot be accomplished if the means we rely on involve political violence.

Whether we are focusing on other human beings or other species, nonviolent forms of change are founded on two interrelated attributes of political life. The first is recognition. Nonviolent means of change are founded on the recognition of others' singularities, whether other refers to human beings or other species. Recognition is not merely passive perception. Rather, recognition of others' singularities founds acts of care, which I have argued found belonging and dwelling vis-à-vis the polis. By contrast, acts of political violence represent distortions of recognition and the absence of care.

There are three other points. First, acts of caring for other human beings and other species, in my view, is a form of political action that, deliberately or not, make inoperative the apparatuses of political-economic violence. As Lewis Mumford remarks, "the re-creation of caring and sustainable human cultures ought to become part of the real work of our time" (in Harvey, 2016, p.209). Second, political caring, as a nonviolent method of change, may include aggressive acts of resistance toward political-economic apparatuses of violence. Aggression is justifiable as long as it does not involve either mis- or non-recognition of one's opponents or actions that deny or disavow the political agency of one's opponents. Third, in a climate emergency, care for those who are proximate (in our polis) should include finding ways to care for and about those who are distant, for we share life on this one earth.

It is important to stress that nonviolent means of political change, which render the apparatuses of political-economic violence inoperative, do not undermine these apparatuses. King and others acted nonviolently to effect change, but they did not undo the apparatuses of white supremacy, which are, sadly, alive and well today. Although important social and political changes ensued, the apparatuses of white supremacy remained powerfully present. When it comes to climate change, to engage in nonviolent resistance, to engage in acts of care that makes inoperative apparatuses of political violence, simply means that individuals and groups decide not to act out of the grammar of political violence and its attending ontological rift. More positively, individuals and groups, in speaking and acting together, construct apparatuses that support not simply interpersonal recognition, but a recognition of the singularities of other species—a recognition that accompanies care for other species and the earth. This care is also at the base of nonviolent resistance in that it acknowledges the necessity of a biodiverse earth for the existence of the polis (aim), even as the varied apparatuses of political violence (sovereignty, capitalism, nationalism, and imperialism) remain seemingly unchanged and unchangeable.

## Change and the Issue of Hope

The discussion in the previous chapter regarding the daunting systemic realities that contribute to climate change and serve as obstacles to climate action, and the discussion above regarding methods of political change, might raise questions about the effectiveness of nonviolent resistance, which, in turn, raises the issue of hope. Given the fierce urgency of now, how effective is nonviolent resistance considering the systemic forces we face? Is there any hope that we will be able to alter the trajectory of climate change by engaging in nonviolent actions, by caring for other human beings and other species? I suspect many of us who are concerned about the climate emergency have days where we walk on the edge of despair. In this section, I briefly address the issue of hope by first locating hope in Erikson's first task of psychosocial development. This enables me to claim that parental care precedes hope, revealing the ethical demand to care. While care is often connected to hope, it is not contingent on hope or the realization of hope, which has implications for those who are concerned about the climate emergency. Included in this discussion is my view that hope is, more often than not, captive to binary thinking (one has hope or one despairs). A postmodern view also provides ways of rethinking this by opting for a complex view of psychic life; namely, that human beings are comprised of multiple self-states, while having the illusion of a unitive self. This has implications for eco-hope and hopelessness vis-à-vis care. That is, one part of me is in touch with despair, though another part of me chooses to care and resist, while not being defined by the self-state of despair.

Erik Erikson (1982) conceptualized the first stage of psychosocial development as a "dialogue" between parents and infants, wherein the parents' "almost unrestricted attentiveness and generosity" give rise to children's basic trust (p.35). On the parents' side of the dialogue, unrestricted attentiveness and generosity represent consistent attunement to infants' assertions, and this attunement includes repairs or "therapeutic adaptations" (Winnicott, 1990, p.127) to inevitable mismatches between parents and infants (see Safron & Muran, 1996, 2000; Tronick & Cohn, 1989). These mismatches can give rise to anxiety and mistrust, but when repaired, trust is restored and deepened. It should be stressed that repair is a mutual effort in that infants signal distress—suggesting a nascent agency—and good-enough parents respond appropriately. A notable feature of this perspective, which is central to the discussion below, is that parents' reliable *care precedes and is foundational to infants' experiences of trust*. Put another way, undergoing an alteration or moving from the potential for trust to actual trust depends on parents' good-enough care.

In Erikson's (1982) schema of the stages of psychosocial development, each stage entails a particular psychosocial "crisis" that, if successfully navigated, gives rise to a strength (pp.32–33). The crisis of the first stage of development is trust-mistrust, and when parents and infants manage to move through this stage success-fully, the resulting psychosocial strength or virtue is hope. Failures in this stage, for Erikson, lead to withdrawal or, from Winnicott's (1971) perspective, the emergence of a false self, which defends against hopelessness. In brief, for Erikson, hope is an "expectant desire" (p.59) that emerges from the successful parent-child naviga-tion of basic trust vs. mistrust (p.79). Put differently, "Hopes derive from infantile impulses for oral and oedipal gratifications and triumphs" (Mitchell, 1993, p.15), and these gratifications and triumphs occur as a result of good-enough parental care vis-à-vis parent-infant dialogue. Naturally, this early form of hope, like trust, is organized semiotically, leading to a globalized or poorly differentiated sense of hope. This stage and its organizations of experience eventually become symboli-cally (e.g., narratives, rituals) reorganized in later stages of development.

It is helpful to expand a bit more on Erikson's view of hope as expectant desire. While infants obviously are unable to conceive of time as past, present, and future, they do have a sense of duration and going on being (Winnicott, 1960), as well as a nascent awareness of time in terms of the gap between need/desire and the need/desire being met. In this gap, there is an expectation or anticipation that one's expressions of needs/desires will be recognized and responded to in a timely man-ner by attentive and generous parents. Here is where we can begin to see some differences between "realistic" hopes and wishful thinking. Infants' hopes, if they are realistic, must be based on past experiences of trust—past experiences of par-ents reliably responding to the infant's assertions of needs/desires (Winnicott, 1990, p.129). The "present" is the experience of the satisfaction of need/desire and the "future" is the anticipation that parents will recognize and meet the desire. This is why trust and hope, while distinct, are intimately connected. Infants trust the environment to respond to their assertions of expectant desires. Wishing, by contrast, is an expectant need/desire that is disconnected from past experiences of having the desire met, which means the future is captive to fantasy. The construc-tion of a false self, for instance, can be seen in light of a child's attempt to manage, by way of wishful thinking, the painful failures associated with parental care. The false self represents not a hope for the real parent, but a desire for the wished-for parent.

So far I have depicted Erikson's view of early hope as arising from "dialogue" between caring parents who recognize and respond to their infants' assertions related to their needs/desires. Connected to this is the nascent agency of infants, which moves the discussion to the relation between hope and the *means* of achieving hope's vision. Children's assertions, which denote budding agency, represent diverse rudimentary methods of attaining various aims. Expectant desire, then, can be seen as connected to infants' *means* of communicating in order to have their desires/needs met. Put another way, good-enough parents are trained by their infants, and infants learn to select the ways of achieving their desires/needs. These methods are "realistic" to the extent that they are based on past experiences where the *means* resulted in the need being met. So, an infant's high-pitched cry represents painful distress and expectant desire. The cry can be understood as the agentic means for obtaining parental attention that accompanies hope for specific relief. If we were to imagine parents' consistent lack of responses to cries, then infants, who have very few options with regard to actions, may, as Erikson suggests, withdraw, forming a false self.

The infant's means are also connected to the actions taken by parents to meet infants' assertions or expectant desires/needs. The process in good-enough parent-child communicative interactions is care or personalizing attunements, which includes repair. Put differently, the process is the "dialogue" that is characterized by parents' reliable caring attunements in relation to infants' expectant desires. As indicated above, parents' consistent care precedes and gives rise to trust (Erikson, 1952, p.250), which is joined to children's hopes or expectant desires. So, we note that the relatively good dialogical match between the means used by both children and parents in this first stage of trust-mistrust results in the psychosocial strength of hope. This said, I emphasize that the foundation of infants' trust *and* hope is parental care, and this suggests *that an existential core of the ethics of hope is care.* Care precedes and founds the possibility of both trust and hope.

In earlier chapters, I discussed transitional objects and their relation to children's movement toward public-political life. Here I simply state that children's use of transitional objects can also be seen in terms of the relationship between trust and hope, which are under children's omnipotent control. During these transitions, children develop greater agency with regard to their expectant desires and the means of realizing these desires (hope). Caring and repairing relational disruptions, then, are part and parcel of these early interactions with TOs. Secondary transitional objects represent the movement toward using cultural meanings and methods vis-à-vis trust and hope. So, if we wanted to understand an individual's trust and hope, we would need to locate this within one's particular cultural context and attending caring interactions. In other words, what comprises the culture's apparatuses of care, as well as vision and means of hope?

Given this, I want to turn to the work of scholar and activist Miguel De La Torre (2017), because his notion of embracing hopelessness vis-à-vis marginalized and oppressed communities highlights the point above regarding care. De La Torre points out that hope is often "responsible for maintaining oppressive structures" (p.xiv). The particular context he is addressing is the hope promulgated by Christian theologians, which, in turn, operates in concert with political apparatuses that marginalize and oppress people (Latin and South America, U.S. people of color). Critiquing Jurgen Moltmann's theology of hope, De La Torre highlights how Western Christian hope is imbricated with the notion of conquering, which is supported by apparatuses of sovereignty and political violence (p.45). Consider, for example, Christian leaders in early America. Their religious hopes for freedom and salvation were connected to the means for achieving their vision—strategies that resulted in horrific forms of political violence, including ethnic cleansings (forms of political violence that excluded native peoples from political life). This continued well into the 19th century, when individuals like Catherine Beecher, Harriet Beecher Stowe (Kaplan, 2002, pp.29, 32), and Senator Beveridge (Johnson, 2004, p.43) hoped the United States, as a putative Christian nation, could "bring civilization to native peoples," like people of the Philippines. Add to this the general fact that Christian (and Western political apparatuses) hopes for human flourishing are wedded to the ontological rift, which accompanies instrumental epistemologies and forms of political violence toward Othered human beings, other species, and the earth.

De La Torre (2017) continues by contending that hope, "as a middle-class privilege, soothes the conscience of those complicit with oppressive structures, lulling them to do nothing except to look forward to salvific futures" (p.5). In their hoping, the middle-class numb "themselves to the pain of the oppressed" (p.5), which I contend includes the sufferings of other species. Hope, then, can serve as a soporific toward the consequences of the means used to achieve hope's vision. For De La Torre, the problem of hope is not resolved by having a more accurate hope. "To hope," he writes passionately, "is to bury one's head in the sands of peace, making us useless to meet the inevitable struggle that is coming" (p.96). Instead, he wants "nothing to do with Christian hope, the protagonist of too many atrocities conducted in its name." "Do not shower me with reminders of God's future promises," he continues,

> show me God's present grace through your loving mercy. Do not tempt me with riches of some afterlife; convince me of your sacrificial agape in the here and now. In the midst of unfathomable sufferings, the earth's marginalized no longer need pious pontifications about rewards of the hereafter. Nor do they need their oppressors providing the answers for their salvation.
>
> (p.96)

In my view, De La Torre rejects the hope tied to oppressors and, instead, demands accountability and care for the oppressed. Care or love in the present is more important than promises of a future that may or may not come to fruition.

De La Torre indicates that marginalized and oppressed people embrace hopelessness, which does not mean they necessarily embrace despair. Two aspects of his provocative title are worth delving into. My interpretation is that De La Torre is not saying that oppressed people actually embrace hopelessness. Rather, like him, they are wary and critical of the hopes of the oppressor, because oppressed people are used as the means to attain the privileges and visions of the sovereign classes. Instead, oppressed peoples, generally speaking, gather in groups and communities where there is mutual-personal recognition and care, which sustains them and their resistance to the visions and desires of those who oppress them. These are groups and communities of ungovernable selves, actualizing but not exhausting their potentialities as human beings, as persons. This actualization depends on interpersonal care— a care that does not depend on the hopes and visions of the oppressors. Of course, some people may succumb to despair. James Baldwin (1990) saw his father succumb to oppressive racist apparatuses of humiliation. He writes, "He was defeated long before he died because, at the bottom of his heart, he really believed what white people said about him" (p.4). Nevertheless, more often than not, oppressed people survive and resist the hopes of the oppressors through acts of mutual recognition and care. To turn to Jonathan Lear (2006), he interprets Plenty Coup's and the Crow people's response to the oppression of white Americans as instances of radical hope. Another way to conceptualize the response of the Crow people is that, in the face of hopelessness, they maintained and relied principally on mutual-personal recognition and care rather than hope. Plenty Coup, in other words, did not have a clear vision or hope for the Crow people, since their ways of being in the world were undermined by white people. While hope was in question, care among the Crow people in the present was not. If this is accurate, then it reinforces my claim that care precedes and is not necessarily contingent on hope.

There is another point to elaborate. De La Torre, like Baldwin and Lear, recognizes that people who are oppressed can give into despair, while many others who have an experience of hopelessness do not. I think we can grasp this complexity of this by turning to postmodern views of the psyche. A modernist view of the psyche is one that affirms a unitive self. Postmodern views tend to conceptualize the psyche as comprised of multiple self-states, though possessing a fiction of a unitive self (Stern, 1997, pp.156–158). A postmodern view of the psyche moves us to reject binary thinking when it comes to hope and despair. By this, I mean that an individual (or group) can be in touch with the self-state of hopelessness, yet choose to act out of a different self-state, such as the self-state associated with care. There are innumerable routine examples this. For instance, a parent who knows there is no hope for their dying child chooses to continue to care. Or the care and love of parents for their children while living in oppressive cultures that show no sign of change.

If we turn to the Anthropocene Age, we might imagine how the problems of hope De La Torre mentions will increase as resources dwindle and nations and groups compete instead of cooperate. Racism, sexism, classism, and speciesism will likely worsen as human beings become increasingly anxious, and transform this anxiety into hostility, hatred, and violence in the pursuit of maintaining the privileges of the dominant group and attending ontological rift. We might feel a sense of hopelessness when we recognize the power of the systemic obstacles to climate action. We might experience eco-despair when powerful nations and their elites seek to secure their futures through varied forms of political violence aimed at governing Othered human beings and other species. All of this is quite daunting and, while I am not against hope as a motivator for political action and change, I prefer to settle on care as the means of and motive for change in the present, in the now. Care for other human beings, other species, and the earth is contingent on neither hope nor hopelessness, though, of course, people can care with the hope that human beings and other species will survive the climate emergency. Nevertheless, one can feel a sense of hopelessness given the realities of the Anthropocene Age, while acknowledging that care precedes hope. This acknowledgment can create a space to operate out of a self-state of care, while being in touch with the self-state of despair. As Valerie Kaur (2020) proclaims, "This is our defiance—to practice love even in hopelessness" (p.243). Or as Martin Luther was alleged to have said, "If I knew the world was going to end tomorrow, I would plant an apple tree today."

Before concluding, it is important to highlight Kaur's "our." Care as a means of political change is intersubjective and made possible by groups and communities. De La Torre, for instance, knows that resistance against the hopes of the oppressors depends on groups and communities that foster relations of care—care that founds and maintains ungovernable selves—selves not captive to the apparatuses of oppression. Sojourner Truth, W. E. B. Dubois, Emma Goldman, Rosa Parks, Desmond Tutu, Susan B. Anthony, Nelson Mandela, Ida B. Wells, and innumerable others found ways to resist, because they were connected to caring communities and groups, however flawed or limited these communities and groups were and are. If *we* are to resist the forces that rely on political violence for change, if we are to acknowledge hopelessness while caring for other human beings and other species in the present, we need to be part of communities and groups that practice care for each other, other species, and the earth. These groups will give rise to and maintain ungovernable selves that make inoperative the grammar of apparatuses of political violence, which creates spaces for care that is not contingent on hope.

## Conclusion

Years ago, when we were first married, I noticed my wife catching spiders and other bugs in the house and releasing them outdoors. My tendency was simply to kill them, which certainly seemed the most efficient manner of dealing with inferior beings. At one point, I realized that killing these bugs was more a sign of my laziness and privilege. It was more labor intensive and time consuming to catch these critters and place them outside. This realization is connected to political violence as the method of political change. It is much easier to destroy things and persons to achieve one's aims. Political violence reveals both human laziness and privilege. It is much more difficult to recognize, respect, and treat human beings as persons; it is more challenging to recognize and respect the singularities of other species; it is much more labor intensive (psychologically and socially) to care and to build. Human beings are incredibly inventive at destroying, but we are also capable of incredible acts of creativity, which requires caring labor. A psychoanalytic political philosophy can help us understand the dynamics of political violence, while also affirming the necessity of care as a method of political change and for dwelling in the Anthropocene Age—a method consonant with the activity of psychoanalysis itself.

## Notes

1  Freud did mention courage and truth as features of psychoanalysis, suggesting the virtues of psychoanalytic exploration. However, Freud wanted psychoanalysis to be a science and was leery of psychoanalysis moving toward "ethical" treatments that were fashionable in the 19th and early 20th centuries.

2  It is important to point out that Fanon had trained with François Tosquelles at a psychiatric hospital in France. Fanon considered Dr. Tosquelles to be a mentor and Fanon his disciple (Gibson & Beneduce, 2017, p.131). Tosquelles believed that "the [psychiatric] institution had to be transformed into a caring community" (p.133). He developed a sociotherapy that understood psychological suffering within the context of a particular social milieu. Fanon carried this with him to Algeria.

3  Because of space constraints, I will restrict myself to political violence within a state, though I consider political violence between states to also be unethical despite the mountains of literature on just war theory.

4  Hannah Arendt (1970) distinguishes between power and violence. As noted in a previous chapter, power is associated with people speaking and acting together, while force is a synonym for violence, which is characterized by its instrumental nature. She writes, "Power is indeed the essence of all government, but violence is not. Violence is by nature instrumental" (p.51).

5  It would take me off course, but it is important to make clear that the origins of capitalism lie in indirect forms of political violence (Woods, 2017). The so-called agrarian reforms in England were the result of political-economic elites who constructed laws and policies resulting in the displacement, suffering, and deaths of thousands of Britons.

6  During the Cold War, some religious leaders and organizations rejected just war theorizing vis-à-vis the use of nuclear weapons, largely because these weapons jeopardize not only human life globally, but also other species. This was, at least, a step in the right direction regarding the inclusion of other species in moral discussions about war.

7  Ruby Sales—Where Does It Hurt?|The On Being Project – The On Being Project, https://onbeing.org/programs/ruby-sales-where-does-it-hurt/#transcript, accessed 9 June 2021.

8  Fanon makes this point when he was asked to help two French policemen who were involved in torturing Algerians. Fanon "made clear the difficulty, or, in fact, the impossibility of healing someone who will not yield to self-reflection" or take accountability (Gibson & Beneduce, 2017, p.238). From a different context, Hannah Arendt (1965) makes a similar point about the lack of the self-reflective (mentalization) and accountability in Eichmann.

9  Let me reiterate, I am not suggesting that the only route to political change is non-violence. I certainly can see that oppressed and marginalized groups may choose violence as a means to attain the just end of freedom. However, by saying that political violence is not justifiable. I am saying that people using violence must take accountability for the harm they do, have remorse for those harmed, and grieve the deaths of opponents. In so doing, there remains a possibility of forgiveness and political repair (see Tutu, 1999).

10  Donna Orange (2017) offers a radical ethics for the climate crisis. While she occasionally references care for "non-human" species, most of the text deals with interhuman relations. I add that "non-human" species are considered because they are important for a biodiverse earth and, therefore, human existence. I do not believe this is radical enough. We need to include other-than-human species in our ethical-political deliberations, not simply because we need them to maintain earth's biodiversity and thus human existence. This retains a kind of instrumental thinking that Orange seeks to overcome vis-à-vis interhuman relations. A more radical view is care for other species in their singularities. This care eschews instrumental epistemologies and types of political-economic violence.

# Part II

# Chapter 6

# Socrates, Tiresias, and Freud

## Reimagining Psychoanalysis and the Public Square

In 1919, Max Weber (2013/1919) delivered a lecture to the Free Students Union in the midst of the German Revolution. Germany had lost the war and was forced to take "responsibility…for causing all the loss and damage to which the Allied and Associated Governments and their nationals have been subjected as a consequence of the war imposed upon them by the aggression of Germany and her allies."[1] In signing the treaty, Germany was required to pay crippling economic reparations ($442 billion in 2023 dollars) that destabilized the society. The future, in Weber's eyes, was bleak and, with the rise of Hitler in 1933, he sadly turned out to be correct. When the polar night and crumbling hopes take hold in a society, how are we to respond, Weber asks. Are we to simply accept the status quo, retreat into mundane boredom, or escape into flights of fantasy? Many people will, but Weber believed and argued for another response, given instability, violence, and polarization. "And even those who are neither leaders nor heroes," he stated,

> must arm themselves with steadfastness of heart which can brave even the crumbling of all hopes. This is necessary right now, or else [human beings] will not be able to attain even that which is possible today. Only he has the calling for politics who is sure that he shall not crumble when the world from his point of view is too stupid or to base for what he wants to offer. Only he who in the face of all this can say 'In spite of all' has the calling for politics.
>
> (pp.79–80)[2]

Interestingly, Weber's focus on the calling of politics was understood in terms of the lawyer, journalist, and party official, leaving aside his own vocation as an academic. Weber, the eminent sociologist, engaged in various social-political and economic organizations throughout his adult life. He was one of the founders of the German Democratic Party and contributed to the making of the Weimar Constitution (Radkau, 2009). Perhaps Weber's political vocation concerns those in academic and other disciplines. Marx would have agreed, believing that philosophers should not simply set out to understand and explain the world, but to change it. More recently, Noam Chomsky, noted linguist scholar, first stepped into the political arena by criticizing the U.S. involvement in Vietnam, which began his

DOI: 10.4324/9781003258827-9

decades-long vocation as public intellectual. Around the same time, psychoanalyst and Marxist Joel Kovel (1988) entered the fray, with his first book on racism (1970). Kovel (1988) was not the first psychoanalyst to engage political issues. Indeed, he initially was an "ardent [follower] of…Wilhelm Reich" (p.11), who was deeply engaged in political matters. And I have already mentioned Frantz Fanon and the staff at the LaFargue clinic, indicating their vocations of politics. Of course, there are any number of scholars and psychoanalysts in each generation who have, in various ways, addressed political issues, which, in my view, indicates that they answered the call of a political vocation.

This said, in previous generations, psychoanalysts, like Joel Kovel, found their way into this vocation *despite* their analytic training/education, which primarily focused on the analytic knowledge/theories, virtues, and skills needed to be effective therapists. The vocation of politics was an add-on and not seen as something connected or integral to the calling to be a psychoanalytically inclined therapist. This left people, like Kovel and Fanon, struggling to integrate a political philosophy with psychoanalysis or to hold them in tension and conversation. Kovel (1988) was asked how he reconciled the significant anthropological differences between Freudianism and Marxism. He responded,

> That is the most difficult question I have to face. It's a fascinating question and I don't have a ready answer. If I had to choose, I would say that I am more Marxist than Freudian. By values. On the other hand, by training…I am more Freudian.
>
> (p.19)

Here we see a struggle to integrate political philosophy and psychoanalytic theories. In other words, there is an apparent uneasy tension between vocations, which I suggest is partly rooted in Freud's construction of psychoanalysis as a science that separates the consulting room from politics and ignores how psychoanalysis has been shaped by Western political philosophies.[3] I wonder if Kovel's psychoanalytic training had included the critical engagement of psychoanalysis with political philosophies, he would have had a ready answer or, better, developed a psychoanalytically informed political philosophy that would support both vocations.

Embracing both vocations, for this generation and the next, is even more urgent given the dire realities of climate change. In this chapter, I consider psychoanalysis in relation to the public-political sphere, arguing that analytically informed therapists can integrate the vocation of therapy and the vocation of politics. To bridge these disciplines depends, in part, on developing a psychoanalytic political philosophy, which has been the focus of Part I of this book. I begin by claiming that, from the earliest origins of the polis, there have been critics, gadflies, and prophets who identified faulty social-political premises, railed against injustices, and sought to awaken the populace and leaders from soporific self-deceptions. The well-being of the polis depended, in part, on those who took up this political vocation, sometimes at their own peril. This sets the stage for arguing that psychoanalytic therapies and institutes are, whether they are aware of it or not, inextricably tied to social, political, and economic realities. This implies an ethical demand to engage political realities—using just means—especially in situations where injustices are occurring and when societies are facing existential crises, such as a climate emergency. From here, using the psychoanalytic political philosophy of the previous chapters, I indicate that this political vocation of analytically informed therapists can take many forms. This has implications for psychoanalytic education and therapy, which I take up in the next chapter. Included in this discussion is my depiction of some political virtues and analytic skills that attend this vocation.

A few clarifications are proffered before beginning. First, the aim of this chapter is to invite more conversation about the role of the analytic therapist in public life. I am, therefore, not proposing or suggesting there is only one way to conceptualize an analytic political vocation. The particular social, cultural, and political context and the individual analyst (and institute) will no doubt shape what this vocation looks like. Second, a key premise in my argument is that a psychoanalytic political philosophy can bridge these vocations, as well as inform one's stance and engagement in the political realm. More precisely, the implicit aim of persons developing a psychoanalytic political philosophy will necessarily be concerned about integrating one's engagement in the consulting room with one's participation in public-political life. This does not imply an identity between the two realms, but it does mean, as indicated in the last chapter, that there needs to be congruence in method. Finally, I liken our present situation to the Titanic. We did not know, for decades, we were steaming toward climate disaster, but we have known for some five decades that we have hit this iceberg. Using this analogy, it seems ludicrous to imagine someone doing therapy in one of the ship's rooms while the ship is sinking. "All hands-on deck" is what is required. This analogy does not entirely fit, because we need to see patients, some of whom are not suffering from eco-anxiety, eco-grief, and eco-despair. But we also have a vocation to engage in larger political spheres, especially in social-political crises and their attending injustices.

## The Polis' Need for Gadflies, Prophets, and Psychoanalytically Informed Social Critics

I suspect most readers are familiar with the story that Socrates was convicted of corrupting Athenian youths and, subsequently, put to death. Socrates had a calling to engage in the routine political life of the polis—speaking and acting together—which was later exemplified in a Roman statesman and philosopher, Cicero. He, like Socrates, believed "philosophy is essential for public life and that philosophers have a duty to serve the public good" (Nussbaum, 2019, p.23). A main feature of this vocation was, for Socrates, raising questions and counterpoints to his interlocutors with the aim of moving toward greater intellectual clarity. This was not a mere academic philosophical activity, closeted in the classroom. For Socrates and Cicero, a philosopher[4] had a calling to aid citizens (in this case, adult males) to think critically in their speaking and acting together. Critical thinking was essential to the polis and not just to a democratic polis.[5] In speaking and acting together, we need clear concepts tied to practical actions toward concise aims. The Greek term "phronesis" means practical wisdom, and practical wisdom vis-à-vis the polis is only possible when there is critical thinking. For Hannah Arendt (1958), referring to the early Greeks, "To be political, to live in a polis, meant that everything was decided through words and persuasion and not through force and violence" (p.26). A feature of persuasion, which is evident in the Socratic dialogues, was critical thinking. And Socrates embodied and lived out this calling in the polis—the polis was his academy.

Unfortunately, Plato, appalled at the death of his beloved teacher, retreated from engaging in public-political life (in the manner of Socrates), which, Hannah Arendt (1958) argued, had a lasting impact on Western philosophy. "The Platonic separation of knowing and doing," Arendt notes,

> has remained at the root of all theories of domination which are not mere justifications of an irreducible and irresponsible will to power. By sheer force of conceptualization and philosophical clarification, the Platonic identification of knowledge with command and rulership and of action with obedience and execution overruled all earlier experiences and articulations in the political realm and became authoritative for the whole tradition of [Western] political thought.
>
> (p.225)

In my view, critical thinking obviously continued, but became associated with the theoretical (versus phronesis) and less as a necessity of the very foundation of the polis. Many later political philosophers contemplated questions of metaphysics and eternity, while leaving the Socratic political vocation to the side for less erudite others to get their hands dirty with political practical wisdom.

Socrates considered himself to be a gadfly because he knew that to live in a polis, to engage in acts of speaking and acting together with the aim of the survival and flourishing of the polis, required critical, constructive discourse. Indeed, Socrates avers that

> God has attached me to this city to perform the office of such a fly (stinging insect or gadfly); and all day long I never cease to settle here, there, and everywhere, rousing, persuading, reproving every one of you. You will not easily find another like me, gentlemen, and if you take my advice you will spare my life. I suspect, however... you will finish me off with a single slap; and then you will go on sleeping till the end of your days, unless God in his care sends you someone to take my place.
>
> (Tredennick, 1984, p.63)

Socrates viewed the role of gadfly as necessary for waking people up and the method of the gadfly was critical thinking, which is not left to the philosopher, but to anyone who lives in the polis and has and develops this capacity. Of course, most of the time, as Socrates knew firsthand, we do not interrogate our concepts. We leave our premises unexplored. The political gadfly is someone who stops us on the street and challenges us to account for our thinking and action. So, what do you mean when you use the word "justice"? What are its methods? Whom does it concern? Who is a citizen and who decides who is or who is not? Yet, in the main, we prefer to sleep, finding it exceedingly annoying when the gadfly tries to awaken us. Any resident of the polis can accept this vocation. Socrates simply happened to be annoyingly exceptional at it.

There was another gadfly in ancient Greece, though he and his followers had different methods, and these methods stemmed from critical thinking. Diogenes the Cynic (Greek *kyon* means dog) was also engaged in the public-political arena, but in decidedly provocative ways. He rejected social conventions, seeking to live according to nature. There are any number of apocryphal stories that detail Diogenes "performative" critique of cultural conventions, such as masturbating in public and living on the street. Anthony Grayling (2019) writes, "He charged his contemporaries with living artificially, their minds befogged…because of the folly desiring wealth, fame, and honour" (p.102). The aims were to reach *eudaimonia* and *atuphia* (clarity of mind) and these aims were blocked by social-political conventions. Socrates, I think, would agree with those aims, but his method was debate, while Diogenes was performative in the sense of trying to show people the errors of their ways of being in the polis, rather than engage in philosophical debates.

The polis may need a gadfly, whether in the guise of Socrates or Diogenes, but, as the adult male citizens of "democratic" Athens reveal, we do not like to be questioned.[6] It is not only frustrating to have our cherished political concepts and premises questioned, it is also painful, even humiliating to find ourselves to be wrong or clueless or unjust, as Socrates' interlocutors discovered. But it was not simply frustration and possible humiliation that stirred Socrates' political opponents to put him on trial. It was fear. The chosen representatives feared that Socrates' public-political method of critical thinking was ostensibly corrupting the youth. They feared that people would begin to question the traditions and apparatuses upon which the leaders believed the polis depended, even though Socrates did not see himself as doing so. The political leaders believed that to undermine these traditions would be to undermine the stability and security of the polis. More aptly, I suspect those in positions of power feared people questioning their power, positions, and prestige, which motivated them to use political violence to suppress critical thinkers and thinking. Arendt argued that the Greeks viewed political violence as pre-political (p.27), but it is clear that, even in so-called democracies (rule of the people—men in this case), violence and the threat of violence are, as noted in a previous chapter, features of sovereignty itself. And most of those who are sovereign are deathly afraid of critical thinking or questioning. Therefore, Socrates was sentenced to death by those who represented the polis and the status quo, and who feared critique and critical thinking. I wonder if his death also quelled the desires of other Athenians who may have felt a calling to be a political gadfly.

What the Athenian council reveals was the totalitarianism that undergirded their democracy or what Christopher Bollas (1995) termed the fascist state of mind. Totalitarian regimes, which obviously include fascist regimes, abhor criticism and will go to incredible lengths to crush any dissent, strangling any voice that questions political authority. One might immediately think of Russia and Putin's regime that brutally smashes dissent regarding the war against Ukraine. We might also mention Iran, Saudi Arabia, China, Hong Kong, Burma/Myanmar, Egypt, and other nations that eschew political gadflies. For putatively democratic nations, the totalitarian tendency is masked by the rule of law (like the Council of Athens), which was evident during slavery and the Jim Crow Era when white supremacy, codified in law and political institutions, was the unquestioned and unquestionable political system. When the rule of law is unmasked—revealing its illusory or false foundation—the totalitarian mindset in democratic regimes shifts to the creation of "alternative realities" or "alternative facts," which exploded with the rise of the conservative members of the Trump cult. When dissent cannot be violently crushed by the despot's henchmen, totalitarian tendencies shift to creating alternative facts. For instance, in Nazi Germany, propaganda minister Joseph Goebbels remarked that if you tell a lie a 1,000 times, it becomes a truth—an adage that Fox has taken to new heights. Those who live out the totalitarian tendencies in the polis, whether it was ancient Athens or present-day United States, abhor and stifle critical thinking and the search for truth/wisdom. Instead, they look for flights of fancy, mystification, and other soporifics that cloud the mind toward the real sources of danger, which is evident in climate denial and rationalizations that support the capitalist, nationalist, and imperialist status quo.

The stability of many societies may suggest that the polis does not really need a gadfly. A society can be quite stable and secure without people called to a political vocation of critical thinking. North Korea has been stable for decades, as has China. I am sure there is a great deal of critical thinking in those societies, but it is neither public nor political. To speak and act publicly would invite political violence. This said, Socrates believed that a polis flourished when spaces of speaking and acting together included critical thinking, which he lived out in the public realm. This flourishing meant the presence of freedom and creativity (for adult male citizens), which can introduce some destabilization and insecurity. Nevertheless, a polis flourishes when, to recall Arendt's (1958) view, power is people speaking and acting together, and the exercise of this power entails creative critical thinking in and about the public square. Totalitarian regimes may be stable and secure, but they corrupt or destroy power and critical thinking through force, suppressing spaces of speaking and acting together, which in the long run destabilizes society. I would argue that when the totalitarian tendency is ascending, as it is in the United States and other democracies (e.g., France, Britain, Hungary, Poland, etc.), then the polis is diminished, becoming more unstable. It does not and cannot flourish, because it is dependent on cultivating falsehoods that masquerade as truths or facts. A society that is overrun by falsehoods cannot face together concrete dangers, like global warming. Yes, it is true that a totalitarian regime like China is flourishing, if we use economics as the only indicator. Similarly, it is also true that the United States, as a democracy, economically flourished in the 19th and 20th centuries at the expense of native peoples, African Americans, and poor people. But these are indecent societies (Margalit, 1996), because they depend on tools of suppression and mystification, sidelining political gadflies that question and confront the king who wears no clothes.

Critical thinking is necessary for a polis, and this is vitally true today as we face the daunting realities of climate change—realities that threaten the very existence of any polis. A polis, however, also needs a prophet. By prophet, I do not mean someone who can predict the future. Rather, I am thinking of the prophets in Jewish scriptures who spoke truth to power regarding injustices. As Michael Walzer (2012) notes, the prophets arrived with the birth of the monarchy (human sovereignty) and established a conflict between political power and the admonitions of God. The prophet Samuel warned the elders of the consequences of enthroning a monarch (1Sam. 8:11–17). Prophets like Amos called political leaders into accountability by emphasizing "the importance of justice and compassion" (Armstrong, 1993, p.46; see also Horsley, 2009, pp.65–79). The prophet Nathan had the temerity to confront King David, who had ordered the killing of one of his generals so that he could marry the general's wife, Bathsheba. Leaving aside Jewish scripture, Tiresias, the blind prophet, confronted King Oedipus with the fact that he had killed his father and married his mother, though one can hardly blame him for not knowing, while kings Laius and David clearly knew. Prophets are demystifiers of the sources of suffering and injustice. Their critical thinking is not focused on conceptual clarity regarding justice, but on pointing out and fighting injustices and their sources. Elizabeth Cady Stanton, Susan B. Anthony, Lucy Stone, and Francis Harper were modern prophets pointing to the marginalization of women in the political and economic spheres. Frederick Douglass, Sojourner Truth, Martin Luther King Jr., Ida B. Wells, Desmond Tutu, and Rosa Parks are examples of modern prophets who demystified the sources of racial oppression. Philosophers like Schopenhauer and Singer are prophets pointing out the pervasive sufferings of other species at the hands of human beings. Giorgio Agamben, who I have relied on in previous chapters, is a prophet in the sense that he demystifies Western political thought— thought and action that create the ontological rift and its attending injustices. Without prophets, the polis remains blind to its failings and its injustices. In the Anthropocene Age, this becomes increasingly important because marginalization and oppression will rise as anxiety, fear, and insecurity soar.

A political vocation as gadfly and prophet pertains to any of a number of psychoanalysts and psychoanalytically informed cultural critics over the last century. In some ways, Freud was a gadfly, because he exposed our illusions and revealed our secret fears and anxieties. I would also mention Alfred Adler, Theodore Reich, Erich Fromm, Donald Winnicott, and many others who sought to identify societal ills and their sources. And I have in the previous chapters mentioned Donna Orange, Sally Weintrobe, Paul Hoggett, Susan Kassouf, and others whose political vocation is revealed in their public concern about the impacts of climate change, as well as their use of psychoanalysis to understand the relation between larger systems and subjects' resistance to engaging in necessary political-economic changes. In my view, the political vocation of psychoanalytic therapists adds to the traditions of gadflies and prophets. To be sure, an analytically oriented political vocation can include the critical thinking associated with clarifying ideas and methods. It can and has included identifying injustices and their sources (e.g., Kovel, 1970). But unlike the gadfly or prophet, a psychoanalytic political vocation entails a critical thinking informed by the hermeneutics of suspicion, to use Paul Riceour's term, with the aims of (1) bringing to consciousness that which is unconscious and (2) exposing our collectively held destructive illusions and delusions. Put another way, a psychoanalytically informed political vocation, like Nathan's vocation as prophet, seeks to expose our self-deceptions, judging when "there is a purposeful discrepancy between the way the individual really is engaged in the world and the story he tells himself" (Fingarette, 1969, p.62).

My contention is that the political life of a community or society needs gadflies, prophets, and analytically inclined social-political critics. Exposing faulty concepts and premises, uncovering injustices, and revealing illusions and self-deceptions invite the possibility of accountability and forgiveness, the development of practical wisdom, and attending constructive changes necessary for human (and other species) to flourish. When it comes to the climate emergency, this political vocation becomes increasingly important. We need to see how Western political premises and concepts create an ontological gap, which underlines our destructive relations to the biosphere. Prophets need to reveal the present and future injustices not only regarding human beings, but toward other species and the earth. We need critics to expose our self-deceptions, such as our anthropocentric beliefs that have excluded other species from our historical and normative consciousness. The Anthropocene Age reveals that a political vocation is not something that we *might* take up, as if it is simply one choice over another. There is, in other words, an ethical demand to take up a political vocation as psychoanalytically inclined therapists. Of course, we can decide to ignore this demand, retreating to the consulting room, but this would be analogous to treating patients who are suffering from horrific oppression as if the sources of oppression can be ignored or sequestered from the work of therapy. As Joel Kovel (1988) writes, "therapy is in itself a political act and can only be grasped in relation to the material conditions it seeks to alter" (p.122). He remarks further: "What should not be tolerated, in therapy any more than life outside, is political unconsciousness and automatism—a politics passively received and blindly reproduced" (p.160).

## Psychoanalytic Vocation of Politics: Further Thoughts

Over 30 years ago, I was a hospital chaplain working primarily with cancer patients and their families. While this was as difficult as it was rewarding, I wanted to find ways to help people work through their psychological struggles, which seemed to me to be better than dealing with the revolving door of good-byes to people I cared about and for. So, I decided to return to graduate school—one which had a clinical portion that was steeped in psychoanalytic theories and concepts. This was an enlightening and exciting time, because psychoanalytic theories (and therapy) helped me develop what Theodor Reik (1998/1948) called a third ear—an analytic ear that facilitates listening in depth. As an analytically oriented therapist, I viewed my vocation as one of facilitating patients' insight, healing, and/or liberation. During graduate school, and later during my sojourn at an analytic institute, my vocation as a therapist was divorced from my interests in political matters, though I was very interested in politics. The absence of texts or discussions regarding politics and therapy by my teachers and mentors left me without the conceptual tools to bridge these. Slowly, I took steps to try to connect psychoanalysis with political issues, but the vocation and consulting room remained segregated. It was while reading Frantz Fanon and Joel Kovel (and others) that I began to see that while there are important distinctions between the analytic vocation of caring for patients and engaging in the political sphere—distinctions do not necessarily require either separation or require compartmentalization. In other words, I began to see that insight, healing, and freedom vis-à-vis the consulting room *cannot* be divorced from the political realm without contributing to collusion and mystification. These teachers, in the form of books and articles, taught me that therapists are obliged to consider a political vocation as part of their work, especially in contexts of social-political and environmental crises. In this section, I expand on what I mean by political vocation vis-à-vis psychoanalysis, holding to the premise that psychoanalytic therapists, like Cicero's philosophers, have a duty to serve the public good, and this public good includes other species and the earth.

First, let me begin by saying that there are varied ways of living out one's political vocation as a psychoanalytically informed therapist. Voting (local, state, and national elections) for and helping candidates who are genuinely committed to climate action and environmental justice, writing to one's representatives, researching and writing for one's discipline regarding climate change and other political, economic, and social issues, writing for popular media or news sources, participating in public actions around climate change and social justice (includes other species) at home and abroad, engaging with (or starting) local, national, and international NGOs and other organizations that address climate change and justice these are just some of the various ways one can live out a political vocation. Absent from this list is political office. This absence is not because I think holding a political office would require getting one's hands dirty and making compromises or deals with capitalists and nationalists. My hesitation is due to the difficulty in continuing to practice one's vocation as a therapist while holding political office, unless perhaps the office does not require one's full attention and time. Instead, I consider ways of living out both vocations.

A question may arise regarding the relation between public-political actions and therapy. What about patients and their discovery of the therapists' political engagements and views? While I will address the issue of therapy and the political in the last chapter, for now let me say it is an illusion, especially today, to pretend that patients do not know or cannot come to know a great deal about us in the absence of self-disclosures. Unless a therapist is completely off the grid, there is a great deal of information a curious patient can find on social media and other sources. For therapists who write, patients can easily access these texts. Over the years, patients have been told about or have sought out articles and books I have written, which has evoked all kinds of thoughts and feelings. Joel Kovel (1988) addresses this: "a question arises," he writes, "as to whether public political activity by the therapist outside the office may affect the transference. Indeed, it may—but so may everything else, including anonymity and the absence of political involvement" (p.160).[7] If these things "become known, they should be acknowledged and then made into an occasion for active confrontation by the patient of his or her own political values and relation to public life" (p.160). I would add that the therapist can also reflect on the patient's comments as a form of critique. For instance, a patient's noting the therapist's lack of political engagement regarding climate change and/or other political issues of injustice is not something simply to explore vis-à-vis the patient's transference. Of course, we do that, but it can also be an occasion for self-exploration as to why we are not living out our political vocation as a therapist.

A couple of decades ago, I came across Phillip Bromberg's (1996) quip that "psychoanalysis is a good profession for someone who wants to do something dangerous without leaving the office" (p.70). Bromberg was referring to Breuer and Freud and the relational messiness that attends the transference-countertransference dynamics. It is hardly dangerous, but it is risky when working with people who are vulnerable and struggling with psychological maladies. This said, the quip reflects the split between the office and the streets. If we take up the vocation associated both with the office and the streets, then we might begin to realize it is indeed more dangerous or, at least, riskier. Frantz Fanon (Hudis, 2015b) certainly experienced this in practicing his vocation as a psychiatrist and political activist. There were occasions when he was watched by the French secret police and, in other cases, he fled and changed his name in order to continue practicing. I am sure that, in other repressive regimes today, therapists who engage in public-political critiques and protests place themselves in danger. For those living in so-called Western democratic societies, the risks are not nearly as frightening, at least for now. The rise of authoritarianism in Western democracies (e.g., the United States, France, Britain, Austria, Italy, and Hungary) does not bode well for the exercise of one's political vocation. In the United States, political violence as a means of change is on the increase.[8] So, as climate change worsens and anxieties increase, leaving the office and exercising one's political vocation may become more dangerous.

So far the reader may presume that a therapist's vocations—therapeutic and political— concern patients and other individuals suffering as a result of political, economic, and cultural oppression and marginalization. This is true, but recall that the polis is inextricably tied to and dependent on a biodiverse earth. A political vocation, whether exercised by a journalist, lawyer, clergyperson, politician, or therapist, entails attending to the needs and sufferings of other species. Stated differently, a political vocation in the Anthropocene Age overcomes or renders inoperative the ontological rift, recognizing that human existence and flourishing are dependent on biodiversity. The biodiversity of the earth does not depend on human beings, but we depend on the earth's biodiversity, which means that to engage in a political vocation requires attending to the protection and furthering of biodiversity. This may have little to do with the office where one conducts therapy, but the office and practice also depend on a biodiverse earth. There are also occasions when this issue may come up in therapy, which I will address in the next chapter.

If one agrees that therapists' primary vocation is to provide excellent psychological care for their patients and *that a political vocation subsists in this*, then it is important to consider what virtues attend this political vocation.[9] While psychoanalytic literature typically avoids the notion of "virtue,"[10] some psychoanalysts have ventured to discuss analytic virtues, such as reliance, consistency, and presence (Wilson, 2018) or constraint, incompletion, and tolerance of unknowing (Clark, 1997). Understandably, for these authors, analytic virtues inhere in the very practice of psychoanalytic therapy. Can we extend these to a psychoanalytic political vocation?

Before doing so, it is important to obtain, if only briefly, a bit more clarity about what virtue means. Alasdair MacIntyre (1983) states that virtue is "an acquired human quality the possession and exercise of which tends to enable us to achieve goods which are internal to practices and the lack of which prevents us from achieving any such goods" (p.191). Virtue, we note, is something that someone possesses and exercises, which, of course, is linked to knowledge, skills, and motivation. If we are concerned about the consulting room, then we can inquire as to the knowledge and skills needed to achieve what is good for patients. When Wilson mentions the virtues of reliance, consistency, and presence, and Clarke mentions restraint, I reframe these as virtues of trustworthiness and compassion. The virtue of trustworthiness depends on reliability in respecting and caring for patients, as well as the willingness to recognize our mistakes and repair relational disruptions. The absence of this virtue means analytic work cannot be done, because patients will not feel safe enough to be vulnerable. The virtue of compassion depends on the capacities of emotional regulation and empathy, which, according to care theorist Daniel Engster (2007), includes three virtues central to caring activities, namely, attentiveness, responsiveness, and respect (pp.30–31). Attentiveness entails knowledge or awareness of the needs and experiences of the patient, as well as self-awareness of the therapist's countertransference. Closely associated with attentiveness is responsiveness, which for Engster "means engaging with others to discern the precise nature of their needs and monitoring their responses to our care" (p.30). Here, responsiveness suggests a collaborative interaction aimed at empathic understanding and meeting the needs of the patient. The third virtue is respect and this, for Engster, involves recognizing the Other as an equal who possesses inherent dignity and is worthy of our attention and care, which, in my view, entails recognizing and treating others as persons—unique, valued, inviolable, and agentic—a central feature of care that grounds the analytic vocation. I add here that Clarke's view that tolerance of unknowing or negative capability "is when a [person] is capable of being in uncertainty, mysteries, doubts, without irritable reaching after fact and reason" (letter John Keats wrote to George Keats, in Bion, 1970, p.125). Negative capability strikes me as the virtue of humility, which entails both emotional regulation and recognition of the limits of one's knowledge, one's theories, and concepts. Put another way, analytic care and the virtue of humility foster a space of learning from the patient (Casement, 1985).

Before shifting to virtues regarding a political vocation, let me say a bit more about what I consider to be psychoanalytic virtues. Socrates was believed to have said that an unexamined life is not worth living, and I am confident that for Plato the principal method for examination was Socratic. Plato's Socrates must have thought that the virtue of critical self-examination was a necessary method for attaining the good of *eudaimonia* or well-being and we need to remember that well-being is not something simply associated with an individual; it includes the social. This is why Socrates practiced the art of examination in public political spaces, as well as in the homes of his friends. I believe this is, in part, evident in the very roots of psychoanalysis. A key feature of analysis is raising to conscious what was previously unconscious, which is for the sake of the patient's healing, freedom, psychosocial well-being, etc. (goods). Naturally, the process can include appropriately and timely empathic confrontation of patients' faulty premises or beliefs, as well as the analyst's coming to awareness of their mistaken perceptions, beliefs, and self-deceptions. Of course, analytic methods of raising the unconscious to consciousness do not necessarily ensure well-being, happiness (for Freud, to live a normally miserable life), or freedom or even becoming a better person. But it does create the possibility of greater freedom and a richer life.

According to McIntyre's notion of virtue, we can consider the practice of critical, constructive examination, which includes psychoanalytic methods, to be a virtue that can contribute to human flourishing. Staying within the context of the consulting room, I am arguing that analytic exploration depends on the capacities for and practices of self-reflexivity and emotional self-regulation, as well as the skills and knowledge necessary for timely, effective interventions and repairs of relational disruptions. Ideally, analytic therapists learn these virtues in their education and their own analysis.

A question arises, given the realities of the Anthropocene Age, whether these virtues are applicable to analysts' engagement in public-political life. It was obviously clear that Socrates had a political vocation and central to that vocation was examination, which he believed was necessary for the well-being of the polis, though his accusers apparently thought otherwise. I certainly think analytic virtues are relevant today for therapists and social-political critics. That is, the virtues mentioned above (e.g., attentiveness, responsiveness, respect, and humility), as well as the knowledge and skills associated with self-reflexivity, emotional regulation, and repair, go a long way to being able to engage in contested public-political spaces.

To my mind, a good way to begin practicing these virtues of an analytic political vocation is at home. By this, I mean in one's analytic institutes and organizations. My experience at a psychoanalytic institute was disappointing in this respect. The two founders of the institute undermined each other, creating factions within the institute. I found it ironic and tragic that these skilled analysts could practice the virtues mentioned above in sessions with patients and analysands, but when it came to the politics of the institute, these virtues were replaced by the political vices of self-certainty and name-calling. These leaders also displayed a complete distortion of the virtue of analytic examination and accountability vis-à-vis the public realm, which has been evident throughout the history of psychoanalytic politics, including Freud's comments about Carl Jung and Sandor Ferenczi. When psychoanalytic diagnoses are used to demean and undermine people, they are no longer a public virtue. This is why I emphasize practicing these virtues at home. In so doing, we are better prepared to exercise them in the varying political contexts in which we choose to engage. This is especially true when we consider the political polarizing discourse in the United States. The eclipse of civil discourse begs for analytic examination, as well as the capacities for humility, critical thinking, self-reflexivity, emotional regulation, and repair.

As Socrates learned, a political vocation that entails examination does not necessarily mean it is effective or that there is an absence of pushback. As he knew, this political vocation is a dangerous one. The Anthropocene Age is one of growing anxiety, fear, and hostility in political spaces, which will undermine persons' capacities for self-reflexivity. We need and will need people who can exercise emotional regulation, thoughtfulness, and respect as necessary to their political vocation. Let me add that Socrates' assumptive world included the ontological rift, which means that his political vocation did not include other species. Of course, one cannot engage in examination with other species, since they do not possess political agency. However, a political vocation today needs to acknowledge not only the necessity of other species for the existence of the polis, for human survival and flourishing, but also the inherent value or singularity of other species. This is where we need to exercise the capacity for repair or reconciliation (Kovel, 1988, pp.288–305)—repair of our relations to other species and the earth. This requires demonstrating respect for the singularities of other species, as well as an ongoing critical, constructive analysis of our political, economic, and social apparatuses that produce and maintain interhuman and interspecies divisions.

Implicit in this discussion of the therapists' political vocation and attending virtues is a question about the role of psychoanalytic institutes regarding the political vocation of psychoanalytic therapists. As noted above, I happened upon the notion of political vocation vis-à-vis analytic therapies. My graduate education and training at a psychoanalytic institute neither provided the conceptual tools to bridge therapy and politics nor teachers to model the political vocation and its virtues. I am going to say more about this in the next chapter, but for now I offer a few thoughts about psychoanalytic institutes and political vocation. First, institutes themselves need to affirm a political vocation by way of their mission statements or information about the institute. Positively, there are any number of institutes that affirm community outreach and have programs to address mental health issues in their communities (e.g., LA Institute) and to use psychoanalytic knowledge for the betterment of the society (e.g., Boston). A third of the institutes I examined also had anti-racism statements, which are clearly political statements. Most institutes affirm the use of psychoanalytic knowledge to address communal and societal issues. In my view, all of this is broadly political, yet in the 31 institutes or centers I explored there is, surprisingly, no mention of the political, which piques my analytic curiosity. Is there some anxiety about including the political in mission statements or information of the center? It may also be that the concept "political" is vague and can have different meanings for various people. But this is also true of concepts like "community" or "society," which may have fewer negative—anxiety-evoking—valences. I also suggest the absence of the concept of the political in mission statements or statements about the institute *is itself a political act*—in my view, an unfortunate one.

Let me stay with this. Psychoanalytic centers rightly need to be concerned about mental health issues in their local community and in the larger society. This moves them away from being preoccupied with the practice of psychoanalytic therapies in consulting rooms or clinics. This is to be commended. However, to be concerned about mental health in society necessarily entails attending to the systemic economic and political structures that are responsible for mental suffering—suffering that cannot be divorced from embodiment. By this I mean, to care about mental health includes being concerned about the material needs and realities of persons. A degraded environment impacts human beings physically and mentally. Similarly, concern for and about community and society includes being motivated to address issues of injustice and while anti-racism statements are important and necessary, they are not sufficient. It is not simply racism that is a political, economic, and social issue. There is also classism, sexism, ableism, and other instantiations of oppression and marginalization—all of which have mental, physical, and relation impacts. Add to this the climate emergency where people are experiencing varied forms of eco-distress (anxiety, guilt, sorrow, depression, despair, etc.), not to mention further stress associated with and exacerbated by political and economic injustices—injustices that impact human beings as well as other species. To my mind, all of this suggests that a psychoanalytic political vocation, expressed in community outreach and concern for society, is no longer a sufficient focus, at least in the Anthropocene Age. Yes, a center located in a city rightly needs to attend to local political and economic issues, but the climate emergency reveals that the local is connected to the universal.

I am in no way suggesting that a psychoanalytic center include all of the above in a mission statement or in their statements about the center. What I am arguing for is some clearer statements about the political vocation of the center/institute and how this political vocation is integral to addressing diverse issues associated with climate change. Naturally, this will require a great deal of thought and conversations among the members, and both are part of what it means to have a political vocation. The process of arriving at a statement that includes the institute's political vocation will serve as a model for those who are in analytic training and for those in the local community. Of course, ideally, mission statements have to be connected to curricula and outreach programs; otherwise, it is mere verbiage. This means that some attention needs to be paid to how the idea of therapists' political vocation is taught (and lived out), which I will say more about in the next chapter.

I wish to add one more thought. Analytic centers, while accredited by varied bodies, typically exist autonomously. Also, while some institutes are eclectic with regard to various analytic theories, some are Freudian, Kleinian, Lacanian, Relational, etc., which can lead to building psychoanalytic enclaves. All of this can result in a lack of collective engagement and cooperation around shared political and social concerns. This is evident in the history of psychoanalysis, which is fraught with mean-spirited divisions, instead of respectful contestations and disagreements that can lead to cooperation. If psychoanalysis and its institutes of learning embrace a political vocation given the climate emergency, it seems to me that we need to find ways to overcome the narcissism of our minor differences so that we can create ways to cooperate with each other, which from my perspective is an essential feature of any political vocation.

If moving to include a political vocation vis-à-vis psychoanalytic institutes seems overwhelming, it is, nevertheless, necessary given the truly terrifying realities of climate change. Psychoanalytic therapists are trained to recognize and metabolize intense affects in their work with patients. Analogously, leaders and members of analytic centers can ideally metabolize the feelings of being overwhelmed, so that an institute can live out its political vocation in the midst of an anxious and fearful world. Moreover, institutes, in affirming and modeling a political vocation, serve to link the political with (1) a particular type of critical thinking that entails raising the unconscious to consciousness, (2) exposing self-deceptions, (3) affirming the centrality of care for psychosocial well-being, and acts of care that precede, but are not contingent on hope, (4) living out anarchic relations (more on this in the next chapter), and (5) upholding nonviolent forms of resistance that render inoperative apparatuses that contribute to oppression and marginalization. Put another way, since psychoanalytic theories are premised on care and respect for patients, as well as care for families and communities, then care is extended to the polis, other species, and the earth.

All of this may strike someone as naïve or idealistic rather than *realpolitik*, whether I am addressing the political vocation of individual therapists or institutes of learning. Perhaps it is both, but for institutes and individual therapists to continue to operate without directly facing and engaging the political-economic and social realities of climate change, strikes me as a kind of tragic madness. It is as if we are caring for the psychological well-being of the passengers while the ship is sinking. We need to care for the psychosocial well-being of patients *and* live out a political vocation, which means, in my view, doing the work to facilitate cooperation within and between institutes (and other organizations) toward addressing the manifold issues associated with climate change.

## Conclusion

The sources for choosing a vocation adhere to the psychoanalytic notions of overdetermination and multiple function. My conscious motivation to be a therapist (and teacher) have familial roots, growing up with a depressed mother (see Roth, 1990) and, on one side of the family, a tradition of writers and scholars. We often gravitate toward the vocation that will provide a remedy for acknowledged and unacknowledged suffering. Yet some vocations are related to external events that beckon us to respond regardless of family history and neuroses. In Martin Luther King's (1998) autobiography, he recalls graduating with a doctorate and having intense conversations with his wife, Coretta, about whether they should return to the south. After living in the northern states, the Kings were reluctant to return to southern apartheid. King clearly felt called to minister and he was entertaining the call to serve as pastor of a Detroit church. Yet, after much discernment, Coretta and Martin felt the call to return to the south, and it was in answering this call that King gradually accepted his political vocation. Malcolm X (Haley, 1964), while in prison, converted to Islam. This conversion accompanied his finding and accepting his political vocation, criticizing racism, and seeking the emancipation of African Americans. In 2011, Gabby Giffords, a U.S. representative, was shot in the head, while meeting voters. Clearly, Representative Giffords had a political vocation prior to the shooting, but afterward she and her husband, Mark Kelly, formed an organization to work toward solving gun violence. Kelly, who was an astronaut, took up his political vocation, largely due to his wife and what happened to her. Today, the event of climate change and its attending environmental disasters call us to accept a political vocation that entails caring for human beings, other species, and the earth—our one and only home. Accepting a political vocation can and should take many forms, precisely because there are manifold needs and contexts. And accepting this vocation does not suggest that we must set aside our analytic vocation. Indeed, I have endeavored to argue that these vocations can go hand in hand and necessarily so in the Anthropocene Age. As Max Horkheimer presciently wrote, "The future of humanity depends on the existence today of the critical attitude" (as cited in Wolin, 2016b, p.231). So, like the Kings, Malcolm X, and the Giffords, taking up this vocation necessitates finding ways to develop a critical attitude, becoming gadflies, prophets, and analysts, and exposing faulty premises, injustices, and self-deceptions. This political vocation also requires creating and engaging in spaces of speaking and acting together, for in doing so we will, in our individual and collective caring, sustain and be sustained by others.

## Notes

1 Treaty of Versailles – Wikipedia, https://en.wikipedia.org/wiki/Treaty_of_Versailles, accessed 26 July 2022.
2 Obviously, Weber was writing during a time when men in Europe dominated political-economic spaces. Moreover, there was binary thinking about gender—men and women. While there have been strides in having women in politics, there remains the prevalence

of binary thinking regarding gender. Hopefully, we are seeing small changes in the West with regard to more inclusive political representation.

3   Donna Orange (2010) notes that Freud initially wanted to be a philosopher. He took a number of classes, though he later "contemptuously claimed that had nothing to contribute to his thinking" (p.3). Freud (1925) was later dismissive of philosophy, making sweeping generalizations that revealed, in my view, his ignorance of the depth and breadth of Western philosophies, as well as how these philosophies influenced his theories (pp.216–217). This may have been a reason why many psychoanalytic therapists have avoided engaging philosophy, which, I believe, is why Orange wrote a book about how philosophy can be used as a resource for clinicians.

4   Martha Nussbaum (2019) points out that Cicero believed there were only a few exceptions for citizens not to be engaged in political action. Otherwise, anyone else "is surely wrong to pursue a life that does not involve service to others through political action" (p.45). To be sure therapists have a clear calling to serve others in their work as therapists, but, as I will argue, they also have a political vocation, which I am confident Nussbaum and some past and present analytic therapists would agree.

5   Donna Orange's (2010) text is an attempt to show clinicians the utility of philosophy for their work as therapists. I could not agree more. However, there is an additional step to be taken, and that is to connect the critical thinking associated with the vocation of a therapist helping patients and the critical thinking needed for the therapist's vocation in and for political life.

6   One may wonder why Diogenes, who lived to be almost 90, was not put to death for corrupting the youth. I suspect it was easier to dismiss and ignore Diogenes because of his outrageous behavior. Perhaps passersby could simply avert their gaze and rush past him, much like many of us do when encountering houseless persons.

7   Jonathan Lear (1998), in exploring the work of Hans Loewald, writes, "transference is of its essence a form of political engagement" (p.132). Here we note the connection between transference in the consulting room and its relation to the polis.

8   Jan 6: New polling shows rising acceptance of political violence 1 year after insurrection|CNN Politics, https://www.cnn.com/2022/01/03/politics/jan-6-capitol-riot-political-violence-what-matters/index.html, accessed 18 July 2022.

9   Max Weber (2013/1919) argued that there are "three pre-eminent qualities" in a political vocation, namely, "passion, a feeling of responsibility, and a sense of proportion" (p.59). These are not necessarily virtues, but they are related to the exercise of the virtues of a political vocation.

10   There are 2,035 uses of the term "virtue" in the Psychoanalytic Electronic Publishing database, which comprises numerous volumes and over 70,000 articles. There are only 7 mentions of psychoanalytic "virtues," all except one coming in the last 20 years. Perhaps this stems from Freud's (one reference to the notion of virtue in his works) reluctance to join ethics to psychoanalysis, wishing to locate analysis in the scientific realm rather than religion or the arts.

# Chapter 7

# Psychoanalytic Education and Therapy in the Anthropocene Age

In Plato's Republic (Rouse, 1956, pp.312–320), Socrates offers Glaucon a parable regarding education, which many of us are now quite familiar. Prisoners are tethered in their chairs facing a wall and behind them is a road and a fire. The "puppet show-men" use varied instruments to project images on the wall, which the prisoners, talking together, name and take to be real. "Now consider," Socrates says, "what their release would be like and their cure from these fetters and their folly" (p.313). Socrates empathically imagines that if a prisoner is "compelled suddenly to stand up and turn his neck round, and to walk towards the firelight; all this would hurt him, and he would be too much dazzled to see distinctly those things whose shadows he had seen before" (p.313). Socrates is not finished. If the prisoner was "compelled to look towards the light, it would hurt his eyes….and would he not be distressed and furious at being dragged" (p.313). Then Socrates imagines the person, who has been freed, going back to his fellow prisoners. These fellow prisoners treat him with scorn and even death at the thought of having their world of images challenged (p.315).

While this parable is about the process and pain of education, Socrates' did not view this as simply something that takes place in the academy. Rather, he uses the parable to address the situation of the polis and those who govern—those who project images on the wall. Individuals who have awakened, who have contemplated painful truths, and who have recognized illusions have an ethical demand to return to the cave.

> Down you must go then, in turn, to the habitation of the others, and accustom yourselves to their darkness; for when you have grown accustomed you will see a thousand times better than those who live there, and you will know what the images are and what they are images of, because you have seen the realities behind just and beautiful and good things.
>
> (pp.318–319)

Lest this strike one as elitist, Socrates believed that those who have seen the light and awakened to the illusions of the images do not return to impart their wisdom to the ignorant. "Our belief," Socrates says,

> about these matters must be this, that the nature of education is not really such as some of its professors say it is; as you know, they say that there is not

DOI: 10.4324/9781003258827-10

understanding in the soul, but they put it in, as if they were putting sight into blind eyes....But our reasoning indicates...that this power is already in the soul of each and is the instrument by which each learns.

(pp.316–317)[1]

Each of us has the capacity for facing our illusions and cultivating wisdom. Those who return are not imparting reality, but educing what is already within a person. This education is necessary for the well-being of the polis.

While this capacity to "see" is within each of us, Socrates also recognized that what is potential needs a guide to facilitate actualizing the capacity. Indeed, Socrates modeled this by engaging in public conversations that were aimed at assisting persons in gaining clarity about their premises, their visions of reality. As noted in the last chapter, human beings need the gadfly, the prophet, and the public critic to be able to see that the images we cling to are mere illusions. And as Socrates knew firsthand, the process of seeing the truth is painfully disruptive.

The allegory of the cave strikes me as relevant with regard to psychoanalytic education and therapy. I remember, early in my first analysis, my training analyst told me that his initial experience of psychoanalytic therapy involved the painful realization that his virtues were not virtues at all. Later, I realized that he was, like Socrates, empathically telling me what lay ahead—the pain of disillusionment. There were occasions when I felt anger, not because I was compelled by my analyst to see, but because the process brought out aspects I did not want to face or work through, which fits with the allegory's point about the pain of seeing the light. There were also times of anxiety—an anxiety related to discovering yet another aspect of myself I had long overlooked. All of this said, it is not simply about the pain that comes from discovering truths. It is also about the potential for actualizing a greater sense of freedom, the pleasure of learning, the existential satisfaction that attends the deepening of one's life, and the taking up the ethical demand to care for others—to accustom ourselves to the plight of others—and the development of what is termed negative capability, which "is when a [person] is capable of being in uncertainty, mysteries, doubts, without irritable reaching after fact and reason" (letter John Keats wrote to George Keats, in Bion, 1970, p.125).

Using this allegory to depict, in part, the process and ends of psychoanalysis and psychoanalytic education seem apt. However, a problem arises when we take the allegory of the cave and separate it from its context, which, for Socrates, was the polis. Put differently, the cave for Socrates was not the individual's unconscious, but the social reality of the polis. In my view, and as indicated in the last chapter, the focus on the *individual* in psychoanalysis has largely been the case of believing the cave was the individual's unconscious.[2] Moreover, the truths of the Anthropocene Age reveal the illusion of simply viewing psychoanalytic education and therapy in terms of what takes place in the consulting room, wherein a therapist facilitates a patient becoming aware of what was previously unconscious. Put differently, the climate emergency invites us to reimagine psychoanalytic education and therapy, which involves a slight adjustment to both. In this final chapter,

I discuss the current status of psychoanalytic education in the United States, which I argue has inherent flaws when one considers the social, political, and economic realities of climate change. This discussion includes suggestions for making adjustments—adjustments that embrace a psychoanalytic political vocation and an attending political philosophy that require alterations in the training and education of analytic therapists. I then move to address how we might reimagine, *in part*, psychoanalytic therapy—at least for some patients.

Let me rush to make some qualifications. First, it is not possible to advance in detail changes to psychoanalytic education. There are individual institutes of learning, as well as governing and certifying bodies, which, no doubt, have differing views on education. Instead, I simply want to get conversations started—conversations (that include students) that can take place at individual institutes, as well as within larger organizations, like the APA (American Psychological Association, Division 39), American Psychoanalytic Association, International Psychoanalytic Association, to name a few. It is urgent that these conversations take place, and I suspect that younger generations of analytic therapists and analysands are eager to engage in these conversations. Second, I have been involved in higher education for over 25 years and, during that time, I spent three or four years at a psychoanalytic institute. I am not an expert in either education or psychoanalytic education, but I have experiences in both and rely on those in approaching this topic. This is to recognize and acknowledge my limits in this subject matter, but also to say that anyone concerned about or involved in learning and practicing analytic therapy should be part of this conversation. We should, in other words, not leave psychoanalytic education simply to the experts (training analysts, teachers) or the leaders (institutes' or organizations' presidents). Students and others ought to be included, especially given that they are the next generation and will bear the brunt of climate disasters. Third, in the following discussion on therapy, I am not claiming that this involves every patient. I am saying that, for some patients, given the appropriate timing, we need to address and discuss systemic realities that are the real sources of patients' suffering. Failing to do so simply colludes with and mystifies these sources.

## Psychoanalytic Education and the Anthropocene

When I started my analytic education at an institute in the late 1990s, I was introduced to the foundational works of Freud, though psychoanalytic literature was part of my graduate education and clinical internship. Each year entailed building on this foundation, exploring other theories that emerged during and after Freud's death. I recall coming home during that first year and talking to my partner about my frustrations with the education I was receiving. I said it felt more like indoctrination or catechism classes where one learns uncritically the dogmas and doctrines of the Catholic Church, and less like a graduate seminar in psychoanalysis, where one engages in critical discourses around the texts. This was all the more surprising because every student had at least a master's degree and most had terminal degrees.

In addition, we were so focused on the theories of various analytic schools that there was absolutely no discussion or attention paid to political issues and never once was climate change mentioned.[3] The latter may be excused considering that mainline media at that time largely ignored climate change, but the former is not excusable, in my opinion. My interpretation now is that the two leaders/educators of the institute (also training analysts) were engaged in intellectual formation of their analysands, focusing on the analysands' understanding (not critiquing) psychoanalytic theories and methods, especially the works of Freud. This institute, like others, was also interested in forming our identities as psychoanalysts, which included intellectual formation and practice—analytic skills and virtues. The success of the institute was measured by gaining certification and graduating students. This is understandable, but perhaps we need to reconsider education, training, and certification, given the dire realities that we face.

I ought not to rely on my experiences of psychoanalytic education from over two decades ago at one institute as a basis for critique or suggestions regarding psychoanalytic education in general. So, I explored and examined the websites of 31 analytic centers in the United States, reading their mission statements, educational programs, and, if available, their syllabi. Let me first acknowledge a great deal takes place in any educational endeavor that is not covered by the syllabi or the institution's stated aims. However, we can learn a great deal by what is stated and what is excluded. Of the 31 centers, as noted in the previous chapter, not one mentioned the term "political" and there was no mention of the climate emergency. To be fair, several institutes mentioned their commitment to dealing with social and communal issues, but this leaves the majority of centers without a word in that direction. Two institutes clearly addressed class, race, and immigration in their curricula. Also, about ten centers had statements about antiracism, which indicates they are taking a political stance. This is to be commended and encouraged, but there are three possible problems and questions. First, do antiracism statements shape analytic education at their respective institutes? Is the issue of racism dealt with in courses analysands take? Since racial biases are embedded in our collective psyches (the United States), are these addressed in training analyses? As far as I could tell by reading the syllabi, the answer is, at best, maybe. Second, does an antiracism stance include issues of environmental racism that are evident in most major cities in which many of these centers are ensconced? Third, while racism is a key issue, why only this issue? Why not sexism, classism, and, of course, the climate emergency? Naturally, someone may respond that institutes cannot do it all. They have to pick their battles. Yet, the NPAP (National Psychological Association for Psychoanalysis) has a vision statement[4] that is brief and broad: "Creating a more humane world through the transformative power of psychoanalysis." Creating a humane world is a large and complicated task, which would include addressing political issues such as racism, classism, sexism, and other forms of oppression and marginalization. And, of course, all of these issues intersect with the climate emergency. I am not saying this has to be the main focus, but the very absence of naming the realities of climate change and attending forms of exploitation of Othered human beings, other species, and the earth is a political and educational stance that is deeply problematic. Let me add, one does not have to be an expert on these issues to include them in mission statements, course schedules, and training analyses.

There may also be systemic issues with psychoanalytic education. When I started, the leaders of the institute, in concert with the accrediting body, developed curricula aimed at obtaining certification. From one perspective, this is all quite logical. Those who have obtained the requisite education/certification and who have been practicing for some years are deemed to have more knowledge and authority for developing the curriculum for intellectual and practical education. Students, then, are deemed to lack the knowledge and skills necessary to function as analysts. Most educational institutions operate out of the master-apprentice or pedagogical epistemological model, which has its obvious truths and advantages. There are, however, two weaknesses of this model and its attending views of authority. First, analysands are not children. As stated above, all have graduate education degrees; more often than not they have certification/licensure and attending professional experiences. Second, a hierarchy is established, which accompanies significant differences in power relations. Teachers and training analysts become the gatekeepers. Using Arendt's notion of speaking and acting together, hierarchies, in varying degrees, diminish spaces of speaking and acting together for those who are considered be on the lower rungs of the hierarchy. Analysands, in other words, have little or no power to decide what issues are relevant in their psychoanalytic education. To be fair, some institutes include a student on their academic committees. The institute I attended did, but this was largely a token, because it had little if any impact on the curricula or structure, let alone the conflicts that emerged between the leaders.

To continue with the issue of hierarchy, there is a subtle air of sovereignty in analytic education.[5] Those on accrediting bodies make sovereign decisions about what analytic educational requirements are needed to obtain certificate/licensure. Leaders of analytic centers determine the curricula and assign training analysts. Together, they decide who is and who is not an analyst. To recall a previous chapter on sovereignty, this analogy seems to fall short since those in leadership do not exercise the state of exception and political violence. But any cursory reading of the histories of psychoanalysis, clearly reveals mean-spiritedness or cruelty directed at those deemed to be apostates. Long before states became involved in licensure (in the United States), the major certifying body allowed only medical doctors to become and be called psychoanalysts. Is that not parallel to the state of exception, wherein the sovereign and sovereign classes decide who is a citizen and who is not? Does not cruelty that creates division and psychological harm (in some instances) represent a kind of political violence evident in some institutes and organizations? The vicious conflict between two leaders of the institute I attended may not be seen as political violence, but in some ways it represented a fight to "rule" over the institute, with no doubt each side possessing legitimate reasons for seeking to assume control.

What does all of this have to do with climate change and psychoanalytic education? First, let me begin with a general claim. We need to ask what is learned, consciously and unconsciously, when students are involved in an educational process where hierarchy exists and thrives? It seems to me that one thing they learn (or is reinforced) is that this is the "natural" state of affairs, which means that (1) the process will continue and (2) imagination is stifled with regard to doing things differently. Put another way, students internalize views of authority and dependency, as if these cannot be questioned. Rebels and heretics are excluded and held up as examples to be avoided. Sometimes, we note in psychoanalytic history, rebels and heretics beginning their own schools, yet bringing along pedagogical, hierarchical models of educating students into their theories. In terms of the issue of climate change, I have anecdotal experience of listening to several analysands who struggle with and in their institutes precisely because leaders are not listening to students' desires to address issues associated with climate change in the institute's mission and curricula. These students, who are colleagues, are the next generation, and they will continue to experience not only the effects of climate change, but also patients who struggle with eco-anxiety, despair, sorrow, etc. As noted above, these are people who have graduate education and professional experiences. They are licensed therapists, who have partners, children, and a great deal of life experience. Nevertheless, they face institutional resistance, which I argue is due in large part because of hierarchical models of leadership/organization and pedagogical learning models and methods.

I recognize that a great deal of collegiality can and does take place between analysands and leaders/teachers. I also acknowledge that there are likely institutes that work diligently to be inclusive to analysands' perspectives. However, the background of hierarchical educational, certifying structures and attending pedagogical models are present, thereby shaping subjectivities and spaces of speaking and acting together. While there is much to value in psychoanalytic institutes of education, they tend to be resistant to change. They are, in other words, like other educational institutions—conservative (in the sense of maintaining a tradition) and sluggish in adapting to a changing world. When we consider the dire realities of climate change, Clayton Crockett's (2012) mandate comes to mind: "We need to experiment radically with new ways of thinking and living, because the current [Western] paradigm is in a state of exhaustion, depletion, and death" (p.165). In reference to psychoanalytic education, this is a bit dramatic, but there is some truth in it. Any educational institution that continues to ignore the political, economic, and cultural issues associated with climate emergency is one that is colluding with the trajectory of the loss of the biodiverse earth necessary for the dwelling of human beings and millions of other species.

This critical perspective elicits a question regarding how psychoanalytic education and training can change. While this is something that analytic centers and accrediting/professional bodies need to engage, I offer a few thoughts for conversation. Recall that in Chapter 3 I critiqued the issue of sovereignty, opting in the end for anarchic ways of organizing belonging, which I contend has developmental roots in good-enough parent-infant relations. By framing anarchic relations and belonging in this way, neither shies away from the reality of asymmetrical power between parent and child nor the responsibility of parental leadership. This analogy breaks down a bit when referring to institutes that are involved in the education of adults. However, some principles can be carried over. In good-enough parent-infant relations, parents gradually cede parts of their leadership role and power as children actualize their potentialities. Eventually, parents are no longer leaders or hold power, because their children are recognized as capable of engaging the world without the parents. Ideally, what remains is cooperation, which includes contestation and repair among equals. The principle here with regard to anarchic relations is that leadership and the exercise of power are fluid—open to the exercise of power and leadership from others. Using this perspective, analytic centers can work to remove educational hierarchies, replacing them with andragogical methods and relations of equality. Students should have a clear voice and power in making decisions about their analytic education and training, which does not mean rejecting expectations and standards, but it does mean being open to amending these. In my view, students can also take on leadership positions, since many may have the qualities and capacities to lead—even though they may not have completed their analytic education or training. When I think back to my time at an institute, I remember two students who should have been in charge. They had more education and more experiences in effective leadership than the established leaders had; they were more thoughtful and possessed virtues that were lacking in the two leaders who were certified analysts with decades of experience. If those students had been the leaders, I am confident that institute would have navigated the conflict and crisis.

A critic may raise the concern that anarchic relations will be messier, even chaotic. Anarchy has been continually tagged as the harbinger of chaos, which strikes fear in those who are dependent on hierarchies to organize belonging. This said, I do think anarchic organizations can be messy because of their dynamic nature, but it is also the case that hierarchically organized institutions can be messy, conflicted, and even chaotic. This said, the messiness of anarchic relations is attributed to their fluidity, which accompanies flexibility in adapting to changing times and crises. Granted, to be effective, psychoanalytic institutes that adopt anarchic structures will require more psychological and relational work, because they cannot rely on hierarchical relations to demand adherence to established rules, expectations, etc. Put another way, more attention may be needed to cultivate cooperation, which will require collective work on the capacities for emotional regulation and repair.

Another feature of anarchic educational and training institutes entails the cultivation of ungovernable selves, which is, in part, a goal vis-à-vis some therapies—more on this below. In an earlier chapter, I noted that Agamben posits that potentiality for human beings includes the ability to not actualize their potentiality. "*Human beings,*" Agamben (2004) writes, "*are the animals who are capable of their own impotentiality*" (p.182). I also indicated that Winnicott (1965) held a similar idea when he claimed that children had a "right not to communicate" (p.179)—to prefer not to communicate. Part of a good-enough parent's discernment is to find ways to recognize, accept, and nurture children's appropriate exercise of their impotentiality, which does not mean that there are no consequences for "preferring not to." By "appropriate," I mean the exercise of impotentiality that does not harm the child or others. An ungovernable self, I argued, is one who has developed the capacity to actualize impotentiality—preferring not to render apparatuses, including psychoanalytic educational apparatuses, inoperative.

Adam Phillips holds an analogous view. He (1993) writes, "With the discovery of transference Freud evolved what could be called a cure by idolatry; in fact, potentially, a cure of idolatry, through idolatry. But the one thing psychoanalysis cannot cure, when it works, is belief in psychoanalysis" (p.121). This is echoed when he writes, "The problem with (and for) psychoanalysts has always been that they had to believe in psychoanalysis" (2021a, p.118). Later, Phillips (2021b) remarks that "Psychoanalytic treatment is an antidote to indoctrination" (p.23).[6] From my perspective, a cure for idolatry or an antidote to indoctrination entails facilitating the development and exercise of the capacity for impotentiality or for an ungovernable self vis-à-vis the analyst. An educational institute, it seems to me, needs to find ways to cultivate this in their analysands and in themselves, if they are to facilitate the ungovernable selves of their patients.

For an anxious reader, let me quickly say that ungovernable selves do not mean this is a Hobbesian state of nature where everyone is an individual acting on their own desires, leading to chaos and violence. Agamben's notion of impotentiality or ungovernable self is simply a key aspect of the capacities for human freedom and creativity. Winnicott's creative use of the psychoanalytic tradition depended, in part, on his critical engagement with this tradition, which, in turn, meant he exercised his capacity for impotentiality, rendering Freud's work inoperative—to a degree. Indeed, I think that Winnicott's notion of play or spontaneity fits well with Agamben's notion of impotentiality. Spontaneity suggests freedom to prefer not to abide by the rules, without destroying the rules. Put differently, impotentiality creates a space for a person to be spontaneous and creative. Winnicott also said one cannot be creative without tradition, but he should have added that the vitality of any tradition requires people exercising their impotentiality. So, an ungovernable self does not blindly rebel against traditions or institutions. An ungovernable self critically, thoughtfully, and creatively engages tradition with the aim of addressing new problems or challenges, which in the Anthropocene Age are many.

In terms of analytic education and training, it seems to me that andragogical education cultivates a critical intelligence that includes choosing to exercise one's impotentiality—an ungovernable self. I contend that this means facilitating freedom, creativity, and change. It is, to my mind, unfortunate when institutes develop loyal disciples of a psychoanalytic school/tradition. Loyal disciples can, of course, be brilliant and creative defenders of orthodoxy, but they are unlikely to exercise their ungovernable selves, which curtails a kind of imagination and freedom to think out of, if not without, a box. Psychoanalytic institutes, I believe, can foster anarchic structures to cultivate students' ungovernable selves, because ungovernable selves are needed to create new paradigms of thinking, belonging, and dwelling.

I need to make two clarifications since I am relying on Agamben's notion of inoperativity. In surveying the works of Agamben, Adam Kotsko (2020) argues that Agamben believed Western

> ideologies and institutions…thoughtlessly, heedlessly, and quasi-automatically produce and reproduce the structures and categories that define the Western world. The term (anthropological machine) highlights at once the artificiality or contingency of the ideology or institution in question and the necessity of stopping it—rather than tinkering with it while it is still in operation, for instance—in order to make space for a substitute.
>
> (pp.108–109)

Impotentiality and the ungovernable self, in this context, seek to render inoperative apparatuses that, for example, produce the ontological rift. On the one hand, cultivating ungovernable selves would mean making inoperative Western traditions that produce and maintain the ontological rift. To make these traditions inoperative, a space is cleared to implement relations where there is no rift. On the other hand, Agamben was not talking about all traditions. So, in terms of analytic education, ungovernable selves are not aiming to stop the psychoanalytic tradition, but rather to tinker with it. What needs to be stopped in the analytic tradition (and its educational institutes) are those aspects of tradition that wittingly or unwittingly support or collude with the ontological rift.

Agamben also views inoperativity vis-à-vis institutions and traditions as making possible a new use of these traditions. When we consider the creativity within the analytic tradition, we observe the emergence of new schools of thought (e.g., Lacanian, Kleinian, British Independents, Adlerian, Relational, Self-Psychology) that were the result of critique and, if you will, inoperativity. In many cases, the creativity that led to the development of these new schools ossified into their own traditions. The point here is that analytic training should nurture persons' capacities for exercising impotentiality, which is, I contend, a necessary feature of both critical awareness and creativity.

Let me add another part of the story. After the third or fourth year at the institute, my partner made an observation. Cindy said, "I thought the reason for your joining the institute was to have fun and for colleagueship. Over the last six months you come home annoyed, frustrated, and sometimes hurt." It was one of those moments when one slaps his forehead. Of course, Cindy was right. After some soul-searching, I decided to exercise my ungovernable self and impotentiality, preferring not to continue, rendering inoperative the institute's (and accrediting) expectations rules, etc. I continued my analysis with a Jungian therapist, who was practicing on his own. He was not, in other words, another training analyst. Moreover, I continue to use psychoanalytic theories to understand the work I do as a therapist, and I have never stopped writing analytic articles and books. According to accrediting bodies, I am not a psychoanalyst, which is a consequence of my preferring not, of exercising my ungovernable self. What really has changed as a result was not much at all. In this example, the institute and its leaders did not cultivate the exercise of impotentiality. Instead, it was a strict hierarchy, where education entailed a catechetical approach to psychoanalytic doctrine/theory. To encourage and nurture inoperativity requires leaders and teachers to metabolize anxiety and fear about change, about people critiquing, playing with, and creating new ideas. I suspect some centers of training are better at this than others.

There is another related area of psychoanalytic education (and professional organizations) to address. As far as I can tell, every institute attends to the issues of ethics regarding analytic therapies. While Freud was wary of engaging ethics directly (Hale, 1971, pp.98–99), analytic institutes and accrediting bodies recognize that ethics is central to the practice of therapy. Yet, Franz Fanon and the staff of the Lafargue clinic did not see the ethics of the psychoanalyst as confined to the consulting room. It is not simply the patient who is invited to decide to act toward the real social sources of suffering; the analyst is as well. Fanon, for example, was very involved in postcolonial movements to liberate people. Would it have been ethical for him to treat patients and do nothing about the very sources that created their suffering? What would it mean to treat people and help them get better so they can go back into the very system that caused the suffering? It would be like treating a shell-shocked soldier so that he could get better and return to the madness of war. At best, this would be ethically ambiguous, at least for some people. If we turn to the present, Donna Orange (2017) offers a radical ethics, which means that analysts do not simply have a responsibility to care for their patients; they also have a responsibility to engage in the social-political-economic realm to address the sources of psychological and material sufferings (regardless of whether evident in their practice) associated with climate change (and related political-economic injustices). I am not suggesting that every therapist or student become an activist or revolutionary, like Fanon, but I am suggesting that institutes include in their education political ethics that embrace acting responsibly vis-à-vis larger systemic realities that are causes of suffering. This is particularly important given the global political, economic, and social issues associated with climate change. Indeed, a psychoanalytic ethics that is focused simply and solely on practice and is disconnected from political-economic realities is an impoverished ethics, if not itself unethical with regard to the education of therapists and the practice of psychotherapy.

Much of psychoanalytic education is understandably insular. Centers and institutes navigate within the epistemological realms of varied psychoanalytic schools. These centers also are focused on what is taking place in their locale, seeing how they might contribute to their communities. All of this is reminiscent of other educational systems, especially those of higher education. Even within these institutions, there is a good deal of creating epistemological silos, with disciplines creating their own language that creates barriers vis-à-vis other disciplines. I am suggesting that, given the complexities of the Anthropocene Age, institutes reach out not only to other analytic institutes, but to other disciplines. As I mentioned in the previous chapter, finding ways to cooperate with other institutes around issues of climate change can result in more effective action as well as mutual support. It would also model for students the importance of creating spaces of cooperation with other organizations. In my imagination, this would include inviting people from other disciplines to speak about climate change. Since climate change impacts all life, we need voices of people from diverse disciplines and locations to participate in conversations and actions.

Most psychoanalytic institutes and centers no doubt do well in educating students and engaging their local community. My sketching out some critiques and offering some thoughts are not meant to suggest these centers are deficient. Instead, I am inviting a conversation about how the realities of climate change might alter how people think about analytic education and training. The Anthropocene Age invites everyone to reconsider the ways we go about work, play, and our ways of dwelling and belonging. To my mind, andragogical methods, anarchic structures, the cultivation of ungovernable selves, climate-informed psychoanalytic ethics, and cooperation with other institutes, organizations, and disciplines are possible avenues in making changes to analytic education and training.

## Psychoanalytic Therapy and Climate Change

In this section, I consider how climate change might emend, if only slightly, how we think about the aims and process of analytic therapies for some patients. I begin by offering some general comments about the key factors associated with the process of psychoanalytic therapy. This lays the groundwork for discussing the aims of psychoanalysis, which are then framed in terms of patients dealing with the present and future impacts of climate change. From here, a couple of illustrations taken from my work are proffered, recognizing that names and details are altered to protect anonymity. As in the previous section, let me stress that the perspective offered here is not definitive, but rather seeks to initiate conversations about the craft of psychoanalytic therapy in the Anthropocene Age.

Psychoanalytic therapies are largely hermeneutical endeavors between therapists and patients, wherein therapists rely on particular analytic theories to understand patient-therapist communications. This process, as Freud (1926) recognized, depends on patients' trust of both the therapist and the process. This trust, which is, at times, imbued with positive and negative transferences (and countertransferences), is necessary for the work of therapy and in moving toward its aims. Put another way, trust is necessary for patients' willingness to be vulnerable and this is necessary for change (Phillips, 2021a, 2021b). A patient's trust depends on a therapist's genuine care for and about the patient, which means that the therapist recognizes and treats the individual as a person—a unique, valued, inviolable, and responsive subject. Care, which is the very condition for this hermeneutical enterprise of speaking and acting together, is foundational, as argued in previous chapters, for individuals to undergo a change—for actualizing their potentiality—potentialities blocked by neuroses, traumas, etc.

Since care is foundational to therapy, then how is this distinguished from other therapies or other forms of caring relationships of speaking and acting together?

A key feature of analytic therapies, going back to Freud, is raising the unconscious to consciousness. This has parallels to Plato's cave, but with obvious differences, the most apparent is that analysis is not claiming to facilitate a process of attaining the contemplation of truth, especially when "truth" is framed in terms of eternal ideal forms. Rather, the analytic process is facilitating, with varying degrees of confidence, patients' coming to terms with what they have repressed, confronting their cherished illusions that were believed to be truths, and facing their self-deceptions. This implies that the therapist is in a position to be able to "see" the unconscious, illusions, and self-deceptions, which needs some qualifications, not the least of which is that therapists also possess unconscious material that shapes and, at times, distorts their perceptions and interpretations. The therapist, then, is neither a guru of truth nor a prophet. Rather, analytic therapists must be willing to engage in their own work of attending to their unconscious, their illusions, and their self-deceptions. This is accomplished by entering into analysis (during and after training—analysis interminable), engaging in supervisory or consultative relationships, attending and being open to patients' stated and unstated cues and corrections (Casement, 1985), and the ongoing cultivation of the discipline of self-analysis and analytic reverie (Ogden, 1997). In this sense, the therapists' care for patients includes doing their own work, which facilitates patients' trust to be vulnerable and to surrender to the analytic process of exploration.

In my view, psychoanalysis is not simply directed toward raising what is unconscious to consciousness. The very context of the emergence of psychoanalysis was individuals' mental sufferings and trying to find ways to alleviate or perhaps to come to terms with this suffering. There is in this also an emancipatory element. By engaging in therapy, patients may be able to put the past in the past, instead of past traumas being alive in the present (Winnicott, 1971) and interfering with their agency and flourishing. In this painful work (one patient called it barbaric), they are mostly liberated from the terrors of the past, which frees them to participate more fully in their relationships and vocations. Freedom may be experienced in terms of having greater insight and differentiation vis-à-vis their motivations and desires. There is also a sense of flourishing when people feel freer to exercise previously restrained potentialities. Bertha Pappenheim leaps to mind as an example. After telling Freud to listen, she initiated a talking therapy that freed her to exercise her agency, which she later developed further in her activism on the behalf of women oppressed by patriarchal societies.

Of course, people may enter analysis with other motivations. People may enter psychoanalytic training and undergo analysis with the aim not of alleviating their suffering, but of experiencing and learning about the analytic process. Others may seek analysis as a process of deepening their lives. Still others may enter analysis to become more adept as marriage and family therapists.

Analytic therapists like Frantz Fanon, Joel Kovel, Andrew Samuels, Lynn Layton, Jessica Benjamin, and the therapists of the LaFargue clinic in Harlem argue that there is more to psychoanalytic therapy than simply or merely exploring a patient's family of origin and unconscious with the aims of psychic freedom and flourishing. When, in Fanon's (2008/1952) context, patients' mental suffering is clearly the result of political, economic, and social forces, the aims of therapy are (a) "to *'consciousnessize'* [the patient's] unconscious, to no longer be tempted by a hallucinatory lactification," and (b) "to enable [the patient] to choose an action with respect to the *real source of the conflict*, i.e., the social structure" (p.80; emphasis mine). Fanon was echoing the therapists of the Lafargue clinic in Harlem who sought "to give each bewildered patient an insight into the relation between his problems and his (racist) environment, and out of this understanding to reforge the will" (Ellison, 1995/1953, p.302). Patients' unconscious, their self-deceptions, and repressions are often the result of systemic political and economic apparatuses that mystify the sources of their suffering (Cushman, 1995, 2019). In some ways, psychological therapies that have focused on individuals and their mental suffering have functioned unwittingly to collude with political-economic apparatuses that are sources of their suffering (Cvetkovich, 2012; Dufour, 2008; Rogers-Vaughn, 2016; Silva, 2013). Add to this Andrew Samuel's (1993) contention that all patients and analysts have political selves—selves developed in relation to the dominant political-economic milieu that also shapes households and parenting. All of this indicates the necessity of paying careful attention to how larger structures and forces shape our subjectivities and, in particular, patients' sufferings.

While the brutality of colonizing nations and the specter of racism and other forms of oppression that Fanon and others experienced continue today, we are also facing climate disasters and their impacts on mental and material suffering of untold millions of people (Andrews & Hoggett, 2019; Antadze, 2020; Clayton, 2020; Clayton & Manning, 2018; Comtesse, Ertl, Hengst, Rosner, & Smid, 2021; Fredericks, 2021; Grouse, 2020; Parenti, 2011; Sassen, 2014). If we ignore the political and economic realities associated with climate change, therapy will then function to collude with political-economic apparatuses implicated in patients' suffering and to mystify the real sources of their suffering. This said, I am not suggesting this is the case for all patients. Some patients' struggles may have little or no relation to larger social-political forces, such as someone struggling with schizophrenia or manic-depressive illnesses. Though, even in these cases, I think it is prudent for therapists to at least reflect on the possibility of some connection, since these illnesses have cultural-political meanings and treatments (see Sass, 1992). The reason for stressing this is because of the long history of Western therapies that are focused on medical-psychological diagnoses, which elide political and economic sources of suffering. To return to the focus of mental suffering and the Anthropocene Age, it becomes clear that, given the varied political-economic apparatuses implicated in the climate emergency and attending mental suffering, analytic therapists need to address these sources when appropriate, as well as consider how these systemic apparatuses are impacting their own psychic well-being.

Let me add to Fanon's view of therapy, which has implications for therapy during the Anthropocene Age. To facilitate patients becoming aware of the real social sources of their suffering so that they can decide to act in relation to these sources can be understood in terms of the ungovernable self, which I contend is an aim of psychoanalytic therapy for some (maybe most) patients. Above I noted that the process of therapy can be seen as assisting patients to actualize their potentialities, which have been thwarted by traumas, family inhibitions, or societal oppressions and marginalization. A trans patient who has been demonized by their family and the culture can actualize their sense of self more fully in relations where they are accepted, understood, and valued, whether that is in therapy or in their participation in an affirming community. Actualizing potentiality includes actualizing one's capacity for impotentiality—preferring not to. The cultivation of the capacity for impotentiality is the process of developing an ungovernable self. This is what Fanon and others were trying to facilitate in their work with patients. An ungovernable self is able to prefer not to actualize the expectations of political, economic apparatuses that are implicated in the suffering of persons—themselves or others. A trans person, for instance, develops the impotentiality of an ungovernable self by preferring not to accept and participate in the larger culture's attempts to marginalize them by forcing them to accept binary understanding of sexuality. In terms of the Anthropocene Age, the cultivation of an ungovernable self depends on identifying the social, political, and economic sources of eco-distress and choosing actions to render these apparatuses inoperative. As mentioned before, this is not to suggest that these apparatuses are rendered ineffective. Rather, the ungovernable self is differentiated from these apparatuses and chooses not to operate out of the apparatuses' grammar. I add here that the emergence of an ungovernable self, whether in therapy or other venues, cannot take place without a corresponding conscious critical awareness of the apparatuses and their functions. When Fanon indicates that the aim of analytic therapy is to raise to consciousness the real social sources of suffering, he is, in my view, referring to facilitating the capacities for critical self-reflection (and differentiation) and impotentiality—the hallmarks of ungovernable selves.

All of this presumes that the analytic therapist possesses the capacities for critical reflection and impotentiality associated with an ungovernable self. If Fanon, for instance, had ignored or colluded with French colonizing apparatuses, he would have not exercised his critical reflective capacity or capacity for impotentiality, which would have meant his interactions with patients would not have facilitated their ungovernable selves. This, of course, does not mean patients cannot develop ungovernable selves on their own. To move to the Anthropocene, therapists who ignore climate change or compartmentalize (separating climate realities and their apparatuses from the therapy room) will likely misdiagnose patients' eco-distress, as well as fail to facilitate patients' critical reflective capacities and their capacities for impotentiality—at least in relation to apparatuses associated with climate change. If this is the case, it is not simply non-optimal therapy; it is unethical. It would be akin to the staff at the Lafargue clinic having set aside the realities of racism or Fanon having ignored the apparatuses of colonization.

I wish to qualify this. Freud's work with Bertha Pappenheim, from my perspective, can be seen, in part, as facilitating Bertha's ungovernable self. However, Bertha's ungovernable self and exercise of impotentiality were evident when she told Freud to listen. If Freud had refused, I suspect therapy would have ended. To his credit, Freud listened, but I am fairly confident he had, at the time, no clue as to the patriarchal social-political apparatuses implicated in Bertha's suffering. Apparently, Bertha did or later recognized the political-economic sources of her suffering, which is evident in her political activism. Therapy with Bertha would have been optimal if Freud had recognized the social-political apparatuses of her suffering and, at an appropriate time, facilitated her recognition of these apparatuses. Let's imagine that Bertha had a good idea, though perhaps it was latent. Failure to address this clearly would have meant colluding with these apparatuses. Freud was not likely aware that patriarchy shaped his work and was linked to Bertha's struggles, yet when Bertha told him to be quiet, she was exercising her capacity for impotentiality, preferring not to submit to the patriarchal grammar of the doctor-patient relationship. Nevertheless, even without Freud's recognition, therapy, while not optimal, was good-enough. This said, if Freud had been aware and had chosen not to explore this, the therapy would be, in part, unethical, even though it might have had positive results. To return to the present, it may be that some therapists have little or no idea of how climate change and associated apparatuses are implicated in patients' distress. Therapy, of course, can still have benefits. However, therapists who are aware of climate change and its sources and do not address this when encountering patients who are suffering eco-distress are mystifying the real social-political sources of patients' sufferings, which is unethical.

One more comment about doing therapy in the Anthropocene. I have been addressing the facilitation of impotentiality and the ungovernable self in relation to apparatuses that are sources of material and psychosocial suffering. As the illustrations below suggest, I am fairly comfortable in doing this when appropriate, depending on the patient and the timing. I am much less confident about addressing a more complicated issue associated with the ontological rift and its attending instrumental relations with regard to other species. As mentioned in previous chapters, the apparatuses that produce and maintain the ontological rift give rise to subjectivities whereby people overlook or legitimate the exploitation of other species and the earth. It seems to me that becoming aware of the sources of psychosocial distress and exercising one's impotentiality would include altering one's relations to other species and the earth, but that is not necessarily the case in many instances. Many people are concerned about climate change and are acting to make changes in their lives to reduce their carbon footprint, while also being active politically in gaining traction in climate action. Yet, many people continue to ignore the sufferings of other species and how their suffering is the result of apparatuses of anthropocentrism and corresponding ontological rift. Factory farms, experimentation on other species, etc., are overlooked, denied, or even justified. This is not surprising given the fact that people who become aware of their own oppression may not extend compassion to others and, worse, even be implicated in their suffering. Conservative Israelis, for instance, rightly recognize and lament the Holocaust and prejudice against Jews, while at the same time oppressing and marginalizing Palestinians. So, a patient may become aware of the social-political sources of their eco-distress, while not developing empathy or compassion toward the sufferings of other species. The lingering question is what to do about this in therapy, and here my answer is on shaky ground, because I have not done so. That said, with those patients who are anxious about climate change, many of them do manifest empathy and compassion toward the sufferings of other species, though, more often than not, they feel helpless or powerless to do anything. When this does come up in therapy, I do address it, not only in terms of the sense of helpless and that it does not have to define whether one acts. This includes exploring the types of actions patients would be motivated to do vis-à-vis the sufferings of other species. That said, I am less confident in bringing up this topic in a direct way, as if I am educating the patient about how they should develop empathy for other species— empathy that involves exercising one's impotentiality regarding the apparatuses that produce and maintain the ontological rift. This said, depending on the person and timing, I feel more confident asking how their critical awareness (and inoperativity) alters how they see and treat themselves, others, and the world. This may or may not open some conversation about actions associated with preferring not to act out of the grammars of apparatuses that produce the ontological rift.

I now turn to two illustrations. Sue (36), a very bright and accomplished woman, was married and had two children (8, 6). The reason for beginning therapy was the stress associated with taking on a new job that demanded more travel and work responsibilities. For the most part, as a couple and as parents, Sue and her husband were finding ways to manage this, yet Sue often felt torn between her career advancement as an engineer and her family life. There is much I could say about her work in therapy, but for my purposes I want to focus on one segment of our time together. After six months, Sue came in the office and seemed anxious and distressed. Over the weekend, she, for reasons she was not sure, started to read a recent climate change report that was published by leading climate scientists. As Sue read the document, she grew more anxious, helpless, and conflicted. It was not that she and her husband were oblivious of the impacts of climate change. Indeed, they had hybrid vehicles, recycled, did not use chemicals on their lawn, planted trees, and had talked about getting solar panels for their house. Most of her anxiety was in relation to her children. Their future looked pretty bleak, and Sue felt helpless about being able to do anything about that. At the same time, Sue felt conflicted, because she traveled frequently and worked for a company that had a large carbon footprint. Indeed, it was an engineering company that did nothing about climate change.

After reading the report, she talked with her husband, Gary. Gary agreed, saying he had similar thoughts, feelings, and concerns. What did not sit well with Sue was Gary's method of coping, even though she completely understood it. Sue said that Gary's approach was to focus on loving their kids and doing what they could in their own lives about reducing their carbon footprint. After acknowledging her feelings, I asked Sue what her method was or what method she would like to develop and implement. "When I am confronted with a seemingly insurmountable problem at work," she responded, "I usually do a deep dive into the issue, believing that a solution will appear with the more data I obtain." "In this situation," she went on, "I am not sure that will work. I would still be anxious and helpless, because the problem is too massive and complicated for one person or a hundred people to solve." I responded that her typical method was aimed at solving an engineering problem and, in this case, she knew it would be a fantasy to hold onto this. I suggested that she might retain the method and let the aim(s) emerge, rather than nurturing her fantasy of solving problems. I also wondered aloud if her fantasies about finding a silver bullet might persist, as if she and others could magically find an engineering solution to our climate ills. This made sense to Sue, because she recognized that her fantasies emerged in relation to her anxiety and helplessness.

Over the next six months, Sue did a great deal of research about climate change, which included identifying systemic political and economic sources of climate change, as well as possible solutions or responses that scientists, engineers, and climate activists were developing. Gary and Sue installed solar panels on their house. Sue also began to explore the possibility of shifting her engineering acumen and skills to a company actively engaged in developing products that addressed diverse climate issues. One afternoon, Sue arrived, declaring with some zeal that she was taking a position in a regional engineering company that was focused solely on engineering issues and products that had to do with climate change. "The icing on the cake is that I will have much less travel and more time with my husband and kids," she remarked. Sue also said that her company supports engineers who get involved in their local communities, which she intended to do, though she was not quite sure what that might look like.

> Some of the research I have done over the past year has revealed how climate change has even more negative impacts on poor persons and persons of color. In our city, there are clear examples of environmental racism, which concerns me.

In our later conversations, Sue acknowledged that the anxiety, helplessness, and conflict remained. The future for her kids was not any brighter, but Sue felt that her actions were constructive (and healthy) responses to managing anxiety, and she also felt a little less helpless and conflicted. In my view, Sue began exercising her ungovernable self, by recognizing the real political-economic sources of her eco-affects and deciding, in part, to prefer not (actualizing impotentiality) to engage in practices and structures/systems that were exacerbating climate change. Of course, it would be impossible to completely "prefer not" to engage in capitalism, but she could work for a company that sought to address issues of climate change. Sue obviously did most of the work in developing an ungovernable self, while my role was facilitating conversation, exploration, and the capacity for impotentiality.

It is necessary to mention that facilitating the development and exercise of the capacity for impotentiality or an ungovernable self is not a remedy for Sue's eco-distress. As Adam Phillips (2021b) notes, "The analyst provides a setting to facilitate growth, as opposed to applying a remedy to solve a problem" (p.29).

In this case, the problem is the eco-distress (anxiety, helplessness, and fear) that is inevitably present when one becomes aware of the existential threat of climate change. While there is no remedy, there nevertheless remains our capacity to act, which in this case is aimed toward the real sources of suffering. Let me stress that this does not mean that the actions will undermine systemic forces associated with climate change, but Sue can still exercise her capacity for impotentiality with regard to the grammar of these forces.

It is clear that Sue and Gary had numerous resources for finding ways to respond to the challenges of climate change, even though the use of these resources (e.g., money to buy solar panels) would have a negligible impact on the trajectory of climate change. Countless others have decidedly fewer economic and political resources. Joe, a 29-year-old burly, thoughtful, no-nonsense man, sought therapy because he was weary and depressed. With a supportive wife, Janet, and two small children, Joe worked 60 hours a week trying to make ends meet. His wife recognized Joe's depression and encouraged him to get help, which he initially resisted, ostensibly for financial reasons and time. I work one day a week at a clinic that has a sliding fee scale, which is how Joe and I met.

Joe grew up in a poor section of the city. His dad worked at a local factory and was a nonviolent, though absent, alcoholic. Joe's mother was an anxious woman, always understandably concerned about finances, which improved slightly when Joe's dad stopped drinking when Joe was 18. After graduating from high school, Joe, having never thought about the possibility of college, joined his father at the factory, until it closed down when he was 21. While working at the factory, Joe met and later married Janet. Once the factory closed down, Joe eventually found a job at the warehouse of a large corporation—a corporation that paid low wages and offered few benefits. Both he and his wife worked, relying on his parents and in-laws to care for their children. Between the two of them, they were able to afford a modest home (a fixer-upper, he said) in the neighborhood where Joe and Janet grew up.

Joe was convinced that the sources of his depression were his family of origin (Dad's alcoholism, Mom's anxiety) and biology, which is a typical perspective for persons growing up in the United States, where sources of psychological suffering are believed to be one's family and/or biology. After several meetings, Joe was willing to see a psychiatrist and was put on a low dose of an SSRI. Naturally, we explored Joe's developmental history and his manifest and latent thoughts and feelings about his dad and mom. When he remembered his father's drinking, he wondered if that was his dad's way of coping with working at a factory. "He was probably depressed, like me," Joe remarked. During that first year, Joe began to have more energy, felt less depressed, and arrived at some insights regarding his early life and his parents. Given this, I decided to invite Joe to explore some other avenues. During one session, I said that we had considered the biological source of his depression and explored his family of origin. I wondered if he was interested in considering other sources. Joe was curious and said yes.

Initially, I framed these other sources in terms of the struggles of his parents when Joe was growing up. I said something to the effect that Joe's recognition that his dad's depression and alcohol use stemmed from working in a factory could also be understood in terms of the larger economic system that denied just compensation and benefits. His Dad, like other men and women in this part of the city, worked hard for little recompense and likely felt powerless in the face of the economic system. This was exacerbated by the lack of governmental recognition or services. Moreover, his mother's chronic anxiety was, in my view, linked to an economic-political system that not only placed significant obstacles in the path of working-class persons, but also had a social safety net that was geared mainly to the indigent. To my mind, I was suggesting that the real sources of Joe's depression were not simply his biology or his growing up, but larger economic and political systems that enervated millions of people. Joe thought about this, though he was not sure how this would be helpful. I replied by telling Joe this was one avenue he could choose to pursue or not: it was up to him.

Over the next seven or eight months, we would, at times, return to this topic, at Joe's initiative. During those months, Joe said he felt greater empathy for his dad's struggle, his mother's anxiety, and their collective helplessness. On Saturdays, it was his practice to take his kids to the public library, giving his wife some time to relax. While they were busy reading or involved in varied programs, Joe began to read more about the history of his city, as well as the labor struggles that went back to the 19th century. This led to conversations with his wife and parents. During a conversation with his wife, Joe lamented that he was powerless in the face of these systems. His wife's reply set him on his heels. She said, "That is exactly what they aim to do." Janet said her friend, an African American woman living down the street, said something similar when talking about how black persons are treated by the police. Joe later told me that he began to think about becoming engaged in his community. Even though he (and his wife) were busy people trying to survive, he now had the energy and motivation to become involved in local organizations.

Much of this has more to do with capitalism and classism, leaving aside issues of climate change. I never broached the subject, because Joe had enough on his plate and I did not want to add any more. This, I later recalled, said more about me and less about Joe. Indeed, as therapy seemed to be winding down, Joe came in and said he had heard in the local news that the area of the city they were in had higher rates of cancer, infant mortality and ill-health, and lower rates of longevity. The reporter indicated that scientists from the local university attributed higher rates of cancer to being downwind of a coal-fired power plant. Joe was outraged and decided to learn more. It was Joe who later raised the issue of environmental racism and classism, since over half of the population in this part of the city were/are poor and working-class black persons. And Joe was also the one to make the connection between these local issues and climate change. In one of our last sessions, Joe said that he no longer felt depressed, except on occasion, though he was more in touch with feelings of helplessness. "You know what comes to mind when I feel that?" he asked.

I remember what Janet said a year ago, 'That's exactly what they aim to do.' Then I begin to think about what I am doing and going to do, even though so much of my time is taken up with my family and work.

Joe, unlike Sue, did not have as many resources in dealing with the varied issues linked to his situation and the larger issue of climate change. Nevertheless, Joe's decision to seek help for his depression initiated, in my view, a journey wherein he developed his capacity for impotentiality and a corresponding ungovernable self. It was not simply that he was not going to be captive to his depression and powerlessness; he was not going to be unwittingly determined by economic and political systems that threw up numerous obstacles. Joe decided to act toward the real social-political-economic sources of his and his community's suffering.

As mentioned above, I did not lean into the issue of Sue's or Joe's relationship to other species. It is likely a rationalization when to posit that therapy is a process that can deepen empathy and compassion, whether that is directed toward oneself, other human beings, and, hopefully, other species. The reality was my failure to bring this up for conversation. Perhaps part of Samuels' (1993) exploration of the political self should include our relationships to other species, since that would suggest the inclusion of other species over and against the ontological rift. It might be that my neglect in these two cases reveals that I am still caught (my counter-transference) in the grips of the rift. In any case, this I hope becomes part of the conversation among therapists of all persuasions.

Good-enough analytic therapy is a process of exploration, of asking new questions, and of arriving at new insights. At its base, good-enough therapy is founded on care—a care that provides a foundation for the trust needed to explore and undergo a change. This change can be understood, in part, as developing an ungovernable self—a self that can actualize one's potentiality for impotentiality. Put another way, an ungovernable self comes to recognize the real sources of suffering and, in so doing, to decide to act toward those sources. For some patients, this entails coming to terms with the sources of their eco-distress (fears, anxieties, grief, and helplessness) and exploring ways not simply on how to manage these difficult emotions and thoughts, but to find ways of preferring not to act out of the systemic forces and structures implicated in producing the climate emergency. In both cases, acting was not simply individualistic. Both Sue and Joe found ways to join with others, which helped them sustain their capacities for acting inoperatively. Joining with other ungovernable selves in this climate crisis does not necessarily mean there is hope, but it does strengthen caring resistance or inoperativity. To recall Joel Kovel's (1988) comment, "Ideally, at the end of therapy, patients are more ready for love and the politics of liberation" (p.145). Perhaps, given the dire realities of the Anthropocene, analysts and patients can arrive at Valerie Kaur's (2020) claim: "This is our defiance—to practice love even in hopelessness" (p.241).

## Conclusion

Analytic training and analytic therapy often sequester political-economic realities from education and practice. In the midst of a climate emergency, this needs to change, but, in my view, to do so requires some attention to the political philosophy that latently (or manifestly) shapes our interpretive frameworks. In this book,

I have also argued that psychoanalysis can contribute to political philosophy, and use this philosophy to reimagine psychoanalytic theories, training, and practice, especially in the dire present and future contexts of the Anthropocene Age. Climate change reveals there is no panacea. No calvary. No rescue ship. We need to find ways to care for other human beings, other species, and the earth. We need to find ways of speaking and acting together toward the well-being of a biodiverse earth, because the well-being of human beings depends on this. Indeed, the very reality and functioning of the consulting room is contingent on a biodiverse earth. Therapists and institutes have a role to play, and we need to engage the political-economic spheres, exploring and developing political philosophies so that we can more clearly participate in critical and constructive conversations with interlocutors from other disciplines. In addition, this necessarily includes changes to how we think about psychoanalytic organizations, training, and therapy so that we may act toward addressing the manifold needs and crises linked to the climate crisis. This book is a small step in this direction.

## Notes

1 It is important to stress two points in my eisegetical interpretation of this section of Plato's work. First, Socrates' view of education is linked to his theory of recollection, which is connected to his belief in reincarnation. So, educing is to bring forth what is already in the soul. I am not ascribing to this view, though I do ascribe to the idea of educing or bringing forth from persons, especially when it comes to insight. Second, as Karl Popper (2002) observed, Plato was clearly an elitist and classist, which shapes any view on education.

2 Clearly some analytic therapists have also used their analytic tools to identify the illusions citizens assume to be real or truth (Cushman, 1995; Weintrobe, 2021).

3 I add here that in my training analysis, to my recollection, we never discussed or explored issues associated with my racial biases, male privilege, class, or, more generally, my political perspectives. Since these issues are features of who I am and shape how I practice, the training analyst, in my view, should have raised these.

4 https://npap.org/vision-mission-values/, accessed 29 August 2022.

5 Adam Phillips (2021b) writes that Winnicott considered the analytic relationship to be without hierarchies (p.30). "Psychoanalysis, evolving out of the mother-child, father-child, and mother-father relationship," he writes, "becomes the model for a new kind of sociability" (p.31). This new sociability is without hierarchies (an anarchic relation), which a reader may recall is addressed more fully in Chapter 3. If we accept this premise, then it would seem to me that analytic training itself will need to model this.

6 I have long enjoyed and benefited from reading the works of Adam Phillips, which includes his most recent books (2021a, 2021b). Yet, in my reading of these and other works, he fails to mention climate change or eco-distress, as if psychoanalysis is divorced from political and economic realities. I suspect that Phillips would agree that political and economic realities shape conscious and unconscious thoughts and feelings, though I think the lacuna is telling.

# References

Adamson, J. (2017). We have never been Anthropos: From environmental justice to cosmopolitics. In S. Oppermann & S. Lovino (Eds.), *Environmental humanities: Voices form the Anthropocene*, 155–174. Rowman and Littlefield.

Adger, N., Barnett, J., Brown, K., Marshall, N. & O'Brien, K. (2013). Cultural dimensions of climate impacts and adaptation. *Nature*, 3, 112–117.

Agamben, G. (1998). *Homo sacer: Sovereign power and bare life*, trans. D. Heller-Roazen. Stanford University Press.

Agamben, G. (1999). *Potentialities: Collected essays in philosophy*, trans. D. Heller-Roazen. Stanford University Press.

Agamben, G. (2000). *Means without ends: Notes on politics*, trans. V. Binetti & C. Casarino. University of Minnesota Press.

Agamben, G. (2004). *The open: Man and animal*, trans. K. Attell. Stanford University Press.

Agamben, G. (2005). *State of exception*. Stanford University Press.

Agamben, G. (2009). *What is an apparatus? And other essays*. Stanford University Press.

Agamben, G. (2011). *The kingdom and the glory: For a theological genealogy of economy and government*. Stanford University Press.

Agamben, G. (2013). *The coming community*, trans. M. Hardt. University of Minnesota Press.

Alexander, M. (2010). *The new Jim Crow*. The New Press.

Altman, N. (2000). Black and white thinking. *Psychoanalytic Dialogues*, 10, 589–605.

Altman, N. (2004). Whiteness uncovered. *Psychoanalytic Dialogues*, 14, 439–446.

Anderson, B. (1983). *Imagined communities*. Verso.

Anderson, C. (2016). *White rage*. Bloomsbury.

Andrews, N. & Hoggett, P. (2019). Facing up to ecological crisis: A psychosocial perspective from climate psychology. In J. Foster (Ed.), *Facing up to climate reality: Honesty, disaster and hope*, 155–171. Green House.

Antadze, N. (2020). Moral outrage as the emotional response to climate injustice. *Environmental Justice*, 13, 21–26.

Arendt, H. (1958). *The human condition*. University of Chicago Press.

Arendt, H. (1965). *Eichmann in Jerusalem: A report on the banality of evil*. Penguin Books.

Arendt, H. (1970). *On violence*. Harvest/HBJ.

Arendt, H. (2005). *The promise of politics*. Schocken Books.

Arendt, H. (2018). *Thinking without a banister*. Schocken Books.

Armstrong, D. (2017). "Psychoanalytic Study" and the ethical imagination: The making, finding, and losing of a tradition. *Organizational and Social Dynamics*, 17, 222–234.

Armstrong, K. (1993). *A history of God*. Ballantine Books.

Atwood, G. & Stolorow, R. (2016). Walking the tightrope of emotional dwelling. *Psychoanalytic Dialogues*, 26, 103–108.

Augustine. (1963). *The confessions of St. Augustine*, trans. R. Warner. Mentor Books.

Augustine. (1972). *City of God*, trans. H. Bettenson. Penguin.

Bacevich, A. (2002). *American empire*. Harvard University Press.

Bacevich, A. (2005). *The new American militarism*. Oxford University Press.

Badiou, A. (2018). *Can politics be thought?* Duke University Press.

Baldwin, J. (1984). *Notes of a native son*. Beacon.

Baldwin, J. (1990). *The fire next time*. The Dial Press.

Baptist, E. (2014). *The half has never been told: Slavery and the making of American capitalism*. Basic Books.

Barker, E. (1971). *The politics of Aristotle*. Oxford University Press.

Barry, J. (2012). *Roger Williams and the creation of the American soul*. Viking.

Beardsworth, S. (2019). Who is the perpetrator/The missing affect in torture's violation of human dignity. In A. Allen & B. O'Connor (Eds.), *Transitional subjects: Critical theory and object relations*, 235–260. Columbia University Press.

Beckert, S. & Desan, C. (2018). *American capitalism*. Columbia University Press.

Beebe, B. & Lachmann, F. (2002). *Infant research and adult treatment*. Analytic Press.

Bell, D. (1996). *The cultural contradictions of capitalism*. Basic Books.

Benhabib, S. (1992). *Situating the self*. Routledge Press.

Benjamin, J. (1995). Sameness and difference: Toward an 'over-inclusive' model of gender development. *Psychoanalytic Inquiry*, 15, 125–142.

Bensaïd, B. (2012). Permanent scandal. In G. Agamben (Ed.), *Democracy in What State*, trans. W. McCuaig, 16–43. Columbia University Press.

Bilgrami, A. (Ed.). (2020). *Nature and value*. Columbia University Press.

Bion, W. R. (1970). *Attention and interpretation*. Tavistock.

Blackburn, E. & Epel, E. (2017). *The telomere effect: Living younger, healthier, and longer lives*. Hachette Book Group.

Bodin, J. (2009). *On sovereignty: Six books on the commonwealth*. Seven Treasures Publishing.

Boer, R. (2009). *Criticism of heaven: On Marxism and theology*. Haymarket Books.

Bollas, C. (1987). *The shadow of the object*. Columbia University Press.

Bollas, C. (1995). *Cracking up*. New York: Hill and Wang.

Bonovitz, C. & Harlem, A. (2018). *Developmental perspectives in child psychoanalysis and psychotherapy*. Routledge.

Bourdieu, P. (1990). *The logic of practice*. Stanford University Press.

Bowker, M. & Buzby, A. (Eds.). (2017). *D.W. Winnicott and political theory: Recentering the subject*. Palgrave.

Bracke, S. (2016). Bouncing back: Vulnerability and resistance in times of resilience. In J. Butler, A. Gambetti, & L. Sabsay (Eds.), *Vulnerability in Resistance*, 52–75. Duke University Press.

Brody, S. (1980). Transitional objects: Idealization of a phenomenon. *Psychoanalytic Quarterly*, 49, 561–605.

Bromberg, P. (1983). The mirror and the mask: On narcissism and psychological growth. *Contemporary Psychoanalysis*, 19, 359–387.

Bromberg, P. (1996). Hysteria, dissociation, and cure: Emmy von N revisited. *Psychoanalytic Dialogues*, 6, 55–71.

Brown, W. (2001). *Politics out of history*. Princeton University Press.

Brown, W. (2010). *Walled states, Waning sovereignty*. Zone Books.

Brown, W. (2015). *Undoing the demos*. Zone Books.

Brunning, H. & Khaleelee, O. (2018). Danse macabre spinning faster. *Organizational and Social Dynamics*, 18, 131–153.

Bubeck, D. (1995). *Care, gender, and justice*. Clarendon Press.

Buber, M. (1958). *I and thou*. Charles Scribner.

Budziszewska, M. & Jonsson, S. (2021). From climate anxiety to climate action: An existential perspective on climate change concerns within psychotherapy. *The Journal of Humanistic Psychology*, 61. https://doi.org/10.1177/0022167821993243.

Busch, F., Nagera, H., McKnight, J. & Pezzarossi, G. (1973). Primary transitional objects. *Journal of the American Academy of Child Psychiatry*, 12, 193–214.

Butler, J. (2004). *Precarious life: The powers of mourning and violence*. Verso.

Butler, J. (2005). *Giving an account of oneself*. Fordham University Press.

Butler, J. (2020). *The force of nonviolence*. Verso.

Camus, A. (1947/2002). *The plague*. Penguin.

Capper, B. (2009). Jesus, virtuoso religion, and the community goods. In B. Longenecker & K. Liebengood (Eds.), *Engaging economics: New testament scenarios and early Christian reception*, 60–80. Eerdmanns Publishing Company.

Caputo, J. (2006). *The weakness of God: A theology of the event*. Indiana University Press.

Casement, P. (1985). *Learning from the patient*. Guilford Press.

Casey, E. (2009). *Getting back into place: Toward a renewed understanding of the place-world*. Indiana University Press.

Castoriadis, C. (1998). *The imaginary institution of society*. MIT Press.

Chakrabarty, D. (2009). The climate of history: Four theses. *Critical Inquiry*, 35, 197–222.

Chalwell, R. (2017). Vulnerability, dependency, sovereignty, and ego-distortion theory: Psychoanalyzing political behaviors in the developing world. In M. Bowker & A. Buzby (Eds.), *D.W. Winnicott and political theory*, 333–356. Palgrave.

Chancer, L. (2020). Feminism, humanism, and Erich Fromm. In K. Durkin & J. Braune (Eds.), *Erich Fromm's critical theory*, 96–107. Bloomsbury.

Chari, A. (2015). *A political economy of the senses: Neoliberalism, reification, critique*. Columbia University Press.

Chomsky, N. (2003). *Hegemony or survival: America's quest for global dominance*. Metropolitan Books.

Chomsky, N. (2005). *Imperial ambitions*. Metropolitan Books.

Chused, J. F. (1991). The evocative power of enactments. *Journal of the American Psychoanalytic Association*, 39, 615–639.

Clarke, B. (1997). Hermeneutics and the "relational" turn: Schafer, Riceour, Gadamer, and the nature of psychoanalytic subjectivity. *Psychoanalysis and Contemporary Thought*, 20, 3–68.

Clayton, S. (2020). Climate anxiety: Psychological responses to climate change. *Journal of Anxiety Disorders*, 74, 102263.

Clayton, S. & Manning, C. (Eds.). (2018). *Psychology and climate change: Human perceptions, impacts, and responses*. Academic Press.

Clough, P. T. (2021). Critical theory and its challenge to psychoanalysis: Response to Katie Gentile's "Kittens in the clinical space: Expanding subjectivity through dense temporalities of interspecies transcorporeal becoming." *Psychoanalytic Dialogues*, 31, 151–159.

Coates, T. (2015). *Between the world and me*. Spiegel & Grau.

Cohen, J. (2017). Posthuman environs. In S. Oppermann & S. Lovino (Eds.), *Environmental humanities: Voices from the Anthropocene*, 25–44. Rowman & Littlefield.

Colebrook, C. & Maxwell, J. (2016). *Agamben*. Polity Press.

Colman, A. (2022). Corporeal schemas and body images: Fanon, Merleau-Ponty, and the lived experience of race. In L. Laubscher, D. Hook, & M. Desai (Eds.), *Fanon, phenomenology, and psychology*, 127–138. Routledge.

Comtesse, H., Ertl, V., Hengst, S., Rosner, R. & Smid, G. (2021). Ecological grief as a response to environmental change: A mental health risk or functional response? *International Journal of Environmental Research and Public Health*, 18, 734.

Cone, J. (2010/1970). *A black theology of liberation*. Orbis Books.

Conradi, E. (2015). Redoing care: Societal transformation through critical practice. *Ethics and Social Practice*, 9(2), 113–129.

Corte, L. (1997). Forms of the sacred. *American Journal of Psychoanalysis*, 57, 337–358.

Covington, C. (2019). New walls to keep the bad out: Populism and the totalitarian psyche. *The International Journal of Forensic Psychotherapy*, 1, 120–130.

Cox, H. (2016). *The market as God*. Harvard University Press.

Crockett, C. (2012). *Radical political theology*. Columbia University Press.

Crutzen, P. & Stoermer, E. (2000). The "Anthropocene." *IGB Global Change Newsletter*, 41, 17–18.

Cushman, P. (1995). *Constructing the self, constructing America*. Addison Wesley.

Cushman, P. (2019). *Travels with the self: Interpreting psychology as cultural history*. Routledge Press.

Cvetkovich, A. (2012). *Depression: A public feeling*. Duke University Press.

Dalal, F. (2002). *Race, color and the process of racialization: New perspectives from group analysis, psychoanalysis, and sociology*. Brunner-Routledge.

Danner, M. (2009). *Stripping the body bare: Politics, violence, war*. Nations Books.

Dardot, P. & Laval, C. (2013). *The new way of the world: On neoliberal society*. Verso.

Davenport, C. (2014). Pentagon signals security risks of climate change. *New York Times*, October 13, 2014, http://www.nytimes.com/2014/10/14/us/pentagon-says-global-warming-presents-immediate-security-threat.html?_r=1, accessed 14 December 2021.

de Beauvoir, S. (2011). *The second sex*. Vintage Books.

DeCaroli, S. (2007). Boundary stones: Giorgio Agamben and the field of sovereignty. In M. Calarco & S. DeCaroli (Eds.), *Agamben: Sovereignty & life*, 43–69. Stanford University Press.

De La Torre, M. (2017). *Embracing hopelessness*. Fortress Press.

Deleuze, G. & Guattari, F. (2003). *Anti-Oedipus: Capitalism and schizophrenia*. University of Minnesota Press.

D'Entreves, M. (1994). *The political philosophy of Hannah Arendt*. Routledge Press.

Desmond, M. (2016). *Evicted: Poverty and profit in the American city*. Crown Publishers.

de Tocqueville, A. (2004). *Democracy in America*. Bantam Books.

Dickinson, C. (2015a). On the 'coming philosophy.' In C. Dickinson & A. Kotsko (Eds.), *Agamben's coming philosophy: Finding a new use for theology*, 21–40. Rowman & Littlefield.

Dickinson, C. (2015b). The absence of gender. In C. Dickinson & A. Kotsko (Eds.), *Agamben's coming philosophy: Finding a new use for theology*, 167–182. Rowman & Littlefield.

Dickinson, C. & Kotsko, A. (2015). *Agamben's coming philosophy: Finding a new use for theology*. Rowman & Littlefield.

Dodds, J. (2011). *Psychoanalysis and ecology at the edge of chaos*. Routledge.

Dodds, S. (2014). Dependence, care, and vulnerability. In C. Mackenzie, W. Rogers, & S. Dodds (Eds.), *Vulnerability: New essays in ethics and feminist philosophy*, 181–203. Oxford University Press.

Drysdale, P. (2012). America's pivot to Asia and Asian akrasia. *East Asia Forum*, November 26, http://www.eastasiaforum.org/2012/11/26/americas-pivot-to-asia-and-asian-akrasia/, accessed 8 June 2022.

Dufour, D. (2008). *The art of shrinking heads: On the new servitude of the liberated in the age of total capitalism*. Polity Press.

Duménil, G. & Lévy, D. (2011). *The crisis of neoliberalism*. Harvard University Press.

Durkin, K. & Braune, J. (Eds.). (2020). *Erich Fromm's critical theory*. Bloomsbury.

Dussel, E. (1985). *Philosophy of liberation*. Orbis Books.

Eagleton, T. (1996). *The illusions of postmodernism*. Blackwell.

Eagleton, T. (2003). *After theory*. Basic Books.

Eagleton, T. (2011). *Why Marx was right*. Yale University Press.

Eagleton, T. (2016). *Materialism*. Yale University Press.

Edkins, J. (2007). Whatever politics. In M. Calarco & S. DeCaroli (Eds.), *Agamben: Sovereignty & Life*, 70–91. Stanford University Press.

Elkins, J. (2017). Being and encountering: Movement and aggression in Winnicott. In M. Bowker & H. Buzby (Eds.), *D.W. Winnicott and political theory: Recentering the subject*, 37–68. Palgrave.

Ellison, R. (1995/1953). *Shadow and act*. Vintage Press.

Emerson, R. (1849). *Nature* (E-Book). James Monroe and Company.

Engster, D. (2007). *The heart of justice: Care ethics and political theory*. Oxford University Press.

Engster, D. & Hamington, M. (2015). *Care ethics and political theory*. Oxford University Press.

Erdoes, R. & Ortiz, A. (1984). *American Indian myths and legends*. Pantheon.

Erikson, E. (1952). *Childhood and society*. W. W. Norton.

Erikson, E. (1982). *The life cycle completed*. W. W. Norton.

Fanon, F. (2008/1952). *Black skin, white masks*. Grove Press.

Fergusson, N. (2004). *Colossus: The rise and fall of the American Empire*. Penguin Books.

Fingarette, H. (1969). *Self-deception*. University of California Press.

Fraisart, S. (2021). *The liberalism of care: Community, philosophy and ethics*. University of Chicago Press.

Fraser, N. (2020). *Fortunes of feminism: From state-managed capitalism to neoliberal crisis*. Verso.

Fraser, N. (2022). *Cannibal capitalism*. Verso Books.

Fraser, N. & Honneth, A. (2003). *Redistribution or recognition?* Verso Books.

Fraser, N. & Jaeggi, R. (2018). *Capitalism: A conversation in critical theory*. Polity Press.

Frazer, E. & Hutchings, K. (2020). *Violence and political theory*. Polity Press.

Fredericks, S. (2021). *Environmental guilt and shame: Signals of individual and collective responsibility and the need for ritual responses*. Oxford University Press.

Freire, P. (2018). *Pedagogy of the oppressed*. Bloomsbury.

Freire, P. (2021). *Education for critical consciousness*. Bloomsbury.

Freud, S. (1900). The interpretation of dreams. *Standard Edition*, 4, ix–637. Hogarth Press.

Freud, S. (1914). The Moses of Michelangelo. *Standard Edition*, 13, 209–238. Hogarth Press.

Freud, S. (1915). Thoughts for the times on war and death. *Standard Edition*, 14, 273–300. Hogarth Press.

Freud, S. (1917). General theory of neuroses. *Standard Edition*, 16, 243–463. Hogarth Press.

Freud, S. (1918). From the history of infantile neurosis. *Standard Edition*, 17, 7–123. Hogarth Press.

Freud, S. (1925). Resistance to psychoanalysis. *Standard Edition*, 19, 213–222. Hogarth Press.

Freud, S. (1926). Inhibitions, symptoms and anxiety. *Standard Edition*, 20, 75–176. Hogarth Press.

Freud, S. (1927). The future of an illusion. *Standard Edition*, 21, 5–58. Hogarth Press.

Freud, S. (1930). Civilization and its discontents. *Standard Edition*, 21. Hogarth Press.

Freud, S. (1933). Why war. *Standard Edition*, 22, 195–216. Hogarth Press.

Freud, S. (1939). Moses and monotheism. *Standard Edition*, 23, 237–137. Hogarth Press.

Freud, S. (1950). *Totem and taboo*. W. W. Norton.

Frosh, S. (2020). Sigmund Freud. In Y. Stavrakakis (Ed.), *Routledge handbook of psychoanalytic political theory*, 19–30. Routledge Press.

Frye, N. (1982). *The great code: The bible and literature*. Harcourt Brace.

Fullbright, W. (1966). *The arrogance of power*. Random House.

Fussell, P. (1983). *Class*. Ballantine.

Galtung, J. (1975). Structural violence and direct violence: A note on operationalization. In J. Galtung (Ed.), *Essays in peace research, volume 1: Peace: Research, education, action*, 135–139. Ejlers.

Gasper, R., Blohm, A. & Ruth, M. (2011). Social and economic impacts of climate change on the urban environment. *Current Opinion in Environmental Sustainability*, 3(3), 150–157.

Gauthier, D. (2011). *Martin Heidegger, Emmanuel Levinas, and the politics of dwelling*. Lexington Books.

Gay, P. (1988). *Freud: A life our time*. Anchor Books.

Geertz, C. (1973). *The interpretation of cultures*. Basic Books.

Gentry, C. (2015). Feminist Christian realism: Vulnerability, obligation, and power politics. *International Feminist Journal of Politics*, 18(3), 449–467.

Ghent, E. (1992). Paradox and process. *Psychoanalytic Dialogues*, 2, 135–159.

Gherovici, P. & Christian, C. (Eds.). (2019). *Psychoanalysis in the barrios: Race, class, and the unconscious*. Routledge.

Gibson, N. & Beneduce, R. (2017). *Frantz Fanon, psychiatry, and politics*. Rowman & Littlefield.

Gilens, M. & Page, B. (2014). Testing theories of American politics: Elites, interest groups and average citizens. *American Political Science Association*, 12(3), 564–581.

Gilligan, C. (1982). *In a different voice: Psychological theory and women's development*. Harvard University Press.

Go, J. (2012). *Patterns of empire: The British and American Empires, 1688 to present*. Cambridge University Press.

Goldberg, D. (2009). *The threat of race: Reflections on racial neoliberalism*. Wiley-Blackwell.

Gray, J. (2013). *The silence of animals*. Farrar, Straus, and Giroux.

Grayling, A. (2019). *The history of philosophy*. Penguin Press.

Grouse, A. (2020). *A guide to eco-anxiety: How to protect the planet and your mental health*. Watkins.

Guess, R. (2017). *Changing the subject: Philosophy from Socrates to Adorno*. Harvard University Press.

Gutiérrez, G. (1985). *A theology of liberation*. Orbis Books.

Hale, N. G. (Ed.). (1971). *James Jackson Putnam and psychoanalysis: Letters between Putnam and Sigmund Freud, Ernest Jones, William James, Sandor Ferenczi, and Morton Prince, 1877–1917*. Harvard University Press.

Haley, A. (1964). *The autobiography of Malcolm X*. Ballantine Books.

Hamilton, C. (2012). History and climate change denial. In S. Weintrobe (Ed.), *Engaging with climate change: Psychoanalytic and interdisciplinary perspectives*, 16–32. Routledge.

Hamington, M. (2004). *Embodied care*. University of Illinois.

Hardt, M. & Negri, A. (2005). *Multitude*. Penguin Books.

Harman, C. (2017). *A people's history of the world*. Verso.

Harvey, D. (2005). *A brief history of neoliberalism*. Oxford University.

Harvey, D. (2016). *The ways of the world*. Oxford University Press.

Hedges, C. (2002). *War is a force that gives us meaning*. Anchor Books.

Held, V. (Ed.). (1995). *Justice and care: Essential readings in feminist ethics*. Westview Press.

Held, V. (2006). *The ethics of care: Personal, political, and global*. Oxford University Press.

Hendricks, O. (2011). *The universe bends toward justice*. Orbis.

Herring, G. (2008). *From colony to superpower: U.S. foreign relations since 1776*. Oxford University Press.

Hillman, J. (2004). *A terrible love of war*. Penguin Books.

Hinshelwood, R. D. (2020). Melanie Klein. In Y. Stavrakakis (Ed.), *Routledge handbook of psychoanalytic political theory*, 31–43. Routledge Press.

Hochschild, A. R. (2012a). *The managed heart: Commercialization of human feeling*. University of California Press.

Hochschild, A. R. (2012b). *The outsourced self*. Metropolitan Books.

Hoens, D. (2020). Jacques Lacan. In Y. Stavrakakis (Ed.), *Routledge handbook of psychoanalytic political theory*, 44–56. Routledge Press.

Hofstadter, R. (1963). *The paranoid style of American politics*. Vintage Books.

Hoggett, P. (2012). Climate change in a perverse culture. In S. Weintrobe (Ed.), *Engaging with climate change: Psychoanalytic and interdisciplinary perspectives*, 56–71. Routledge.

Hoggett, P. (2013). Governance and social anxieties. *Organizational and Social Dynamics*, 13, 69–78.

Hoggett, P. (2019). *Climate psychology: On indifference to disaster*. Palgrave Macmillan.

Honneth, A. (1995). *The struggle for recognition*. MIT Press.

Honneth, A. (2007). *Disrespect: The normative foundations of critical theory*. Polity Press.

Honneth, A. (2012). *The I in We*. Polity Press.

Honneth, A. (2021). *Recognition: A chapter in the history of European ideas*. Cambridge University Press.

Horsley, R. (2009). *Covenant economics: A biblical vision of justice for all*. Westminster John Knox Press.

Hudis, P. (2015a). *Marx's concept of the alternative to capitalism*. Haymarket Books.

Hudis, P. (2015b). *Frantz Fanon: Philosopher of the barricades*. Pluto Press.

Illouz, E. (2007). *Cold intimacies: The making of emotional capitalism*. Polity Press.

Illouz, E. (2008). *Saving the modern soul: Therapy, emotions, and the culture of self-help*. University of California Press.

Irwin, T. (2019). *Nichomachean ethics*. Hackett Publishing.

Isenberg, N. (2016). *White trash*. Viking Press.

James, W. (1918/1956). *The principles of psychology*, vol. 1. Henry Holt.

Jepson, P. & Blythe, C. (2022). *Rewilding: The radical new science of ecological recovery.* MIT Press.

Johansen, B. (2020). *Environmental racism in the U.S. and Canada.* ABC-Clio.

Johnson, C. (1999). *Blowback.* Owl Books.

Johnson, C. (2004). *Sorrows of empire.* Owl Books.

Johnson, C. (2006). *Nemesis: The last days of the American republic.* Metropolitan Books.

Johnson, C. (2010). *Dismantling the empire.* Metropolitan Books.

Johnson, M. (1987). *The body in the mind: The bodily basis of meaning, imagination, and reason.* University of Chicago Press.

Jones, S. (2012). *Masters of the universe: Hayek, Friedman, and the birth of neoliberal politics.* Princeton University Press.

Kant, I. (1963/1784). *Idea for a universal history from a cosmopolitan point of view,* trans. L. White. The Bobbs-Merrill Co.

Kaplan, A. (2002). *The anarchy of empire in the making of U.S. culture.* Harvard University Press.

Kassouf, S. (2017). Psychoanalysis and climate change: Revisiting Searles the nonhuman environment. *American Imago,* 74(2), 141–171.

Kaur, V. (2020). *See no stranger: A memoir and manifesto of revolutionary love.* One World.

Keller, C. (2018). *Political theology of the earth: Our planetary emergency and the struggle for a new public.* Columbia University Press.

Kendi, I. (2017). *Stamped from the beginning: The definitive history of racist ideas in America.* Bold Type Books.

Kerber, J. (2017). Up from the ground: Living with/in petrocultures in the US and Canadian Wests. *Western American Literature,* 51(4), 383–389.

Kerven, R. (2018). *Native American myths: Collected 1636–1919.* Talking Stone.

Kessler, L. & Kessler, R. (2019). Neuropyschoanalytic explorations. *Psychoanalytic Inquiry,* 39, 582–595.

Kestenberg, J. & Weinstein, J. (1978). Transitional objects and body image formation. In S. Grolnick & L. Barkin (Eds.), *Between reality and fantasy,* 75–96. Aronson.

Khalfa, J. (2022). My body, this skin, this fire. In L. Laubscher, D. Hook, & M. Desai (Eds.), *Fanon, phenomenology, and psychology,* 48–64. Routledge.

King, M. L. (1998). *The autobiography of Martin Luther King,* C. Carson (Ed.). Grand Central Publishing.

Klein, M. (1949). *Contributions to psychoanalysis.* Hogarth Press.

Klein, N. (2007). *Shock doctrine: The rise of disaster capitalism.* Henry Holt and Company.

Klein, N. (2014). *This changes everything: Capitalism vs. the climate.* Simon and Schuster.

Koggel, C. & Orme, J. (2015). *Care ethics: New theories and applications.* Routledge.

Koivunen, A., Kyrölä, K. & Ryberg, I. (2019). *The power of vulnerability: Mobilizing affect in feminist, queer, and anti-racist media cultures.* Manchester University.

Kolbert, E. (2014). *The sixth extinction: An unnatural history.* Henry Holt.

Kompridis, N. (2020). Nonhuman agency and human normativity. In A. Bilgrami (Ed.), *Nature and value,* 240–260. Columbia University Press.

Kotsko, A. (2020). *Agamben's philosophical trajectory.* University of Edinburgh Press.

Kovel, J. (1970). *White racism: A psychohistory.* Pantheon Books.

Kovel, J. (1988). *The radical spirit: Essays on psychoanalysis and society.* Free Associations Books.

Lakoff, G. & Johnson, M. (1999). *Philosophy in the flesh: The embodied mind and its challenges to western thought.* Basic Books.

LaMothe, R. (2009). The problem of patriotism: A psychoanalytic and theological analysis. *Pastoral Psychology*, 58(2), 151–166.

LaMothe, R. (2018). The market society and psychological suffering: A Fanonian approach. *Free Associations: Psychoanalysis and Culture, Media, Groups, and Politics*, 70, 48–69.

LaMothe, R. (2021a). *A radical political theology for the Anthropocene Age*. Cascade Books.

LaMothe, R. (2021b). Psychoanalysis and the ungovernable self: Further explorations. *Psychoanalytic Review*, 108(1), 27–50.

LaMothe, R. (2021c). Illusions, political selves, and responses to the Anthropocene Age: A political-psychoanalytic perspective. *Free Associations: Psychoanalysis and Culture, Media, Groups, Politics*, 84,1–18.

Lane, M. (2014). *The birth of politics: Eight Greek and Roman political ideas and why they matter*. Princeton University Press.

Larsen, S. (1990). *The mythic imagination*. Inner Traditions International.

Latour, B. (2004). Whose cosmos, which cosmopolitics? Comments on the Peace terms of Ulrich Beck. *Common Knowledge*, 10(3), 450–462.

Laubscher, D., Hook, D. & Desai, M. (Eds.). (2022). *Fanon, phenomenology, and psychology*. Routledge.

Layton, L. (2020). *Toward a social psychoanalysis: Culture, character, and normative unconscious processes*. Routledge.

Layton, L., Hollander, N. & Gutwill, S. (Eds.). (2006). *Psychoanalysis, class, and politics: Encounters in the clinical setting*. Routledge.

Lear, J. (1998). *Open minded: Working out the logic of the soul*. Harvard University Press.

Lear, J. (2006). *Radical hope: Ethics in face of cultural devastation*. Harvard University Press.

Lechte, J. & Newman, S. (2015). *Agamben and the politics of human rights*. Edinburgh University Press.

Lejeune, J. (2017). Adults in the playground: Winnicott and Arendt on politics and playfulness. In M. Bowker & A. Buzby (Eds.), D. W. *Winnicott and political theory*, 247–268. Palgrave.

Lepore, J. (2018). *These truths: A history of the United States*. Norton.

Levin, F. & Trevarthen, C. (2000). Subtle is the Lord: The relationship between consciousness, the unconscious, and the executive control network (ECN) of the Brain. *Annual of Psychoanalysis*, 28, 105–125.

Levinas, E. (1969). *Totality and infinity*. Duquesne University Press.

Levinas, E. (1998). *Otherwise than being*. Duquesne University Press.

Levi-Strauss, C. (1995). *Myth and meaning: Cracking the code of culture*. Schocken.

Lincoln, B. (2000). *Theorizing myth: Narrative ideology, and scholarship*. University of Chicago Press.

Linzey, A. (2009). *Why animal suffering matters: Philosophy, theology, and practical ethics*. Oxford University Press.

Løgstrup, K. (1997). *The ethical demand*. Notre Dame University Press.

Longenecker, B. & Liebengood, K. (Eds.). (2009). *Engaging economics: New testament scenarios and early Christian reception*. Eerdmanns Publishing Company.

Lord, C. (1987). Aristotle. In L. Strauss & J. Cropsey (Eds.), *History of political philosophy*, 3rd Edition, 118–154. University of Chicago Press.

Lukács, G. (1968). *History and class consciousness*. MIT Press.

Lundestad, G. (1990). *The American "Empire."* Oxford University Press.

Machin, A. (2020). Nationalism. In Y. Stavrakakis (Ed.), *Routledge handbook of psychoanalytic political theory*, 285–295. Routledge Press.

MacIntyre, A. (1983). *After virtue*. University of Notre Dame Press.

MacIntyre, A. (2007). *Ethics in the conflicts of modernity*. Cambridge University Press.

MacIntyre, A. (2016). *Ethics in the conflicts of modernity: An essay on desire, practical reasoning, and narrative*. Cambridge University Press.

MacKinnon, C. (1991). *Toward a feminist theory of the state*. Harvard University Press.

Macmurray, J. (1961). *Person in relation*. Humanities Press International.

Macmurray, J. (1991). *The self as agent*. Humanities Press International.

Macmurray, J. (1992). *Reason and emotion*. Humanity Books.

Macmurray, J. (2004). The conception of society. In E. McIntosh (Ed.), *John Macmurray Selected Philosophical Writings*, 95–108. Imprint Academic.

Maldonado-Torres, N. (2022). Fantz Fanon and the decolonial turn in psychology. In L. Laubscher, D. Hook, & M. Desai (Eds.), *Fanon, phenomenology, and psychology*, 89–99. Routledge.

Malpas, J. (1999). *Place and experience: A philosophical topography*. Cambridge University Press.

Malpas, J. (2006). *Heidegger's topology: Being, Place, World*. MIT Press.

Malpas, J. (2012). *Heidegger and thinking of place: Explorations in the topology of being*. MIT Press.

Mander, J. (2012). *The capitalism papers: Fatal flaws in an obsolete system*. Counterpoint Press.

Mann. G. (2013). *Disassembly required: A field guide to actually existing capitalism*. AK Press.

Mantena, K. (2018). Showdown for nonviolence: The theory and practice of non-violent politics. In T. Shelby & B. Terry (Eds.), *To shape a new world*, 78–104. Belknap press.

Marable, M. (2011). *Malcolm X: A life of reinvention*. Viking Press.

Marcuse, H. (1964). *One-dimensional man: Studies in the ideology of advanced industrial society*. Beacon Press.

Margalit, A. (1996). *The decent society*. Harvard University Press.

Marris, P. (1996). *The politics of uncertainty*. Routledge Press.

Marx, K. (1964). Inaugural address of the working men's association. *Marxists Internet Archive*, http://marxengels.public-archive.net/en/ME1400en.html, accessed 29 August 2022.

McAfee, N. (2008). *Democracy and the political unconscious*. Columbia University Press.

McCarroll, P. (2020). Listening for the cries of the earth: Practical theology in the Anthropocene. *International Journal of Practical Theology*, 24, 29–46.

McCarroll, P. (2022). Embodying theology: Trauma theory, climate change, pastoral and practical theology. *Religions*, 13, 294–305.

McGuire, D. (2011). *At the dark end of the street: Black women, rape, and resistance*. Random House.

McKibben, W. (2010). *Eaarth: Making life on a tough planet*. Henry Holt & Company.

McLaren, P. (2015). *Pedagogy of insurrection: From resurrection to revolution*. Peter Lang.

McLoughlin, D. (2016). Agamben on the post-fordist spectacle. In D. McLoughlin (Ed.), *Agamben and radical politics*, 91–114. Edinburgh University Press.

Mei, T. (2006). *Heidegger's topology: Being, place, world*. MIT Press.

Mei, T. (2017). *Land and the given economy: The hermeneutics and phenomenology of dwelling*. Northwestern University Press.

Meijer, E. (2019). *When animals speak: Toward an interspecies democracy*. New York University Press.

Meijer, E. (2020). *Animal languages*. MIT Press.

Meltzer, D. (1975). Adhesive identification. *Contemporary Psychoanalysis*, 11, 289–311.

Miéville, C. (2018). *October: The story of the Russian revolution.* Verso.

Mignolo, W. (2011). *The darker side of western modernity: Global futures, decolonial options.* Duke University Press.

Miller, A. (1998). *For your own good: The hidden cruelty in child-rearing and the roots of violence.* Farrar, Straus, Giroux.

Mills, C. (1983). *Black Marxism: The making of the black radical tradition.* UNC Press.

Mills, C. (1997). *The racial contract.* Cornell University Press.

Mills, C. (2017). *Black rights/White wrongs.* Oxford University Press.

Mitchell, S. (1993). *Hope and dread in psychoanalysis.* Basic Books.

Mitchell, S. (2000). *Relationality: From attachment to intersubjectivity.* Analytic Press.

Moltmann, J. (1973). *The gospel of liberation.* Word Books.

Moore, J. (2016). Name the system! Anthropocene & the Capitalocene alternative, https://jasonwmoore.wordpress.com/tag/capitalocene/, accessed 21 August 2021.

Murdoch, I. (2001). *The sovereignty of the good.* Routledge.

Neihardt, J. (2014). *Black Elk speaks.* University of Nebraska Press.

Nichols, K. & Gogineni, B. (2020). The Anthropocene dating problem. In A. Bilgrami (Ed.), *Nature and value.* Columbia University Press.

Niebuhr, R. (1957). *Love and justice,* J. Robertson (Ed.). Westminster John Knox Press.

Noddings, N. (1984). *Caring: A feminine approach to ethics and moral education.* University of California Press.

Northcott, M. (2014). *A political theology of climate change.* SPCK.

Northcott, M. (2017). On going gently into the Anthropocene. In C. Deane-Drummond, S. Bergmann, & M. Vogt (Eds.), *Religion in the Anthropocene.* Cascade Books.

Nussbaum, M. (2019). *The cosmopolitan tradition: A noble but flawed ideal.* Harvard University Press.

O'Brien, K., Eriksen, S., Sygna, L. & Naess, O. (2006). Questioning complacency: Climate change impacts, vulnerability, and adaptation in Norway. *AMBIO: A Journal of the Human Environment,* 35(2), 50–56.

Ogden, T. (1986). *The matrix of the mind.* Jason Aronson.

Ogden, T. (1997). *Reverie and interpretation.* Jason Aronson.

Oksala, J. (2012). *Foucault, politics, and violence.* Northwestern University Press.

Oliner, P. & Oliner, S. (1995). *Toward a caring society.* Praeger.

Orange, D. (2010). *Thinking for clinicians: Philosophical resources for contemporary psychoanalysis and humanistic psychotherapies.* Routledge.

Orange, D. (2017). *Climate crisis, psychoanalysis, and radical ethics.* Routledge.

Orpana, S. (2021). *Gasoline dreams: Waking up from petroculture.* Fordham University Press.

Paavola, J. (2017). Health impacts of climate change and health and social inequalities. *Environmental Health,* 113, https://doi.org/10.1186/s12940-017-0328-z.

Parenti, C. (2011). *Tropic of chaos: Climate change and the new geography of violence.* Nation Books.

Paterson, M. & Newell, P. (2010). *Climate capitalism: Global warming and the transformation of the global economy.* Cambridge University Press.

Patterson, O. (1982). *Slavery and social death.* Harvard University Press.

Paulsen, M., Jagodzinski, J. & Hawke, M. (Eds.). (2021). *Pedagogy in the Anthropocene: Re-wilding education for a new earth.* Palgrave.

Payne, L. & Payne, T. (2020). *The dead are arising: The life of Malcolm X.* Liveright Publishing Corporation.

Phillips, A. (1993). *On kissing, tickling, and being bored: Psychoanalytic essays on the unexamined life*. Harvard University Press.

Phillips, A. (2021a). *On wanting to change*. Picador.

Phillips, A. (2021b). *On getting better*. Picador.

Pihkala, P. (2019). The cost of bearing witness to the environmental crisis: Vicarious traumatization and dealing with secondary traumatic stress among environmental researchers. *Social Epistemology*, November, 86–100, https://doi.org/10.1080/02691728.2019.1681560.

Piketty, T. (2014). *Capital in the 21st century*. Belknap Press.

Piketty, T. (2020). *Capital and ideology*. Harvard University Press.

Pistor, K. (2019). *The code of capital: How the law creates wealth and inequality*. Princeton University Press.

Plessner, H. (2018/1931). *Political anthropology*. Northwestern University Press.

Plumwood, V. (2008). Shadow places and the politics of dwelling. *Australian Humanities Review*, 44, 139–150.

Popper, K. (2002). *The open society and its enemies*. Routledge.

Porter, E. (2020). *American poison: How radical hostility destroyed our promise*. Alfred A. Knopf.

Prozorov, S. (2014). *Agamben and politics*. Edinburgh University Press.

Radkau, J. (2009). *Max Weber: A biography*. Polity Press.

Rank, O. (1929/2014). *The trauma of birth*. Routledge.

Ransom, J. (1997). *Foucault's discipline: The politics of subjectivity*. Duke University Press.

Reich, R. (2007). *Supercapitalism: The transformation of business, democracy, and everyday life*. Vintage Books.

Reich, R. (2015). *Saving capitalism: For the many, not the few*. Random House.

Reik, T. (1998/1948). *Listening with the third ear*. Farrar, Straus, & Giroux.

Richardson, J. (2019). *Place and identity: The performance of home*. Routledge.

Rigby, K. (2017). Religion and ecology: Towards a communion of creatures. In S. Oppermann & S. Lovino (Eds.), *Environmental humanities: Voices from the Anthropocene*, 273–294. Rowman & Littlefield.

Roazen, P. (1999/1968). *Freud: Political and social thought*. Transaction Publishers.

Robinson, F. (1999). *Globalizing care: Ethics, feminist theory, and international relations*. Westview Press.

Robinson, F. (2011). *The ethics of care: A feminist approach to human security*. Temple University Press.

Robinson, C. (2016). *Black Marxism: The making of the Black radical tradition*. University of North Carolina Press.

Rogers-Vaughn, B. (2016). *Caring for souls in a neoliberal age*. Palgrave.

Roth, S. (1990). *Psychotherapy: The art of wooing nature*. Jason Aronson.

Rouse, W. H. D. (Trans.). (1956). *The great dialogues of Plato*. Mentor Books.

Rousseau, J. (2016). *Discourse on inequality*. Sovereign.

Rousseau, B. (2016). In New Zealand ands and rivers can be people too (legally speaking). *The New York Times*, July 13, 2016, https://www.nytimes.com/2016/07/14/world/what-in-the-world/in-new-zealand-lands-and-rivers-can-be-people-legally-speaking.html.

Ruggiero, V. (2020). *Visions of political violence*. Routledge.

Rustin, M. (1991). *The good society and the inner world*. Verso.

Rustin, M. (2001). *Reason and unreason: Psychoanalysis, science, and politics*. Continuum.

Rustin, M. (2013). How is climate change an issue for psychoanalysis. In S. Weintrobe (Ed.), *Engaging with climate change: Psychoanalytic and interdisciplinary perspectives*, 170–185. Routledge.

Ryan, A. (2012). *On politics: A history of political thought*. Liveright Publishing.

Ryn, C. (2003). *America the virtuous*. Transaction Publishers.

Safron, J. & Muran, J. (1996). The resolution of ruptures in the therapeutic alliance. *Journal of Consulting and Clinical Psychology*, 64, 447–458.

Safron, J. & Muran, J. (2000). *Negotiating the therapeutic alliance*. Guilford Press.

Saïd, E. (1979). *Orientalism*. Vintage Books.

Saïd, E. (1994). *Culture and imperialism*. Vintage Books.

Salamon, G. (2022). "The place where life hides away": Merleau-Ponty, Fanon, and the location of bodily being. In L. Laubscher, D. Hook, & M. Desai (Eds.), *Fanon, phenomenology, and psychology*, 151–161. Routledge.

Samuels, A. (1993). *The political psyche*. Routledge.

Samuels, A. (2001). *Politics on the couch: Citizenship and the internal life*. Karnac Books.

Samuels, A. (2004). Politics on the couch? Psychotherapy and society—some possibilities and limitations. *Psychoanalytic Dialogues*, 14, 817–834.

Samuels, A. (2015). *A new therapy for politics*. Karnac Books.

Sandel, M. (1998). *Liberalism and the limits of justice*. Cambridge University Press.

Sandel, M. (2005). *Public philosophy*. Harvard University Press.

Sandel, M. (2012). *What money can't buy: The moral limits of markets*. Farrar, Straus and Giroux.

Sass, L. (1992). *Madness and modernism*. Harvard University Press.

Sassen, S. (2014). *Expulsions: Brutality and complexity in the global economy*. Belknap Press.

Sayer, A. (2005). *The moral significance of class*. Cambridge University Press.

Schafer, R. (1990). *Aspects of internalization*. International Universities Press.

Schell, J. (2020). The human shadow. In A. Bilgrami (Ed.), *Nature and value*, 13–24. Columbia University Press.

Schiller, B. (2018). Disillusioning gender. *Journal of the American Psychoanalytic Association*, 63, 241–263.

Schmitt, C. (1996). *The concept of the political*, trans. G. Schwab. Chicago University Press.

Schmitt, C. (2005). *Political theology: Four chapters on the concept of sovereignty*, trans. G. Schwab. University of Chicago Press.

Schore, A. (2003). *Affect regulation and the repair of the self*. W. W. Norton.

Searles, H. (1960). *The nonhuman environment in normal development and schizophrenia*. International Universities Press.

Sevenhuijsen, S. (1998). *Citizenship and the ethics of care*. Routledge Press.

Silva, J. (2013). *Coming up short: Working class adulthood in the age of uncertainty*. Oxford University Press.

Singer, P. (1975). *Animal liberation*. Harper Collins.

Singer, P. (2016). *Ethics in the real world*. Princeton University Press.

Skinner, Q. (2009). A genealogy of the modern state. *Proceedings of the British Academy*, 162, 325–370.

Smith, A. (2003). *The wealth of nations*. Bantam Books.

Soss, J., Fording, R. C. & Schram, S. (2011). *Disciplining the poor: Neoliberal paternalism and the persistent power of race*. University of Chicago Press.

Sroufe, A. (1995). *Emotional development*. Cambridge University Press.

Stern, D. (1985). *The interpersonal world of the infant*. Basic Books.

Stern, D. N. (1997). *Unformulated experience*. Analytic Press.

Stiglitz, J. (2012). *The price of inequality*. W. W. Norton.

Stiglitz, J. (2015). *The great divide: Unequal societies and what we can do about them*. W. W. Norton.

Stolorow, R. D. (2014). Undergoing the situation: Emotional dwelling is more than empathic understanding. *International Journal of Psychoanalytic Self Psychology*, 9, 80–83.

Stone, O. & Kuznick, P. (2012). *The untold history of the United States.* Gallery Books.

Strauss, L. & Cropsey, J. (1987). *What is political philosophy?* Chicago University Press.

Sulloway, F. (1992). *Freud: Biologist of the mind.* Harvard University Press.

Swartz, S. (2018.) Counter-recognition in decolonial struggle. *Psychoanalytic Dialogues*, 28:520–527.

Szeman, I. (2017). Conjectures on world energy literature: Or, what is petroculture? *Journal of Postcolonial Writing*, 53(3), 277–288.

Szeman, I. (2019). *On petrocultures: Globalization, culture, and energy.* University of Virginia Press.

Tauber, A. (2010). *Freud, the reluctant philosopher.* Princeton University Press.

Taylor, C. (1992). *Multiculturalism and the politics of recognition.* Princeton University Press.

Taylor, C. (2007). *Modern social imaginaries.* Duke University Press.

Taylor, D. (2014). *Toxic communities: Environmental racism, industrial pollution, and residential mobility.* New York University Press.

Thompson, M. (2020). Erich Fromm and the ontology of the social. In K. Durkin & J. Braune (Eds.), *Erich Fromm's critical theory*, 23–42. Bloomsbury.

Thorpe, C. (2020). Escape from reflexivity: Fromm and Giddens on individualism, anxiety, and authoritarianism. In K. Durkin & J. Braune (Eds.), *Erich Fromm's critical theory*, 166–193. Bloomsbury.

Timperly, J. (2021). The broken $100-billion promise of climate finance — and how to fix it, *Nature*, October 20, The broken $100-billion promise of climate finance — and how to fix it, nature.com, accessed 20 May 2022.

Tollemache, R. (2019). We have to talk about…climate change. In P. Hoggett (Ed.), *Climate psychology: On indifference to disaster.* Palgrave.

Tonner, P. (2018). *Dwelling: Heidegger, archeology, morality.* Routledge.

Tredennick, H. (Trans.). (1984). *Plato: The last days of Socrates.* Penguin.

Trevarthen, C. (1993). Playing into reality: Conversations with the infant communicator. *Winnicott Studies*, 7, Spring. Karnac Books.

Tronick, E. & Cohn, J. (1989). Infant-mother face-to-face interaction: Age and gender differences in coordination and the occurrence of miscoordination. *Child Development*, 60, 85–92.

Tronto, J. (1993). *Moral boundaries: A political argument for an ethic of care.* Routledge Press.

Tronto, J. (2013). *Caring democracy: Markets, equality, and justice.* New York University Press.

Turner, C. (2020). Wilhelm Reich. In Y. Stavrakakis (Ed.), *Routledge handbook of psychoanalytic political theory*, 57–66. Routledge Press.

Turner, L. & Neville, H. (Eds.). (2020). *Frantz Fanon's psychotherapeutic approaches to clinical work.* Routledge.

Tutu, D. (1999). *No future without forgiveness.* Doubleday.

Valencia, S. (2018). *Gore capitalism.* Semiotext(e).

Valverde, M. (2017). Have deportations increased under Donald Trump? Here's what the data shows. *Politifact*, December 19, https://www.politifact.com/truth-o-meter/article/2017/dec/19/have-deportations-increased-under-donald-trump-her/, accessed 25 April 2021.

Van Dooren, T. & Rose, D. (2017). Lively ethnography: Storying animist worlds. In S. Oppermann & S. Lovino (Eds.), *Environmental humanities: Voices from the Anthropocene*, 255–272. Rowan and Littlefield.

Varner, G. (2010). *Ghosts, spirits, and the afterlife in Native American folklore and religion*. OakChylde Books.

Vogt, M. (2017). Human ecology as a key discipline of environmental ethics. In C. Deane-Drummond, S. Bergmann, & M. Vogt (Eds.), *Religion in the Anthropocene*, 235–252. Cascade Books.

Wacquant, L. (2009). *Punishing the poor: The neoliberal government of social insecurity*. Duke University Press.

Waggoner, M. (2018). *Unhoused: Adorno and the problem of dwelling*. Columbia Books.

Wagner, G. & Weitzman, M. (2015). *Climate shock: The economic consequences of a hotter planet*. Princeton University Press.

Wallace-Wells, D. (2020). *The uninhabitable earth: Life after warming*. Duggan Books.

Walzer, M. (2012). *In God's shadow: Politics and the Hebrew bible*. Yale University Press.

Watts, A. (1957). *The way of Zen*. Vintage Books.

Weber, M. (2013/1919). *Politics as vocation*. FNF Publishing.

Weil, S. (1952). *The need for roots*. Routledge and Kegan Paul.

Weintrobe, S. (2010). On links between runaway consumer greed and climate denial: A psychoanalytic perspective. *Bulletin Annual of the British Psychoanalytic Society*, 1, 63–75. Institute of Psychoanalysis.

Weintrobe, S. (Ed.). (2013). *Engaging with climate change*. Routledge.

Weintrobe, S. (2021). *The psychological roots of the climate crisis*. Bloomsbury.

Westcott, G. (2019). Attitude to climate change in some English local authorities: Varying sense of agency in denial and hope. In P. Hoggett (Ed.), *Climate psychology: On indifference to disaster*. Palgrave.

White, L. (1967). The historical roots of our ecological crisis. *Science*, 155, 1203–1207.

Whyte, J. (2013). *Catastrophe and redemption: The political thought of Giorgio Agamben*. SUNY Press.

Wilkerson, I. (2020). *Caste: The origins of our discontents*. Random House.

Wilson, E. O. (2005). *The future of life*. Abacus.

Wilson, M. (2018). The analyst as listening-accompanist: Desire in Bion and Lacan. *Psychoanalytic Quarterly*, 87, 237–264.

Wilson, S., Carlson, A. & Szeman, I. (2017). *Petrocultures: Oil, politics, and culture*. McGill-Queen's University Press.

Winnicott, D. (1960). The theory of parent-infant relationship. *International Journal of Psychoanalysis*, 41, 585–595.

Winnicott, D. (1965). *The maturational processes and the facilitating environment: Studies in the theory of emotional development*, M. Khan (Ed.). Hogarth and the Institute of Psychoanalysis.

Winnicott, D. (1971). *Playing and reality*. Routledge.

Winnicott, D. (1975). Through paediatrics to psychoanalysis. *The International Psychoanalytic Library*, 100, 1–325. Hogarth Press.

Winnicott, D. (1990). *Deprivation and delinquency*. Routledge Press.

Wolff, R. (2012). *Occupy the economy: Challenging capitalism*. City Light Books.

Wolff, R. & Resnick, S. (2012). *Contending economic theories*. MIT Press.

Wolin, S. (2008). *Democracy incorporated*. Princeton University Press.

Wolin. S. (2016a). *Fugitive democracy*. Princeton University Press.

Wolin, S. (2016b). *Politics and vision*. Princeton University Press.

Wollstonecraft, M. (1996). *A vindication of the rights of women*. Dover Publications.

Wood, D. (2019). *Reoccupy the earth: Notes toward another beginning*. Fordham University Press.

Woods, E. (2017). *The origins of capitalism*. Verso.

Young, M. (2005). Imperial language. In L. Gardner & M. Young (Eds.), *The new American empire*, 32–49. The New Press.

Zaretsky, E. (2015). *Political Freud*. Columbia University Press.

Zeddies, T. J. (2002). Behind, beneath, above, and beyond: The historical unconscious. *Journal of the American Academy of Psychoanalysis*, 30, 211–22.

Zimring, C. (2017). *Clean and white: A history of environmental racism*. New York University Press.

Zinn, H. (2003). *A people's history of the United States*. HarperPerrenial.

# Index

Note: Page numbers followed by "n" denote endnotes.

Atwood, G. 76n17
aura of sovereignty 91, 99
autobiography 49n22, 53, 92, 166

Bacon, F. 40
Badiou, A. 61, 93
Baldwin, J. 38, 146
Baptist, E. 58
barbarians 7, 44, 47n7, 55, 82, 85, 121
Beardsworth, S. 33
Beebe, B. 27
Beecher, C. 145
beliefs 6, 7, 9, 27, 28, 36, 40, 43–46,
    51n31, 62, 63, 68, 70, 82, 83, 88–
    91, 93, 94, 96, 97–99, 100n10, 104,
    105, 113–116, 135, 162
belonging 3, 17, 18n8, 23, 31, 55, 56,
    60–66, 73, 75n9, 77, 85–87, 93–99,
    102, 104, 106, 107, 116, 118,
    119–122, 124, 135, 136, 139–141,
    173–175, 178
Beneduce, R. 128
Benhabib, S. 24, 25
Benjamin, J. 26, 60, 179
Beveridge, Senator 145
Bilgrami, A. 18n10
black inferiority 38, 39
Black Lives Matter movement 84, 133
Bodin, J. 79–80, 86
Boer, R. 74n1
Bollas, C. 35, 68, 156
Bourdieu, P. 60
Bracke, S. 75n13
Bretton Woods agreement 110
Breuer, J. 160
British Empire 108
Bromberg, P. 160
Brown, W. 58, 63, 74n1, 85–86, 100n7, 115
Buber, M. 68, 97
Buddhism 55
Butler, J. 47n6, 136
Butler, S. 109

Calvin, J. 96
Camus, A. 102
capacity 14, 29, 31, 33, 35, 36, 49n18, 59,
    64, 68, 93, 118, 122, 126n19, 130,
    137, 154, 163, 169, 175, 181, 182,
    184, 185, 187
*Capital in the 21st Century* (Piketty) 92
capitalism 72–74, 103–107, 110–112, 115,
    120, 121, 123, 140

capitalistic colonization 44
capitalistic markets 106
capitalist system 107, 115
Capitalocene Era 18n10, 72, 110
Carver, G. W. 30
Casey, E. 55, 60, 75n2, 75n5
Castoriadis, C. 53
centralized economic power 120
central political authority 108
central political principles 24
Chancer, L. 78
Chari, A. 115
Chomsky, N. 151
Christians: notions of divine sovereignty
    97; scriptures 55, 120;
    theologians 144
Chused, J. 138
citizenship: political agency/identity 12;
    state apparatuses and notion of 11
civic care/recognition 10–12, 29, 35, 36,
    38, 41, 47, 49n18, 56, 63, 70, 95,
    123, 136, 139
civic mutual-personal trust 9
civic trust for children 9–12, 41, 49n18,
    118–122, 133, 139
civilization 3, 4, 40, 52, 77, 78, 84, 87, 88,
    90, 91, 100n9, 100n10, 101n10,
    104, 145
civilized peoples 90, 91
Civil Rights Movement 83
Clarke, B. 162
classical capitalism 104, 105
classism 1, 5, 27, 44, 58, 61–63, 65, 70, 74,
    91, 102, 107, 112, 119, 131, 133,
    146, 164, 171, 186
climate action 2–4, 15, 16, 18n10, 72,
    74, 103, 129, 133, 142, 146, 159,
    182; psychoanalysis and systemic
    obstacles to (*see* psychoanalysis
    and systemic obstacles, to climate
    action)
climate change 1–5, 16, 18n10, 46, 62,
    74, 75n4, 78, 83, 111, 121, 142,
    158, 159, 173, 178, 183, 184, 188,
    188n6; psychoanalytic therapy and
    178–187
climate crisis 2–3, 40, 148n10, 187, 188
climate discourse 1
climate emergency 2, 142, 153, 158, 171
climate obstacles 118–123
Clinton, B. 9, 19n13
Coates, T. -N. 28, 38, 39, 49n20, 70

psychosocial distress 182
psychosocial strength of hope 143, 144
psychosocial sufferings 3, 4, 125n17, 182
PTO *see* primary transitional object (PTO)
public-political discourse 3
public-political institutions 6
public-political interlocutors 3
Putnam, J. J. 127–128

*qua:* care 45; human construction 102; person 67

racism 5, 70, 74, 91, 152, 171
racist society traditional therapy 128
Rancière, J. 93
Rank, O. 66
rational political philosophy 53
*realpolitik* 165
recognition 7, 9–12, 25–30, 33, 34, 37–39, 41, 44, 45, 47n6, 48n18, 49n18, 56, 60–62, 66, 70, 85, 89, 94, 96, 97, 118, 122, 123, 134–142, 146, 162, 182, 185, 186
Reich, R. 125n17
Reich, T. 157
Reich, W. 152
Reik, T. 159
religious narratives 45
Republicans In Name Only (RINOs) 86
responsiveness 26, 161, 162
revolutionary violence 84, 139
rhizome 50n27
Ricardo, D. 104
Riceour, P. 158
RINOs *see* Republicans In Name Only (RINOs)
Rio Conference 111
Roazen, P. 5, 78
Robinson, C. 58
Rousseau, J. -J. 4, 10, 34, 52, 77, 93, 107, 124n2; *Discourse on Inequality* 77
rule of law 156
Rustin, M. 2, 3, 113

Salamon, G. 49n20
Sales, R. 28, 70, 94, 95, 137, 148n7
Samuels, A. 179, 180, 187
Sanctuary Movement in the United States 86
Sassen, S. 119
Schafer, R. 112, 114
Schell, J. 66, 93

Schmitt, C. 50n29, 52, 74n1, 79–80, 85, 86, 91, 100n1
Schore, A. 27
Schram, S. 58
scientific methodology 3
scientific racism 27
Searles, H. 39, 44, 45
secondary transitional objects (STO) 32–33, 36, 69, 96, 144
self-deception 8, 16, 89, 90, 152, 158, 162, 165, 166, 179, 180
sexism 27, 44, 61, 62, 65, 91, 102, 112, 131, 146, 164, 171
shared ethos 60
shared identity 60, 85, 86, 106
shared national identity 12
Silva, J. 115
Singer, P. 49n25; *Animal Liberation* 75n11
singularity 26, 28, 30, 31–33, 36–39, 41, 44, 49n18, 58, 60, 66, 91, 92, 94–96, 122, 137, 138, 140, 163
Sioux and Yurok peoples 23
Skinner, Q. 19n16
Smith, A. 104, 105, 124n2
social-cultural milieu 112
social death 7, 38, 39, 59, 81, 136
social imaginaries 106, 118
socialism 49n24, 107, 124n5
social justice 159
socially constructed practices 106
social-political apparatuses 2, 96, 136, 182
social-political conventions 155
social-political critics 158, 162
social-political fabric 9
social-political humiliation 27
social-political institutions 106
social-political recognition 61
sociopolitical formation 108
sociotherapy 148n2
Socrates 5, 55, 56, 153–155, 162, 163, 168, 169, 188n1; dialogues 154; methods 56; public-political method 155
Soss, J. 58
sovereign classes 77, 81, 82, 84, 86, 87, 91–92, 101n10, 103, 104, 107, 111, 145, 172
sovereignty 77, 90, 100n7, 103; apparatuses 85; and attributes of 79–87; aura of 91, 99; political violence 91; psychoanalytic rendering of 87–93; psychological sources of 91

For Product Safety Concerns and Information please contact our EU
representative GPSR@taylorandfrancis.com
Taylor & Francis Verlag GmbH, Kaufingerstraße 24, 80331 München, Germany

www.ingramcontent.com/pod-product-compliance
Lightning Source LLC
Chambersburg PA
CBHW050645280326
41932CB00015B/2792